# CHANGING
# PERSPECTIVES
# ON
# MAN

# THE MONDAY LECTURES

THE UNIVERSITY OF CHICAGO

*Selected Lectures, 1966 and 1967*

Bruno Bettelheim
Kenneth E. Boulding
Noam Chomsky
Theodosius Dobzhansky
Brian A. Farrell
Ralph W. Gerard
Robert Gomer
Lawrence S. Kubie
Richard McKeon
William H. McNeill
John R. Platt
Sherwood L. Washburn
John A. Wilson

Edited by Ben Rothblatt

# CHANGING
# PERSPECTIVES
# ON
# MAN

THE UNIVERSITY OF CHICAGO PRESS
CHICAGO AND LONDON

*Library of Congress Catalog Card Number: 68-16714*

THE UNIVERSITY OF CHICAGO PRESS, CHICAGO 60637
THE UNIVERSITY OF CHICAGO PRESS, LTD., LONDON W.C.1

# PREFACE

In the summer of 1964, a small group of faculty members at The University of Chicago met to consider ways of increasing communication within the university, both across disciplinary boundaries and among members of the entire university community at all levels—faculty, graduate students, undergraduates, and interested members of the general community. These men, themselves scholars of considerable distinction in a variety of fields, shared the concern felt by many that the accelerated production of specialized knowledge contributes to intellectual isolation within increasingly minute substantive areas; on the other hand they were also struck by the apparent paradox that important developments within the special disciplines are of increasing relevance to the general discussion of intellectual, social, and moral problems that has been carried on across the centuries.

It was decided to initiate a series of lectures that would address itself to these broad intellectual and moral concerns from the points of view of all of the major scientific and scholarly disciplines. This series, to be called the Monday Lectures, would be established in the Spring of 1965 as a permanent part of the intellectual life of the universtiy. The organizing principle of the series involved bringing new knowledge developed within the special disciplines and reflecting perspectives and methods characteristic of those disciplines to bear upon a range of general intellectual issues often termed "philosophical." These issues include, but are not limited to, the definition of man, the relationship between the individual and society, and man's place in the physical universe. The lecturers were invited to choose

their own topics within the very broad general boundaries described above. It was the hope, if not the conviction, of the
organizers of the Monday Lectures that the diversity of topics,
disciplines, and points of view, and the new knowledge which
emerged, often illuminating corners remote from traditional
intellectual concerns, would nevertheless converge upon the
general issues established as the basis for discussion and would
have important effects on that discussion. To a perhaps surprising degree this hope was realized, as was shown by the first
published collection of Monday Lectures, *New Views of the
Nature of Man*, edited by John R. Platt and published in 1965
by The University of Chicago Press, and as the present collection further demonstrates.

The present volume assembles the majority of Monday Lectures delivered between Winter, 1966 and Spring, 1967; a
group of papers whose subject is the physical universe will be
published separately.

The subject of this volume is man, and the dominant theme
is change: change in the nature of man himself, change in man's
environment, and change in our knowledge and understanding
of man. Within this general framework the subjects of particular
lectures exhibit a wide range of concerns. The opening lectures
by Noam Chomsky, Brian A. Farrell, and John Platt bring
recent developments in linguistics, philosophy, and biophysics
to bear in new and quite different ways on a cluster of problems
traditionally dealt with in the philosophy of mind, as well as in
empirical psychology: the acquisition of knowledge, the nature
of consciousness, and the problem of perception. Dr. Ralph
Gerard describes the possibilities opened up by the new technology for manipulating the environment to effect changes in
the human organism. The concept of personality change is
discussed by Dr. Lawrence S. Kubie in the essay which follows.
In the next lecture, also by an eminent psychoanalytic practi-
tioner, Dr. Bruno Bettelheim turns the discussion to the social
context in analyzing the concepts of alienation and autonomy.

Theodosius Dobzhansky enlarges the discussion of man, examining man's position in the process of universal evolution as a whole and his special role as the only rational being aware of the evolutionary process itself. Sherwood Washburn's paper emphasizes the various forms of knowledge which contribute to an understanding of human evolution, and, in the light of new knowledge of primate behavior, focuses on the problem of man's coming to the ground. Kenneth Boulding shifts the terms of the discussion to man's social evolution, with particular attention devoted to economic development and the role of revolution in that process. William H. McNeill discusses the process of development from the perspective of historical changes in the economic relationship between town and country. The discussion of change is given added point by John A. Wilson's analysis of the importance of historical perspective in the understanding of change and by Robert Gomer's essay which underlines the distinction between the concept of change and the idea of progress. Finally, Richard McKeon analyzes the reflexivity of man's study of man and the consequent interconnectedness of all knowledge and discusses the development of the concept of man and the related concepts of mankind, culture, and the humanities.

Despite considerable diversity of subject matter and the multiplicity of backgrounds and special concerns of the contributors to this volume, the integration of this collection around a set of central themes comes as somewhat of a surprise even to the optimistic organizers of the Monday Lectures. But the unity of science and scholarship is better exhibited than merely stated, and for evidence of that unity it is necessary to turn to the lectures themselves.

A special note of thanks is due to John R. Platt, currently acting director of the Mental Health Research Institute of the University of Michigan and formerly professor of physics and biophysics at the University of Chicago, and to Sol Tax, professor of anthropology and dean of University Extension at the

University of Chicago, who jointly originated the Monday Lectures. Talmage Gornto, of the staff of University Extension, ably assisted with the administration of the series.

BEN ROTHBLATT

# CONTENTS

1

# LANGUAGE AND MIND

NOAM CHOMSKY

NOAM CHOMSKY *is Ward Professor of Linguistics at Massachusetts Institute of Technology and has been a member of the Institute for Advanced Study at Princeton and the Cognitive Study Center at Harvard.* Cartesian Linguistics, Current Issues in Linguistic Theory, *and* Aspects of the Theory of Syntax *are his most recent works.*

# 1

# LANGUAGE AND MIND

*Noam Chomsky*

Toward the end of the sixteenth century, the Spanish scientist-philosopher Juan Huarte composed an important study of what in modern terms might be called "physiological psychology," in which he inquired into the nature of human intelligence. As an afterthought, he asked himself the question why the word for "mind" or "intelligence"—"wit," in the contemporary translation—is *ingenio* (Latin, *ingenium*). He proposes that *ingenio* is derived from the root meaning "engender" or "generate." Thus "one may discover two generative powers in man, one common with the beasts and plants, and the other participating of spiritual substances. . . . Wit is a generative power . . . the understanding is a generative faculty." Man shares with animals the capacity of procreation, but he is uniquely capable of the second type of generation, of creative intelligence and imagination and the free and creative use of language. "As wit is the ornament of a man, so eloquence is the light and beauty of wit. In this alone he distinguishes himself from the brutes. . . ."

Huarte's etymology is not very good, but his insight is excellent. There is, in fact, good reason to begin a discussion of language and mind with a reference to early modern philosophical speculation. Many of the questions that seem critical today were raised and discussed, with insight and understanding, in the seventeenth, eighteenth, and early nineteenth centuries,

This work was supported in part by the Joint Services Electronics Program under Contract DA36-039-AMC-03200(E); and in part by the National Science Foundation (Grant GK-835), the National Institutes of Health (Grant 2P01MH-04737-06), the National Aeronautics and Space Administration (Grant Nsg-496), and the United States Air Force (ESD Contract AF19(628)-2487).

and then largely forgotten as this tradition, for various reasons, came to an end. What is more, much of the understanding that is being achieved in current work was foreshadowed and anticipated during the same period in the speculative psychology and linguistics of rationalism and romanticism.

Huarte analyzes intelligence into three major categories. The lowest level—the level of animal intelligence—is that of the "docile wit" satisfying the empiricist maxim that nothing is in the mind that has not been passed through the sense. For this kind of subhuman intelligence, ideas are merely impressions of sensory images recorded in the brain; and knowledge, presumably, can be nothing but a network of associations, developed, perhaps, through training and conditioning. But normal human intelligence cannot be described in these terms. It is a second type of wit, capable of engendering within itself, by its own power, the principles on which knowledge rests, and capable of expressing itself, in speech, in entirely novel ways. Normal human minds are such that they will, "without the help of any body, produce a thousand conceits they never heard spoke of," "inventing and saying such things as they never heard from their masters nor any mouth." It is in this dual sense that "wit is a generative power," a power that reveals basic principles, and that forms and expresses new thoughts. As a physician, Huarte is interested in pathology. The most severe disability of wit is that of the docile wit that functions in accordance with the empiricist principle. Under this tragic condition, the mind suffers from a disability which "resembles that of Eunuchs . . . unable for generation"; "neither the lash of the rod, nor his cries, nor method, nor time, nor experience, nor any thing in nature can sufficiently excite him to bring forth any thing." The mind can neither discover first principles, nor innovate in the normal human fashion; with this defect, "men differ not at all from brute beasts."

In addition to animal intelligence and normal human creative intelligence there is still a third kind of wit "by means of which some have without art or study spoke such subtle and surprising things, and yet true, that were never before seen, heard, or writ, no nor ever so much as thought of." The first type of wit involves only memory; the second, understanding; the third, true creative imagination. Both the second and the third type of wit are based on some generative principle, but only the third involves true artistic creativity that goes beyond mere innovation.

I have quoted from Huarte at length because the framework that he provides is quite useful for a discussion of psychological theory in the ensuing period and, in fact, until the present. In particular, his reference to what might be called the "creative aspect of language use" as a distinctive feature of normal human intelligence is characteristic of subsequent discussion. Rationalists were concerned with the distinction between the first and second types of wit—with those aspects of human intelligence that go beyond mere recording and association of sensory images. Romantics were primarily concerned with the third type of wit, with genius and true creativity. The contributions to psychology and linguistics that emerged from these concerns are considerable, and merit careful study.

The study of mind becomes very quickly the study of acquisition of knowledge, of perception and learning. In both connections we can distinguish an "active" and a "passive" view. The distinction is in terms of the role attributed to intrinsic processes in determining the nature of what comes to be known —to central processes in perception, and to innate ideas and principles in the case of learning. The empiricist view was that sensory images are transmitted to the brain as impressions which remain as ideas that will be associated in various ways, depending on the contingencies of accidental experience. Thus Hume states quite clearly his view that "all this creative power of the mind amounts to no more than the faculty of compounding, transposing, augmenting, or diminishing the materials afforded us by the senses and experience," these materials being ultimately impressions "which copy their objects truly," the mind being "a faithful mirror." Impressions on the sensory organs and certain techniques of data processing, which he enumerates, provide all of our knowledge, when we add the unconscious, instinctive, inductive principles, shared with animals, which provide "the part of our knowledge" that comes "from the original hand of nature." A language, in this view, is an adventitious construct, a collection of words and phrases and pronunciation habits. To use the formulation of one distinguished contemporary philosopher, knowledge of a language (and, in fact, knowledge in general) can be represented as "a fabric of sentences variously associated to one another and to non-verbal stimuli by the mechanism of conditioned response."[1] Acquisition of knowledge is, in the first place, a matter of gradual construction of this fabric; when given sensory experience is interpreted, the already established network may be activated in some fashion. In its essentials, this view has been predominant in modern "behavioral science," and it has been accepted with little question by many philosophers as well.

The rationalist view was quite different. For Descartes, corporeal motions in the sense organs are not simply mapped onto the mind as "ideas"; rather, they provide the occasion on which the mind forms certain ideas that do not "resemble" these corporeal motions. It is, for example, an intrinsic property of the mind that regular geometrical figures are more easily conceived than the complex figures actually drawn on paper; thus a presented sensory triangle will be interpreted with reference to an ideal, true triangle rather than the "composite figure" of sense, although there is nothing in experience to support this particular interpretation. This is what Descartes means when he speaks of the idea of a triangle as innate, as embedded in the system of "common notions" which, a consistent rationalist would maintain, constitutes a precondition for intelligible experience. It is in this sense that the innate idea

[1] W. V. O. Quine, *Word and Object* (Cambridge, Mass.: M.I.T. Press, 1960).

of a triangle enters into "that part of knowledge with which we were endowed in the primeval plan of nature" (Herbert). For the English neoplatonist Ralph Cudworth, the mind has certain intrinsic properties that enable it to interpret scattered and degenerate data of sense in terms of objects and their relations, cause and effect, whole and part, symmetry, gestalt properties, functions, and so on. Sense is like "a narrow telescope" that provides only fleeting and meaningless images. It is the "active and comprehensive power of the intellect" that determines the unity of objects, the "one comprehensive idea of the whole" that is the typical product of normal perceptual processes, and that evidently is much underdetermined by sensory experience. Sensation is degenerate and particular; knowledge is rich in structure, is of universals, is highly organized. "We have an infinite amount of knowledge of which we are not always conscious"; the innate general principles that underlie and organize this knowledge "enter into our thoughts, of which they form the soul and the connection, . . . although we do not at all think of them" (Leibniz).

This "active" view of acquisition of knowledge runs through the romantic period, as is well known. With respect to language, in particular, it achieves its most illuminating expression in Wilhelm von Humboldt's profound investigations, in his theory of speech perception as involving the activity of a generative system of rules and principles that underlies the production of speech as well as its interpretation, a system that provides for infinite use of the finite means of which it disposes. Similarly, acquisition of language, in his view, is largely a matter of maturation of an innate language capacity in directions that are determined by internal factors, by an innate schematism that is sharpened and differentiated and given its specific realization through experience. As a consequence, he holds that all languages will be found to be very similar in their grammatical form, when studied not superficially but with respect to their deeper inner structure. These innate organizing principles determine the class of possible languages just as the *Urform* of Goethe's biological theories defines the class of possible plants or animals. These principles provide the preconditions for the acquisition of language and for linguistic experience.

The active and passive views regarding perception and learning that have been elaborated with varying degrees of clarity since the seventeenth century can be made precise in several different ways and confronted with empirical evidence. Recent work in psychology and neurophysiology has been highly suggestive in this regard. Thus there is some physiological evidence for the existence of central processes in perception, specifically, for control over the functioning of sensory neurons by the brain-stem reticular system,[2] and behavioral counterparts of this central control have been investigated by psychologists for quite a few years. Furthermore, there is evidence for innate organization of the perceptual system of a highly specific sort at every phyletic level. The studies of the visual system of the frog by Lettvin and his associates,[3] the discovery of specialized cells, responding to angle and motion, in the lower cortical centers of cats and rabbits,[4] and the somewhat comparable investigations of the auditory system of frogs[5] are all relevant to the classical questions mentioned earlier. These studies indicate that there are highly organized, innately

[2] See R. Hernández-Peón, "Reticular Mechanisms of Sensory Control," in W. A. Rosenblith, ed., *Sensory Communication* (Cambridge, Mass.: M.I.T.–Wiley, 1961). For discussion of additional relevant material, see H. L. Teuber, "Perception," in J. Field, H. W. Magoun, and V. E. Hall, eds., *Handbook of Physiology—Neurophysiology* (Washington: American Physiological Society, 1960).

[3] J. Y. Lettvin *et al.*, "What the Frog's Eye Tells the Frog's Brain," *Proceedings of the Institute of Radio Engineers*, vol. 47, 1940–51, 1959.

[4] D. H. Hubel and T. N. Wiesel, "Receptive Fields, Binocular Interaction and Functional Architecture in the Cat's Visual Cortex," *Journal of Physiology*, 160 (1962): 106–54; and H. B. Barlow, "Selective Sensitivity to Direction of Movement in Ganglion Cells of the Rabbit's Retina," *Science*, 139 (1963): 414–15.

[5] L. S. Frishkopf and M. H. Goldstein, "Responses to Acoustic Stimuli from Single Units in the Eighth Nerve of the Bullfrog," *Journal of the Acoustical Society of America*, 35 (1963): 1219–28; and R. R. Capranica, *The Evoked Vocal Response of the Bullfrog* (Cambridge, Mass.: M.I.T. Press, 1965).

determined perceptual systems that are closely adapted to the animal's "life space," and that provide the basis for what we might call "acquisition of knowledge" in a quite specific way. Also relevant are certain behavioral studies of human infants, for example those of Fantz, on preference for faces over other complex stimuli,[6] and Bower, on the innate character of shape and size constancy as factors in perception.[7] These and other studies indicate that it is by no means absurd to suppose that complex intellectual structures are very narrowly determined by innate mental organization, and that what is perceived may be heavily determined by mental processes of considerable depth. Insofar as speech perception is concerned, the Humboldtian idea that the generative processes underlying speech production are involved in the interpretation of signals as well has reappeared in several different forms in recent years; and so-called "analysis-through-synthesis models" of speech perception are by now a commonplace.[8] There is, in fact, fairly good evidence that when a trained phonetician attempts to give a very accurate record of what he hears—a phonetic transcription of a perceived speech signal—this record is heavily influenced by his knowledge of the syntax of the language and by phonological rules of considerable abstractness and complexity, and is, to this extent, independent of the physical signal. And as far as language learning is concerned, it seems to me that a rather convincing argument can be given in support of the view that "first principles," intrinsic to the mind and quite

---

[6] R. L. Fantz, "The Origin of Form Perception," *Scientific American*, 204 (1961): 66.

[7] T. G. R. Bower, "Slant Perception and Shape Constancy in Infants," *Science*, 151, no. 3712 (1966): 832–34.

[8] M. Halle and K. Stevens, "Speech Recognition: A Model and a Program for Research," *I.R.E. Transactions in Information Theory*, vol. IT-8 (1962), pp. 155–59 (reprinted in J. Fodor and J. Katz, eds., *Structure of Language: Readings in the Philosophy of Language* [Englewood Cliffs, N.J.: Prentice-Hall, 1964]). See also much important work from Haskins Laboratories in New York. For a recent review, see A. M. Liberman *et al.*, "Some observations on the Efficiency of Speech Sounds," *Status Report on Speech Research*, November, 1965. See also P. Lieberman, "Intonation, Perception, and Language," Ph.D. diss., M.I.T., 1965.

independent of experience—a kind of universal *Urform*— provide an invariant schematism that is a precondition for linguistic experience and that determines the properties of the language that is learned in surprising detail. In the course of this lecture, I would like to sketch some of the ways in which such conclusions might be clarified and firmly established.[9]

Let us consider the question how investigation of language might provide evidence bearing on the mechanisms of perception and learning. One might adopt the following research strategy for the study of human mental processes through the use of linguistic evidence. A person is presented with a physical stimulus that he interprets in a certain way. Let us say that he constructs a certain "percept" that represents certain of his conclusions (unconscious, in general) about the source of stimulation. To the extent that we can characterize the percept, we can proceed to investigate the process of interpretation. We can, in other words, proceed to develop a model of perception that takes stimuli as inputs and assigns percepts as "outputs," a model that will meet certain given empirical conditions on the actual pairing of stimuli with interpretations of these stimuli. The perceptual model itself may incorporate a certain system of beliefs concerning the perceptual field, and certain strategies that are used in interpreting stimuli. We may also isolate other factors—e.g., organization of memory. Proceeding in these terms, we may try to construct a perceptual model such as (1):

(1)         stimulus →  | system of beliefs
                        | perceptual strategies  | → percept
                        | other factors

[9] For recent discussion of these issues, see N. Chomsky, *Aspects of the Theory of Syntax* (Cambridge, Mass.: M.I.T. Press, 1965) and J. Katz, *The Philosophy of Language* (New York: Harper and Row, 1966), and references in these books. For additional historical background, see N. Chomsky, *Cartesian Linguistics*, (New York: Harper and Row, 1966).

Concentrating on the system of beliefs, we can then inquire into the means by which it was acquired and the basis for its acquisition. We can, in other words, attempt to construct a second model, a learning model which takes certain data as input and gives, as "output," the system of beliefs which is one part of the internal structure of the perceptual model. Such a model must also have an intrinsic structure of some sort, and we may isolate for special study certain factors analogous to those which are appropriate to a perceptual model: specifically, a set of constraints on the nature of the system of beliefs that can be acquired, innate inductive strategies, and other factors such as, again, organization of memory. Proceeding in this way, we may seek to construct a learning model (2):

(2)     data  →  | constraints on form of belief-system
                 | inductive procedures
                 | other factors

                                    → system of beliefs

The percepts that are formed by the perceptual model are first-order constructs; we determine their properties by experiment and observation. The system of beliefs that underlies the formation of a percept is, then, a second-order construct, and the innate constraints and inductive strategies that must be postulated to account for the acquisition of this system, third-order constructs. At each level of abstraction we can proceed to formulate substantive hypotheses to the extent that we have achieved a degree of clarity on earlier levels. Under additional conditions that are interesting, but not here relevant, we can think of both the perceptual and learning models just described as attempts to analyze the processes of acquisition of knowledge (rather than belief) and the conditions under which they operate.

Returning to the notion of active and passive theories, we

can now distinguish these, in the case of perceptual theories, on the basis of the relative importance attached to systems of belief and to analytic mechanisms in a particular domain. Classical examples might be Cudworth and Coleridge at one extreme, James Mill or David Hartley at the other. Analogously, in the case of the theory of learning, we can distinguish between an empiricist and a rationalist view in terms of the relative importance assigned to initial constraints on the form of belief and to inductive procedures. Charles Sanders Peirce, for example, expresses a typical rationalist view when he points out the hopeless inadequacy of inductive procedures, observing that severe innate limitations on the set of admissible hypotheses are a precondition for successful theory construction, and that the "guessing instinct" that provides plausible hypotheses makes use of inductive procedures only for "corrective action."[10] On the other hand, an empiricist might hold that (apart from properties of the receptor system) only certain inductive procedures are innate, and that the mind is otherwise a *tabula rasa* at birth, all knowledge arising from sensation, association, analogy, and generalization. Particular views of this sort can be confronted with empirical evidence at the several levels of abstraction that I have just outlined.

Consider first the problem of constructing a perceptual model such as (1), that is a system that takes a physical signal as input and associates with it a percept, making use of its system of beliefs and its perceptual strategies. In the case of language, the input stimulus is a speech signal and, idealizing away from many complications that are here irrelevant, the "percept" will be a structural description of a linguistic expression—in interesting cases, a sentence—of which the input is interpreted as a realization. This structural description will contain the phonetic, syntactic, and semantic information associated with the input signal by the process of interpretation (it goes without

[10] C. S. Peirce, "The Logic of Abduction," in V. Tomas, ed., *Peirce's Essays in the Philosophy of Science* (New York: Liberal Arts Press, 1957).

saying that the processes involved are in general unconscious or beyond the level of consciousness, and that the information contained in the structural description may not be directly available to introspection).

Within the space of this lecture, I cannot give a precise account of how phonetic, semantic, and syntactic information is represented in a "percept." A few examples, however, should make the matter fairly clear. Consider the three sentences:

(3)
    (i) I persuaded John to leave.
    (ii) I expected John to leave.
    (iii) I told John to leave.

For each sentence, the associated percept will contain phonetic, semantic, and syntactic information. The phonetic information will be essentially that given in a good dictionary, for the individual words (adjusted with respect to dialect), along with a record of the intonational features and other modifications associated with the sentence structure as a whole. The semantic information must meet certain empirical conditions on paraphrase, implication, presupposition, necessary truth, and so on.

More interesting, for our purposes, is the syntactic information contained in the percept that is intuitively constructed by anyone who understands these sentences. At one level, these three sentences are the same in syntactic structure. In traditional terms, each contains the subject "I" and a predicate: "persuaded John to leave," "expected John to leave," "told John to leave," respectively. The predicate, in each case, consists of a verb ("persuaded," "expected," "told"), the noun phrase "John," and the embedded predicate phrase "to leave." Apart from questions of terminology, this description is quite accurate, at one level, and represents a part of the syntactic information—what we may call the "surface structure" of the sentences in question. The three sentences are very similar in surface structure. But if we think about these sentences more carefully, we see that they differ significantly in certain other aspects of syntactic structure—in what we may call their "deep structure." That the sentences differ in syntactic structure is evident from a consideration of their behavior under certain formal operations. For example, in normal conversational English the sentence "I told John to leave" can be roughly paraphrased as: "What I told John was to leave." But we cannot say: "What I persuaded John was to leave" or "What I expected John was to leave." Furthermore, the sentence "I expected John to leave" differs from the other two in that it can be paraphrased by: "It was expected by me that John would leave." But we cannot say: "It was persuaded by me that John would leave" or "It was told by me that John would leave."

The first two sentences differ from one another syntactically in a somewhat more subtle way. Thus "John" is the direct object of "persuade" in "I persuaded John to leave" but it is not the direct object of "expect" in "I expected John to leave." We can see this by considering the slightly more complex sentences: "I persuaded the doctor to examine John" and "I expected the doctor to examine John." Each contains the embedded proposition: "the doctor to examine John." Suppose, in each case, that this embedded proposition is replaced by its passive: "John to be examined by the doctor." The operation of passivization preserves meaning (in a narrow, but important sense of this term). Thus "I expected the doctor to examine John" and "I expected John to be examined by the doctor" are paraphrases. But consider the analogous pair: "I persuaded the doctor to examine John; "I persuaded John to be examined by the doctor." Obviously, these are not paraphrases.

If we think through what is implied by such examples, we see that in such sentences as "I persuaded John to leave," "John" is both the object of "persuade" and the subject of "leave"; whereas in "I expected John to leave," it is only the subject of "leave." These facts must be represented in the percept since, clearly, they are known unconsciously by the person who understands the speech signals in question. The knowledge

is unconscious and by no means available to immediate introspection—it has, in fact, escaped the attention of generations
of excellent and careful grammarians. But it is surely quite real,
as examples of the sort just mentioned clearly show. When presented to the native speaker, these sentences are interpreted,
instantaneously and uniformly, in accordance with principles
of structural organization that are known tacitly and intuitively, though not consciously; no training or instruction is
necessary to enable the native speaker to understand these
examples, although they may be quite new to him.

Such examples as these illustrate two significant points: first,
the surface structure of a sentence, its organization into phrases
of various types, does not necessarily reveal its deep syntactic
structure, which is in general abstract and not represented in
the physical form of the signal; second, the rules that determine
deep and surface structure and their interrelation, in particular
cases, must themselves be highly abstract, and are surely remote
from consciousness. In fact, there is no reason to suppose that
these rules and the formal structures that they manipulate can
be brought to consciousness.

Examples of this sort can be multiplied easily. They are
characteristic of all human languages that have been studied
with any care. A study of such examples constitutes the first
stage of linguistic investigation, as outlined above, namely the
study of the "percept." The percept contains phonetic and
semantic information, related through the medium of an underlying syntactic structure. This underlying syntactic structure
has a double aspect. It consists of a surface structure that is
directly related to the phonetic form, and a deep structure that
underlies the semantic interpretation. The deep structure defines a network of grammatical relations that, except for highly
simple cases, is obscured in the form and surface organization
of the signal. We may think of a language as a set of such percepts, hence as determining a certain sound-meaning correlation, the correlation being mediated through an intervening

syntactic structure of the kind just illustrated. The English language correlates sound and meaning in a particular way; the Japanese language provides a different sound-meaning correlation; and so on. The general properties of percepts and the mechanisms by which they are formed and related are, however, remarkably similar for the languages that have been carefully studied.

Insofar as evidence can be obtained regarding percepts, we can turn to the deeper question of formulating a perceptual model such as (1) that associates percepts with input signals; in particular, we can take up the problem of formulating the system of beliefs that is a central component in perceptual processes. In the case of language, the "system of beliefs" is what in technical terms would be called the "generative grammar" of the language in question; the system of rules that specifies the sound-meaning correlation for this language—the system of rules that generates the class of structural descriptions (potential percepts) that constitutes the language in question. Since the language has no objective existence apart from the internalized grammar, we can speak of the system of beliefs in this case as the speaker-hearer's knowledge of his language, and, with systematic ambiguity, we can speak of the "grammar of the language" as, on the one hand, the internalized unconscious knowledge and, on the other, the linguist's representation of this internalized system of rules.

This internalized grammar must assign structural descriptions to an infinite number of sentences. It must, in other words, provide for the fact that every language makes infinite use of finite means, in Humboldt's terminology. It is important to recognize, with Huarte, with the entire rationalist and romantic tradition of linguistic theory, that normal human use of language is characteristically innovative; that for the most part the sentences to which one is exposed in ordinary life are new, and are not related to those which have previously been used, in one's experience, in terms of any well-defined notion of "analogy" or "generalization." It is important to emphasize this truism, because this classical insight has been lost under the impact of the behaviorist mythology of the past half-century. But one can easily convince oneself of the truth of this remark by unbiased observation of facts that are readily available. For example, a careful look at today's newspaper should suffice to convince anyone that the range of sentences and sentence-forms (in any significant sense of this term) used in normal discourse is so astronomical in scope that repetition or "analogy" must be rather a marginal phenomenon. It is erroneous to describe language as a "habit structure" or as a network of associated responses, as it is to suppose that knowledge of a language is developed by analogy or generalization. Such assumptions, which have achieved the status of dogma through constant re-iteration, do not seem consistent with the empirical facts.

By investigating sentences and their structural descriptions, speech signals and the percepts to which they give rise, we can arrive at detailed conclusions regarding the generative grammar that is one fundamental element in linguistic performance, in speech and understanding of speech. Turning then to the next higher level of abstraction, we can raise the question of how this generative grammar is acquired. What, in other words, is the internal structure of a device, such as (2), that is capable of developing a generative grammar of the required sort, given the empirical conditions of time, data, and access?

From a formal point of view, it would be correct to describe the grammar that is internalized by every normal human as a theory of his language and, as noted earlier, a theory of a highly intricate and abstract form. This theory determines a sound-meaning correlation for an infinite array of sentences. It provides an infinite set of structural descriptions, each containing a surface structure that determines phonetic form and a deep structure that determines semantic content. This pairing of phonetic and semantic interpretations underlies actual performance, although obviously there are many other factors.

From a formal point of view, it would, therefore, be accurate to describe the child's acquisition of knowledge of a language as a kind of theory construction; and if we wish to understand how this acquisition of knowledge takes place, we should, I think, formulate the problem in these terms. Given highly restricted data, the child discovers the theory of the language of which this data is a sample. The child's knowledge of the language obviously extends far beyond any data that has been presented to him. His " theory of the language " has a predictive scope of which the data on which it is based constitutes a negligible part. What is more, the theory that he constructs actually leads him to reject a great deal of the data on which it is based. Thus the sample of language on which the child bases his intuitive conception of sentence structure is degenerate, in the sense that much of it must be characterized as irrelevant or incorrect. Normal speech consists, quite substantially, of fragments, false starts, blends, and other distortions of the underlying idealized forms. But it is remarkable that what the child learns, nevertheless, is the underlying idealization; and quite obviously he learns this without explicit instruction. The child acquires rules of sentence formation that identify much of what he has heard as ill-formed, and rules of semantic interpretation that identify much of his linguistic experience as inaccurate and inappropriate. It is this idealized system of rules that he uses for interpreting the fragments and distortions of normal speech, in everyday life. Furthermore, he acquires this knowledge at a time of life when he is not capable of a high level of intellectual achievement in other respects, and this particular accomplishment is, within a very wide range, independent of intelligence or of the particular and accidental course of experience. These are facts that a theory of learning must face.

A scientist who approaches phenomena of this sort without prejudice or dogma would conclude that the knowledge that is acquired must be determined in a rather specific way by intrinsic properties of mental organization, and he would then set himself the task of discovering the "innate ideas and principles" that make such acquisition of knowledge possible. Returning to Peirce's argument on induction and "abduction," mentioned earlier, we may ask: "How is it that man was ever led to entertain that true theory? You cannot say that it happened by chance, because the . . . chances are too overwhelmingly against the single true theory in the twenty or thirty thousand years during which man has been a thinking animal, ever having come into any man's head." Peirce is speaking of discovery of scientific theories. A fortiori, the chances are even more overwhelmingly against the true theory of each language having come into the head of every four-year-old child. Just as "if man had not the gift . . . of a mind adapted to his requirements, he . . . could not have acquired any knowledge," so if a child did not have a very severe restriction on the form of grammar, independent of any experience, he could not possibly acquire knowledge of a language—a grammar. The innate restriction on the form of grammar is a precondition for linguistic experience and is surely the critical factor in determining the course and result of language learning. Though the child cannot know, at birth, which language he is going to learn, he must know that it is one of a very restricted set of possible human languages, that its grammar must be of a predetermined form that excludes many imaginable "languages." His task, then, is to select the appropriate hypothesis from this restricted class; having selected it, he can use inductive evidence to confirm the choice, but it seems quite clear that no inductive principles could have led to this choice. Once the hypothesis is sufficiently well confirmed, the child knows the language defined by this hypothesis; consequently, his knowledge extends enormously beyond his experience, and, in fact, invalidates much of his experience—more correctly, characterizes much of his linguistic experience as deviant and not in accord with linguistic rules.

This formulation is, to be sure, somewhat metaphorical and

highly oversimplified. This language learning is obviously not an instantaneous process, as implied in this account, which must be understood only as a crude first approximation to a highly intricate course of events. Furthermore, I am using such terms as "know" and "confirm" in a somewhat special way. But there is, I think, no more appropriate terminology than this, and I think that this formulation does properly convey the flavor of what the child has accomplished and what we must suppose to be the basis for this accomplishment. In any event, the matter of terminology is of little importance. What is important is that we make every attempt to give a precise account of the innate principles that serve as a precondition for experience, of the "infinite amount of knowledge of which we are not always conscious" of which Leibniz spoke, and of the unconscious innate principles that determine the character of the acquired knowledge.

I might mention, incidentally, that Peirce saw nothing absurd about the supposition that a chicken, for example, "rummages through all possible theories until it lights on" the right one—although he rejects this view on empirical grounds and concludes that the chicken has "no faculty of thinking anything else." I am not, of course, suggesting that this way of talking is reasonable and enlightening because it is employed by a great philosopher, but rather, in this case, the converse.

The property of grammatical structure that is of primary importance in connection with the topics that I have been discussing is its abstractness—the fact, that is, that both the form and meaning of a sentence are determined by syntactic properties that are not directly represented in the signal, and that are related to the signal only by a long sequence of interpretive rules. It is this property of language on which the inferences I have suggested concerning mental processes ultimately rest. It is therefore important to be clear about just what is being proposed. Not many years ago, it would have been generally supposed that the process of sentence interpretation could be described in approximately the following way. A signal is received and is segmented into successive phonetic segments (with perhaps some overlap at the "edges"). Each phonetic segment is assigned to a phonological category in terms of certain invariant properties detected in it. The resulting sequence of phonological categories is again segmented into minimal semantic units of some sort, and successive operations of segmentation and classification will give, finally, an analysis into phrases of various types: nouns, verbs, noun phrases, predicates, and so on.

On the syntactic level, what can be derived in this fashion is what I have called "surface structure"—an analysis of a sentence into phrases, which can be represented as a proper bracketing of the sentence, with the bracketed units assigned to various categories. Thus the expression "The old man on the corner was waiting for the bus" would be analyzed into its successive words which would be categorized as article, adjective, noun, etc. It might then be resegmented into the four phrases "the old man," "on the corner," "was waiting," "for the bus," which are noun phrase, prepositional phrase, verb, and prepositional phrase, respectively. It would then be further analyzed into the subject phrase "the old man on the corner" and the predicate phrase "was waiting for the bus," and then the whole expression would be assigned to the category, sentence. On the phonological level, each word would be analyzed into successive segments, each identified in terms of certain invariant properties. This would be an exhaustive analysis of the structure of this sentence.

With such a conception of language structure, it made good sense to look forward hopefully to certain engineering applications of linguistics: for example, to voice-operated typewriters capable of segmenting an expression into its successive phonetic units and identifying these, so that speech could be converted to some form of phonetic writing in a mechanical way; and to mechanical analysis of sentence structure by fairly straightforward and well-understood computational techniques. But these hopes have by now been largely abandoned with the realization that this conception of grammatical structure is inadequate at every level. At the level of sound, phonetic representations are themselves in part a projection of surface structure, determined by complexly organized interpretive rules, and even insofar as they are directly related to the signal, it is not simply in terms of segmentation and criterial attributes. At the level of syntactic organization, surface structure indicates semantically significant relations only in extremely simple cases; in general, deeper aspects of syntactic organization are not representable by labeled bracketing, or by any formally marked feature of utterances. Rather, deep structures are related to surface structures by a sequence of certain formal operations, operations now generally called "grammatical transformations." Both at the level of sound and the level of syntax and meaning, the significant structural features of sentences are thus highly abstract and not recoverable by elementary data-processing procedures. It is this fact that motivates the search for central processes in speech perception and for intrinsic, innate structure underlying language learning.

The central notions of syntax, as can be seen from these considerations, are "deep structure," "surface structure," and "grammatical transformation." I should like to say a word about each of these notions.

Labeled bracketing of the sort just mentioned is an adequate representation of surface structure. The evidence for assignment of surface structure is largely phonetic; the surface structure must be assigned in such a way that the projection onto a phonetic representation by the interpretive phonological rules corresponds to the "perceptual reality"—to the representations that are provided by careful impressionistic phonetics. There is also evidence of another sort, from experimental psychology. For example, several years ago Ladefoged and Broadbent demonstrated experimentally that if a click is super-imposed on a speech signal and the subject is asked to identify the syllable on which the click falls, he will make consistent and rather curious errors.[11] An explanation for this fact was pro-posed by Jerry Fodor, and has been confirmed experimentally in experiments by Fodor and Bever.[12] Fodor proposed that what is involved in perceptual click displacement is a kind of gestalt principle, namely, that a coherent unit will resist disruption by an external physical event. In the case of speech, the coherent units are phrases of the surface structure; therefore, clicks should be perceptually displaced toward the boundaries of phrases, and the deeper the phrase boundary—the greater the number of phrases that terminate at this particular point in the labeled bracketing—the greater should be the attraction for the superimposed click. Subsequent experimental work showed, indeed, that one can read the bracketing of surface structure directly from the data on click displacement, in many cases.

In short, there is evidence of various sorts that labeled bracketing is an adequate representation of surface structure. But now consider the grammatical transformations that deter-mine surface structure from underlying deep structures. Consider, for example, the operations of passivization and interrogation in English. The sentence "John was examined by the doctor" has virtually the same deep structure as its paraphrase "The doctor examined John"—the same network of grammatical relations determines the semantic interpreta-tion in each case. One of the grammatical transformations of English is the operation of passivization which forms such structures as "John was examined by the doctor" from a deeper structure which also, in its essentials, underlies "the doctor examined John." Similarly, the sentence "Did the doctor

---

[11] P. Ladefoged and D. E. Broadbent, "Perception of Sequence in Auditory Events," *Quarterly Journal of Experimental Psychology*, 12 (1960): 162–70.

[12] J. A. Fodor and T. G. Bever, "The Psychological Reality of Linguistic Segments," *Journal of Verbal Learning and Verbal Behavior*, 4 (1965): 414–20.

examine John?'' exemplifies the same system of grammatical
relations, and is derived from a rather similar deep structure by
an interrogative transformation. Surface structure is a labeled
bracketing. Therefore, it follows that such operations as passivization and interrogation must produce labeled bracketings,
since each can form a surface structure (virtually—actually a
few further operations are involved). But notice that these
operations can apply in sequence; thus we can form the passive
question "Was John examined by the doctor?" by passivization followed by interrogations. Since the result of passivization
is a labeled bracketing, it follows that the interrogative transformation must operate on a labeled bracketing and must form
a new labeled bracketing. By a similar argument, we can show
that each of the many grammatical transformations of English
must be a mapping of labeled bracketings onto labeled bracketings. Just as many transformations may be terminal in some
sequence, so many may be initial in some sequence. We conclude, then, that the deep structures that underlie all sentences
must themselves be labeled bracketings. And, in fact, a labeled
bracketing is a very natural representation for the semantically
significant grammatical relations. It is a straightforward matter
to define such notions as subject, predicate, object, and so on,
in a very general way, in terms of formal properties of labeled
bracketings.

This argument is somewhat oversimplified, but it is roughly
correct, and when made precise and fully accurate, it strongly
supports the view that deep structures, like surface structures,
are formally to be taken as labeled bracketings, and that grammatical transformations are mappings of such structures onto
other structures of the same sort.

Of course, the labeled bracketing of a sentence that constitutes its deep structure will in general (in fact, invariably) be
different from its surface structure. For example, in the case
of the sentence "John is an easy person for us to please," the
surface structure will be a labeled bracketing of the sequence

of words as given, but the deep structure will have to indicate that "easy" is actually predicated of the proposition "we please John," or "we please that person," or something of this sort. Thus "easy" does not modify "person"—it is senseless to speak of a person as being easy; rather, the sentence "John is an easy person for us to please" asserts that for us to please the particular person, John, is easy. This fact must be indicated in the labeled bracketing constituting deep structure. It is, however, completely masked in the surface form.

Whenever a substantive proposal is made concerning the nature of grammar, it is possible to draw empirical conclusions about the class of possible and impossible languages. If it is correct to conclude that grammatical transformations map labeled bracketings onto labeled bracketings, many consequences follow at once. For example, we can conclude that a language may form interrogatives, as does English, by permutation of certain types of phrases, regardless of their internal complexity; but there cannot be a language that forms interrogatives by such formal operations as reflection of a string of symbols, that is, by reading the corresponding declarative from right to left. That there is no such language is certainly true. It is by no means obvious, however, on any a priori grounds. In fact, one might very well argue that structure-dependent operations such as passivization and interrogation, and all grammatical transformations, are inherently more complex than structure-independent operations such as reflection. It is therefore a non-trivial fact that natural languages use the principle of structure-dependent operations for relating deep and surface forms. This is a very simple example of an empirical consequence of some assumption about grammatical form. Continuing along these lines, one can draw highly restrictive conclusions about what can and what cannot be a human language, conclusions which must, of course, be tested against empirical evidence from a variety of languages.

It is possible to explore the empirical consequences of hypotheses about the form of grammar in a totally different way. During the past few years, very interesting investigations have been initiated, largely under the direction and influence of George Miller, exploring behavioral correlates of grammatical structure. For example, Miller proposed that the amount of memory used to store a sentence should reflect (to first approximation) the number of transformations used in deriving it. This assumption has been investigated in quite a number of experimental studies. For example, Savin and Perchonock presented to subjects a sentence followed by a sequence of unrelated words, and determined the number of these unrelated words correctly recalled when the sentence plus the sequence of words is repeated.[13] This number, they suggest, provides a measure of the amount of memory used in storing the sentence. The results showed a remarkable correlation of amount of memory and number of transformations; in fact, in their experimental material, shorter sentences took up more "space in memory" than longer sentences that involved fewer transformations.

Recently, Savin has extended this work, and has shown that effects of deep structure and surface structure can be differentiated, in recognition and recall, by a similar technique. He considered paired sentences with the same deep structure but different surface structures, one being more complex than the other in surface structure in a well-defined sense; and he showed that under the experimental conditions just described the paired sentences were indistinguishable, whereas if the sequence of unrelated words precedes rather than follows the sentence being tested, then the more complex member of the pair is more difficult to repeat correctly than the simpler member. His quite plausible inference is that sentences are coded in memory in terms of deep structure, although obviously surface structure must be analyzed in perception. When the unrelated words

---

[13] H. B. Savin and E. Perchonock, "Grammatical Structure and the Immediate Recall of English Sentences," *Journal of Verbal Learning and Verbal Behavior*, 4 (1965): 348–53.

precede the sentence being tested, these words use up a certain amount of immediate short-term memory; the sentence which is more complex in surface structure cannot be analyzed with the amount of memory remaining. But if the sentence to be tested precedes the unrelated words, it is, once understood, stored in terms of its deep structure, which is identical in the two cases. Therefore the same amount of memory remains, in the paired cases, for recall of the following words. This is an impressive example, highly tentative, of course, of how creative experimental studies can interweave with theoretical work in the study of language, and of mental processes in general.

Summarizing these remarks, if we investigate the form and meaning of sentences and if we pay careful attention to the characteristic creative aspect of language use, we are led to the conclusion that a person's knowledge of his language is representable as a generative grammar that is organized in the following way: it contains a set of *base rules* that define deep structures and a set of *transformational rules* that convert a deep structure into a surface structure. The grammar will then contain rules of semantic interpretation, which determine the meaning of a sentence on the basis of the intrinsic semantic content of its lexical items and the grammatical relations represented in the deep structure,[14] and it will contain rules of phonetic interpretation, which determine the phonetic form on the basis of the intrinsic phonological content of its minimal elements and the grammatical organization represented in the surface structure. The rules that form and manipulate these structures are highly abstract and, furthermore, meet certain formal conditions and satisfy certain principles of organization of a quite specific sort. One would certainly suppose that much of this structure is universal, and what information is presently

---

[14] Conceivably, these principles of interpretation are language-independent and therefore not part of particular grammars, but, rather, part of universal grammar. So little is known about this matter in detail today that it is pointless to hazard a guess.

available from detailed investigation of language structure seems consistent with this supposition.

Turning from the study of language as such to the study of mental processes, we can now see why it is reasonable to maintain that the linguistic evidence supports what I called earlier a strongly "active" theory of acquisition of knowledge. When we interpret sentences of the sort that I have given as examples, we are manipulating structures that have no point-by-point correspondence—indeed, nothing approaching such a correspondence—to speech signals and their parts. As I noted before, there is evidence that even on the level of phonetic representation, much of what is "heard" is determined by the system of rules and is, in this sense, partially independent of the signal, a conclusion that will hardly surprise anyone who attends to the fact that even highly degraded signals are, under normal conditions, interpreted instantaneously and with no consciousness of departure from idealized norms. Thus it seems to me accurate to say that the study of speech perception and of understanding of sentences leads to a perceptual theory of a classical rationalist sort, as represented, for example, by the seventeenth-century "Cambridge Platonists," mentioned earlier, who were impressed by the fact that our perception is guided by notions that originate from the mind on the "impulse from sense," and that provide the framework for the interpretation of sensory stimuli. I emphasize again that this is not a matter of conscious reasoning about ideas or impressions of sense; I refer, rather, to the most primitive form of interpretation of external stimuli. Furthermore, it is clearly not sufficient to postulate a store of "neural models" or "schemata" which are in some manner applied in perception (as in certain current active theories of perception). We must go well beyond this assumption and return to the Humboldtian view which attributes to the mind a system of rules that generates such models and schemata, on the occasion of sensory stimulation, the content of the percept so formed being determined, in significant respects, by the system of rules itself. We need not content ourselves with this vague and metaphoric account. A generative grammar, and a theory of speech perception that makes essential use of it, gives a concrete specification of the rules that operate and the mental objects that they construct and manipulate. Physiology is very far from being able to suggest physical mechanisms that may carry out the functions abstractly described in these terms, but to my knowledge neither psychology nor physiology provides evidence that calls this account into question or that suggests an alternative. In fact, as mentioned earlier, current work in the physiology of perception shows that even the peripheral systems provide an analysis in terms of complex properties of objects, and that central processes may significantly affect the information transmitted by the receptor organs.

Similarly, in the case of the theory of learning, it seems to me that the study of language supports a typically rationalist view and offers empirical evidence that empiricist theories of learning are incorrect. There has, in fact, been a very serious effort in recent years to develop principles of induction, generalization, and data analysis of various kinds, that would account for knowledge of a language—that would show how a grammar can be derived from a corpus. I think it is quite beyond doubt that this effort has been a total failure; that the methods and principles that were considered fail not for any superficial reason (e.g., lack of time or data), but rather, that they are intrinsically incapable of giving rise to a system of rules of the type that must be presumed to underlie the normal use of language. On the other hand, what evidence is now available supports the view that all human languages share deep-seated and highly abstract properties of organization and structure. These properties—these linguistic universals—can plausibly be assumed to be an innate mental endowment rather than the result of learning. If this is true, then study of language sheds light on certain issues in the theory of knowledge that are of very ancient vintage. Once again, I see little reason to doubt that what is true of language is true of other forms of human knowledge as well.

I have tried to suggest how one can move, in successive steps of increasing abstractness, from the study of percepts to the study of grammar and perceptual mechanisms, and from the study of grammar to the study of universal grammar and mechanisms of learning. There is one further question that might be raised at this point, namely, how the human mind comes to acquire the innate properties that underlie acquisition of knowledge. Here, linguistic evidence obviously provides no information at all. In the essay by Peirce from which I quoted earlier, he does go on to offer a speculation regarding this matter. He argues that "nature fecundates the mind of man with ideas which, when these ideas grow up, will resemble their father, Nature." Man is "provided with . . . certain natural beliefs that are true" because "certain uniformities prevail throughout the universe, and the reasoning mind is [it]self a product of this universe. These same laws are thus, by logical necessity, incorporated in his own being." Here, however, it seems to me that Peirce's argument is totally unconvincing, and offers little improvement over the pre-established harmony that it was presumably intended to replace. The fact that the mind is a product of natural laws does not imply that it is equipped to understand these laws, or to arrive at them by "abduction." There is no difficulty in designing a device (e.g., programming a computer) which is a product of natural law but which, given data, will arrive at any arbitrary absurd theory to "explain" these data. In fact, the processes by which the human mind has achieved its present state of complexity and its particular form of innate organization are a complete mystery—as much of a mystery as the analogous questions that can be asked about the physical and mental organization of any other complex organism. It is perfectly safe to attribute this to evolution, so long as we bear in mind that there is no substance to this assertion—it amounts to nothing more than a belief that there is some naturalistic explanation for these phenomena. The laws that determine the organization and structure of complex biological systems are unknown. In the case of evolution of mind, we cannot guess to what extent there are physically possible alternatives to, let us say, transformational generative grammar, for an organism meeting certain other physical conditions that humans satisfy. Speculation about such matters, for the time being, is likely to be rather vacuous.

There are, however, important aspects of the problem of language and mind that can be sensibly studied within the limitations of present understanding and technique. I think that, for the moment, the investigations that can be most productively pursued are those having to do with the nature of particular grammars and the universal conditions met by all human languages—what traditionally was called "universal grammar." Furthermore, I have tried to indicate how one can investigate the role of particular grammars in perception and the role of universal grammar in acquisition of knowledge of a language. In this area of convergence of linguistics, psychology, and philosophy, one can, I think, look forward to much exciting work in coming years.

# 2

# SOME REFLECTIONS ON THE NATURE OF CONSCIOUSNESS

BRIAN A. FARRELL

BRIAN A. FARRELL, *Wilde Reader in Mental Philosophy and Fellow of Corpus Christi College, Oxford, was visiting professor of philosophy at The University of Chicago in 1966. Much of his recent work has been concerned with the logical status of psychoanalytic theory.*

2

# SOME REFLECTIONS ON THE NATURE OF
# CONSCIOUSNESS

*Brian A. Farrell*

I PROPOSE to touch on certain aspects of a very large subject.
Consider the motorcyclist, Henry Smith. He came off his
cycle at speed and suffered a head injury, which resulted in a
loss of consciousness. Suppose that when we inquire at the hospital a few days later, we are told, "Yes, Mr. Smith has recovered consciousness fully; he is quite normal and there seems
to be no permanent damage." Suppose we pass on this information to Smith's friends and acquaintances, and in particular we
say, "Smith has recovered consciousness." What are we saying
when we say this?

It seems evident that what we are saying is that Smith is now
able to see, hear, and feel things in the usual way again, to tell
us where he is, to understand what is going on, to think and
imagine in his normal manner again, and so on and so forth.
And all this seems very straightforward. If this is what we are
saying—in telling everyone that Smith has recovered consciousness—then what we are saying seems quite unmysterious.
We are merely saying that Smith has recovered the ordinary
powers of seeing, feeling, thinking, and so on, which he possesses
and exercises as a human being.

But precisely *what* are we saying when we say *this*? What is
it to say that Smith can see and think again, and so on? What
*sorts* of powers are we here ascribing to Smith, and by implication to human beings in general? Obviously they are very complex powers indeed, and they differ considerably among
themselves. So let me cut down this vast and unmanageable
question to more tractable proportions. I shall do this by concentrating on *one* of these powers. The one I choose is that of

35

sight. This evening I am interested in our powers insofar as they can throw light on the nature of consciousness. I hope that, in spite of oversimplifying the question by concentrating on sight, we will be able to come sufficiently close to the essence of the problem to be able to notice what steps may help us to deal with it.

When, then, we say that Smith has recovered consciousness, one of the things we would ordinarily mean to say, in this context, is that Smith has recovered his power of sight—he is now able to see again. But what is it to say this? Now there is more than one way of answering this question. In this lecture I shall dare greatly. I shall consider one of these ways—namely, that which is likely to be offered by some workers in science. When asked what it is to say, "Smith is now able to see again," they are likely to answer by describing what we have good reason to believe is in fact the case *now* about Smith, which was *not* the case when he was unconscious. In giving this answer they would describe what, as a matter of fact, is now functioning and going on again in Smith's body which was out of action when he was unconscious; and what, as a matter of fact, happens when Smith actually exercises this power on any occasion and sees something. For ease of reference let us give this answer a name. Let us call it the biological-*cum*-psychological answer to the question, or the BP answer or story, or BP, for brevity.

I shall now try to indicate (repeat "indicate") what the bio-psychological answer looks like to our question about Smith's power to see. I need hardly tell you that there are different ways of doing such indicating; and that the particular way one chooses is bound to be somewhat arbitrary. However, my choice is controlled by the fact that we are concerned with the problem of consciousness, and hence I must present the BP answer in a way that helps to show how it is relevant to our problem. When I have given an indication of the BP answer, I shall go on to ask: How good an answer is it? How good is the answer that the scientific world presents to the problem of consciousness? I shall do this by stating and examining a very well-known, and even orthodox, *objection* to the BP answer—an objection that comes from some contemporary philosophers. I shall end with a brief reassessment of the scientific answer, and an indication of a road along which we may be able to resolve this fundamental issue in Western culture.

First, then, the BP answer. Consider a natural remark we may make to Smith's friends, "Smith is now able to see again." Let us refer to this for brevity as statement R, or R; and let us suppose for simplicity that it is true. What are we saying when we say R? A worker in the biological-*cum*-psychological fields may be inclined to answer this question in the following way.

Let us suppose that, before his accident, Smith had gone along to have a thorough medical examination. At a certain stage the physician came to the neurological part of the business, and at a certain point told Smith that he was now going to show him some familiar objects and ask him to say what they were. He then presented Smith with some familiar objects, one at a time, by bringing them into Smith's field of view. Thus, he showed Smith a pen, and asked, "What is this?" Smith answered, "A pen," or "It's a pen," or something of this sort. Likewise, when the physician presented him with an orange, or any other familiar object. The report of the physician would give us every reason to assert, or say, that "Smith saw a pen," or "Smith saw an orange," and so forth, when the respective object was presented to him. Let us call the statement "Smith saw an orange" statement S or S.

Now, given that S and R are both true, what in fact happened when Smith saw the orange, and what in fact is the case now that Smith is able to see again is a very long and involved story. It is a BP story with many quite crucial gaps in it, which we (BP workers) hope we may be able to fill in some day. But at present it is *very* incomplete, and in outline *could* run something like this.

When Smith was told in his medical examination that he was

going to be shown some familiar objects and asked to name them, this information prepared his central apparatus to handle or process the visual input in a certain sort of way. It set the apparatus, in the first instance, *to match* the input properties which are admitted via the sensory machinery. That is to say, Smith's apparatus is set to run over the pigeonholes, or classification boxes or categories that the central apparatus has acquired and or possesses; and it is set to find a category which fits the property or properties of the input. (If we take an empiricist line at this point, we will stress the acquisition of the categories; if, on the other hand, we take a rationalist and innate dispositional line on the matter [as Professor Chomsky did in talking about a child learning a language], then we will stress that the apparatus already possesses the categories in some form.) When, then, the object (say, an orange) was presented, Smith's central apparatus went into action in the way just outlined. As the orange was intended to be, and no doubt was, a familiar object to Smith, it was easy for the apparatus to find a fit—so easy, probably, that Smith seemed to the physician and to himself to say, "It's an orange," or "Orange" with smooth immediacy. Furthermore, the fit was such that it did not set off a hunt by the apparatus—with the aid of the sensory mechanism—for further features of the input source to test (or check) the categorical fit. In short, the fit achieved here was a good one.

Suppose, in contrast, that Smith had been presented with an object of which we would ordinarily say, "It looks very much like a small, orange-colored balloon." Then, in all probability, if the *first* fit that Smith's apparatus achieved of the input was "an orange," this first fit would have lacked the properties of a good fit; and it would have set off a hunt for further features of the input to test this classification. Now the central apparatus is so arranged, by its own self-controlling devices, as to aim at removing any incongruity between the features of the input and any classification made by the apparatus. So the apparatus would start a hunt for further features of the input with the aim of removing any incongruities between the features of the input and this first classification, "an orange." There are various ways in which it can do this. For example, by placing the input in a different category (ordinarily expressed by saying, for example, "It's really a balloon"); by categorizing the incongruent feature itself so as to make it normal and congruent (ordinarily expressed, for example, by "looks like a balloon, but it is really a very smooth orange"); or by amending and enlarging the system of classification boxes (or categories) available to the apparatus (and hence to Smith) so that the input is now congruent with the amended set of categories available.

When, therefore, we examine what in fact was the case and what occurred, when Smith saw an orange in front of him, we find that Smith's perceptual achievement here represents the outcome of what psychologists call "a decision process." Given a set of input features from the related object or source, Smith's internal apparatus has to decide whether the object is an orange, a balloon, a piece of yellow soap, or what not. We can make it intuitively obvious to the ordinary person that there is *some* sort of decision process at work by presenting him with an *un-familiar*, incongruity-producing object under poor illumination, or some other substandard conditions. We then ask him to tell us what he sees. His apparatus will begin by making some very indeterminate category fit; and he will see it as, for example, perhaps, "something round," "something wobbly," or "transparent," or the like. Then his machinery will start a feature hunt, plus test cycle, with the aim of achieving a good fit. It will probably decide next on a more determinate classification, which it fits provisionally (for instance "a round yellow solid-looking thing"). It will then hunt for further features to test this fit, and to approach a better one. The rest of the hunt-decision-test cycle may then be as follows: uneven surface and orange color—decide, "an orange"—test for incongruity feature of roundness—decide, this feature of input recategorized as "round but squashed look." The apparatus has now achieved a good fit, since testing is completed, and the hunt-decision-test cycle stops. What, therefore, Smith sees at the end of any one moment of achievement is the end product of the decision of his central apparatus at that moment. To begin with, he saw something round; at the end of the decision process, he sees an orange, And of course most of what constitutes one decision process goes beyond his own powers of self-scrutiny.

But all this (our biopsychological storyteller could continue) still presents a very inadequate picture of our psychological view of this problem. It is inadequate in more ways than one. It leaves out the developmental part of the story. We have concentrated so far on simple category placements, such as an orange; and hence on simple perceptual achievements. If Smith happened to be an orange buyer, it is quite possible that, when presented with an orange in his medical examination, he would classify it at once as "an early Outspan from South Africa," and hence see it as one. Here the decision process has led smoothly to fitting the input features into a small highly-determinate category box or pigeonhole. Next, observe that our presentation has underemphasized and not made clear what role the acquisition of speech and language plays in all this. Now, whatever the full and adequate answer here will turn out to be, one thing does seem to be clear. It is not possible in fact for Smith, or anyone else, to acquire and use the system of categories we have been speaking about—without also acquiring a mastery of the language involved in learning and applying these concepts. In this sense the system of categories or concepts is psychologically dependent on language. What does *not* seem to be clear, however, is the role of language *after* Smith has acquired the categories and is required to fit them on any given occasion. Thus, when his apparatus enables him smoothly to categorize an object as an orange, did it *first* have to get the word "orange" out of store *before* it could do the fitting, or did the two operations go on together, or can the category fit take place before the word "orange" is got out of store? This is a topic that is the subject of psychological investigation at the present time.

Such, then, is the barest outline of the biopsychological story we can offer at present—the story that tells what happened when Smith saw the orange. As we have emphasized, the story is very incomplete. One of the respects in which it is incomplete is that we cannot fill it out at present so as to describe in detail how the central apparatus does what our story says it does. Of course, we do know a great deal about the ways in which our central nervous system works; and especially do we know a great deal about the input end of the visual system. But we do not yet know how the central nervous system does the job of classifying the input in the various ways in which our story asserts it does. Nor, as we have already noted, are we at all clear how the category store is related to the verbal store that the apparatus can call upon. Hence, in its essential respects our story about what happens is at present neurophysiologically uninterpreted for the most part.

Well, now, what is our short answer to the original question? We were asked: What is it to say, "Smith is now able to see again"? (statement R); and we were also asked: What is it to say, "Smith saw an orange"? (statement S). Given that S is true of Smith, what happened was that, at his medical examination, Smith exercised his powers, in the way we have outlined, of handling visual input, and in such a way as to achieve the categorizing of one of the presented objects on this occasion as an orange. And this is *all* that we are saying in S. Smith's accident put his powers of handling and categorizing input out of action, in some way or other, for a time. Given that R is true of him, what is now the case about him is that he is once more able to exercise these powers of handling visual input in his usual way. And this is *all* that we are saying when we say, "Smith is now able to see again."

This answer to the original two questions has an additional merit. It can be generalized to some extent to cover powers *other* than sight. Thus, it seems likely that a similar story to the one outlined for sight can also be given of our power to hear, and, with modifications, no doubt, to all our other powers of handling sensory input. To say, however, that Smith has recovered consciousness is not only to say that he has recovered his powers of sight, hearing, etc. It is also to say that he has recovered his powers of thought, of imagination, and so forth. But these powers differ very considerably in character from the sensory ones. Thus, and very obviously, when Smith thinks out a problem or goes into a daydream, his central apparatus is not handling external input in the close way it does when it helps him to see an orange. But the story we have outlined for Smith's power of sight is strong enough to suggest how the story can be elaborated to cover these other powers of thought, imagination and the like. For instance, we can elaborate the story to include the shuttling and passing of input from one part of the central apparatus to another, and to allow for this input to be processed in various parallel and higher order ways. It is possible that we will be able to show at some future date that some specific elaboration of our original story along these lines is reasonably well-attested. If this happens, then we will be in a position to give a better answer to the question: What is it to say that Smith has recovered consciousness? We will then answer that it is to say that Smith has recovered his usual powers of processing and categorizing input, external and internal, in the ways made clear in our elaborated and well-attested story.

This, then, is a biopsychological (or BP) outline of an answer to our initial problem, which I said I would indicate to you. The next step in the argument is obviously for me to ask: Just what light, if any, does the BP answer really throw on the problem of consciousness? How good an answer is it? Many contemporary philosophers may be tempted, more or less strongly, to give the following reply here: the BP answer is a weak one, and not worth spending too much time on. When we assert S, they may say, we are obviously ascribing to Smith what would normally be called a "mental" achievement (he saw an orange). The concept of see that is used, or applied, here is obviously a mental concept. When we look at what the BP story is asserting, it is clear that it is ascribing to Smith a very complex bodily state and sequence of bodily events. The concepts of input processing, category fitting from store, and the rest are ways of referring (in structural and functional terms) to certain sorts of bodily reactivity—of which the full neurophysiological interpretation cannot yet be given.

Now, our philosopher may continue, there is one thing that is perfectly clear about the relation between S and the BP story. The relation between S and the BP story as a whole, or any part of it, is a purely contingent one. It may well be the case that, when it is true, the BP is also true, and conversely. But it is *not* the case that S entails the BP story or any constituent statement or statements in it; and it is also *not* the case that the BP story, or any constituents of it, entail S. That is to say, it is not the case that the BP story, or any statements of it, follow logically from S (in the way that the statement, "Socrates is mortal" follows logically from the statements, "All men are mortal," and "Socrates is a man"). Conversely, S does not follow logically from the BP story. Now these features of S and BP are very important. The scientific answer merely says that, if S, then in fact BP, and conversely. This answer does succeed in telling us *something* about what we are saying in S. It tells us what went on before and at the same time, what to expect when S is true, and what may lead us to doubt whether it is true. But these points apart, the BP answer does not tell us much about *what we mean to say* when we utter S. It does not do so because, and in particular, it is *sense* to assert S and yet deny BP. Clearly, if we are puzzled by what we are saying in S ("Smith saw an orange"), it does not help us much to be told that in fact Smith's central apparatus went through a certain performance—if it is *also* sense (as it is) to assert S along with, for example, "Smith has no central apparatus at all," or "Smith's brain consists of excellent ravioli." So the relation between statements S and BP is only a contingent one. The scientific answer tells us, in effect, that S implies BP. Accordingly, it does not do much to help us elucidate the puzzling nature of mental concepts, such as see and consciousness. Of course, we have considered a BP story that is admittedly very incomplete and inadequate; but a little further thought will show that the *same* objections would apply to any *future* BP story coming from the scientific world, no matter how definitive it may be.

This weakness in the scientific answer is apt to be overlooked. Hence, it is apt to come along with an apparent force that it does not really possess. Its weakness is apt to be overlooked just because we are inclined to take it as asserting a mutual entailment. When we are told that to say, "Smith saw an orange," is just to say that the BP story was the case, we are inclined to take this as asserting that S entails BP, and conversely. But this is just manifestly quite false. There is no identity or equivalence of meaning between them. It is perfect sense (as we have just noted) to assert S and yet deny BP, in part and in whole. So S does not entail BP. And it is also perfect sense to assert BP and deny that Smith saw anything, whether it be an orange or anything else. Thus, for example, it is easy to imagine some man-built hardware machine going through a BP process, and yet having no consciousness whatever, and hence not seeing anything either. In short, to say that Smith has recovered consciousness (statement R) is not *logically* to say anything about Smith's nervous system, its processing of input, or anything of the sort. And conversely. Likewise for statement S (Smith saw an orange). Hence the weakness of the BP answer from the world of science on the nature of human sight and consciousness.

Now this objection from some philosophers has almost been elevated into the status of an orthodoxy. Well, is this orthodoxy *in*vulnerable, unlike other orthodoxies? Or is there something just a bit preposterous about it somewhere, or somehow? From now on, and for convenience of reference, I shall refer to this objection as the orthodox objection, or the orthodoxy.

It is evident that it has two arms. The first is that S does not entail BP; the second is that BP does not entail S. Suppose we challenge orthodoxy to defend the first arm, not merely to proclaim it. Orthodoxy has some well-known moves it can make here—by way of defense—to exhibit the force of this first arm. I shall mention just two of them. Orthodoxy can invite us to play the game of the "historical suppose." Suppose we were all living in the days of Good Queen Bess. Suppose that I am the dear Virgin Queen herself, and that our chairman is Cecil. Cecil hands me a pen with which to sign some document that I do not wish to sign. I then turn to him and say, in my usual rasping and impolite way, "I see the pen. What wouldst thou have me do with it, dolt?" Now in the days of my reign, my good people did not know anything, or anything much, about nerve fibers, electrical impulses, category fitting, and the rest. When, therefore, Elizabeth makes this remark to Cecil, "I see the pen," she could not possibly have meant to say anything whatever about nerve fibers, etc. Yet we today do obviously understand her, and when Smith said, "I see a pen," he means the same today by the verb "see" as she did then. Hence it just cannot logically be the case that to say S (Smith saw . . .) entails BP.

Another and more sophisticated move by orthodoxy is this. BP purports to be a scientific story. Therefore, it is open to constant modification and amendment in the light of further scientific discoveries, like any other scientific theory. If S were to entail BP, it would follow that the meaning of S would alter with every modification of BP. But it is plain that the meaning of S does nothing of the kind. Hence what BP says is not part of the meaning of S.

Suppose we challenge orthodoxy to defend the second arm— that BP does not entail S. A well-known move here is to invite us to take another, closer look at S. When we do so (it is said), we will see that to assert S is also logically to assert statements such as the following:

(a) Smith was aware of an orange;
(b) Smith was conscious of an orange in front of him;
(c) Smith had the experience of seeing an orange.

That is to say, statement S entails statements (a), (b), and (c), and others of the same sort. Now consider some reactive system, say the machine which we have built to replicate ourselves, and to apply for the next vacant instructorship in the Department of Philosophy. It is perfect sense to say that a BP story is true of it when an orange is presented within the field of view of its visual receptors, and yet deny that statements (a), (b), and (c) are true of it. That is, BP here does not entail statement (a) or (b) or (c). These statements, therefore, are not part of the *meaning* of BP—they are not logically involved in it. But as we have seen, they *are* logically involved in the meaning of S. Therefore BP does not entail S. The full scientific story does not entail that "Smith saw an orange." Consequently, to assert S is *not just* to assert a BP story about Smith. It is *also* to assert, for example, statement (a) (Smith was aware of an orange), and so on. Hence, "to see an orange" is not just to go through a BP process. It is also to achieve other things as well—an awareness of an orange, the experience of seeing it, and the like.

These, then, are some of the moves that orthodoxy can make in its own defense. How strong is the orthodox objection to the BP answer? How good are these moves in defense of orthodoxy, and in criticism of the BP answer? It seems very doubtful whether the orthodox objection is anything like as strong as it looks, and very doubtful whether its defenses are good enough. Let us consider it by concentrating on the second arm (BP does not entail S), and on the defensive move that I have just outlined.

Orthodoxy tells us that BP does not entail S, because, e.g., to assert S is also logically to assert (a), namely, that Smith was aware of an orange. But when we assert BP of Smith, we are not logically committed to assert that Smith was aware of an orange. Now just what is it in this context to say that S entails (*a*)? Presumably, when we assert (*a*) in this context, we wish to say that some psychological matter of fact was the case—namely, that Smith was aware of an orange. Presumably, we want to say that Smith was in a certain psychological state—that of being aware of an orange—which he achieved at a certain time. So, quite clearly, (*a*) functions here as an empirical statement. Now the BP story tells us, *inter alia*, that what Smith did was to categorize the visually presented object as an orange. But it does not, apparently, tell us how it came about that *in addition* Smith was also aware of the orange as a matter of psychological fact. Very well, then, what *further* powers should we ascribe to Smith to accommodate this additional psychological fact—that of Smith's awareness? How should we modify and extend the BP story for this purpose? To these questions there is no obvious answer. Smith's awareness is an empirical matter —a psychological fact. Smith (according to the BP story) has the power to categorize the visually presented orange as an orange, along with related powers. But the BP story is alleged to be not enough to incorporate Smith's awareness. What, then, will be enough? Suppose we develop BP into a definitive story at some time in the future—will it then be enough? No, because (as we have seen) no BP story, however good—and therefore no scientific story—will entail (*a*), and the other statements. The same difficulty, therefore, will arise about any improved version of BP

The answer, then, is that *nothing* will logically be enough or sufficient to meet the objection of philosophical orthodoxy. It is not logically possible to do anything to extend our biopsychological story to accommodate Smith's power of becoming and being aware of an orange. Likewise for this power of being conscious of, of experiencing what it is like to see an orange, and so on.

But by now it is becoming plain that the statements (*a*), (*b*), and (*c*) are functioning very queerly indeed in this context. It is now far from clear just what the orthodox objector is saying when he says that S entails (*a*), for example. He appears to treat (*a*) as an empirical statement, which ascribes a psychological state or achievement or both to Smith. But yet it is a state or achievement which is *not* open to empirical investigation, and whose relations with Smith's ordinary psychological states, etc., are necessarily left in complete darkness in perpetuity.

It may help us to appreciate the queerness of the use of "aware of" in this context if we contrast it with a use of this expression in an ordinary context in everyday life. Suppose, for example, that we are at a party and you think that Brown has had too much to drink. Someone has dropped an orange in the middle of the floor, and at one point Brown stumbles across the room just missing treading on the orange. You say, "Look at that—Brown did not even see the orange." To this I may reply, "No, no, you're wrong. Brown was aware of the orange." In this context I am saying that, in spite of your belief to the contrary, Brown did actually see the orange when he crossed the room. I make this point by saying, "No, Brown was aware of the orange." There is nothing puzzling about *this* use of the expression "was aware of." But when the defender of orthodoxy uses the expression "aware of" in statement (*a*), he is trying to make a very different point. He is using it to contrast Smith, when the relevant BP story is true of him and he is *unaware* of an orange, with Smith when the BP story is again true of him and he is *aware* of an orange. But this now seems to be an empty contrast, and therefore a bogus one. When we threw out the request: "Do tell us about this *additional* empirical psychological state, or achievement, by Smith when he is aware of an orange, in contrast with when he is not," we found ourselves being plunged into darkness. Naturally so, if there really is no further, genuine psychological state or achievement to add.

There is another related way—and to philosophers a very

familiar way—of bringing out the oddity, the queerness of statement (*a*) in this philosophical context. Consider again the ordinary context I mentioned where I say of Brown at the party, "No, no, he was aware of the orange." Suppose you are doubtful about the truth of my remark. You can then check it (typically) in the usual ways. By asking Brown himself, by asking others whether they noticed if Brown had looked at all in the direction of the orange, and so on. Now consider the philosophical context. Suppose that we all know that the relevant BP story is true of Smith. Then we are told that statement (*a*) is *also* true of him. What steps can we take to find out whether it is or not? Suppose we do the obvious thing we can do with Brown. We *ask* Smith; and he says, "Yes, of course, I was aware of an orange." This answer from him *looks* just like the answer we had from Brown, and so looks like a helpful answer. But this is a mistake. Smith's answer will not help us at all. Why not? When we ask Brown and he says, "Yes," etc., what we obtain from him is evidence that he did notice the orange as he crossed the room, that he distinguished it from its background and untidy surroundings, that he realized what it was, and so on. In other words, what we obtain from Brown is evidence that he did categorize the object in his field of view as an orange. In short, we obtain further evidence that the BP story is true of him. However, when we ask Smith, and he says: "Yes," etc., what have we obtained from him? It looks very much as if all we have obtained from him is further evidence of the same sort as we obtained from Brown. It is evidence to the effect that Smith was going through the relevant BP process at the time. But if this is so, if this is all we have obtained from Smith, then this answer from Smith is useless to orthodoxy. For orthodoxy wants evidence that, *in addition* to going through a BP process, Smith was also aware of an orange. It seems logically impossible to extract evidence to this effect from his "Yes" answer. His answer, therefore, is very different from Brown's and does not help orthodoxy.

This result suggests a very obvious conclusion. The concept of "aware of" in the philosophical context of statement (*a*) is meant to function as an empirical concept; and statement (*a*) itself is meant to function as an empirical statement. Yet, when we try to establish or verify whether (*a*) is true of Smith, it seems to be logically impossible for us to do so. Clearly, there is something very queer, if not downright incoherent, about an empirical concept whose putative application in any instance we can do nothing to establish or verify. And what applies to statement (*a*) also applies, *mutatis mutandis*, to statements (*b*) and (*c*), and any other similar statements in defense of orthodoxy.

At this point a supporter of orthodoxy has an important retort. "If we are tempted to think that statement (*a*) in the philosophical context really ascribes nothing to Smith, then our temptation probably arises from the fact that the argument has so far concentrated almost exclusively on statements in the third person. We have spoken of Smith and Brown seeing oranges, and so forth. But I, too, under appropriate circumstances can truly say, 'I saw an orange.' So can you, and so can all those of us with normal vision. Now because we can each and all say this truly, we each and all know full well what it is to be aware of something. Hence we know full well what the orthodox position is referring to by its use of the expression 'aware of.' It is using the expression to refer to a mental state with which we are all acquainted—one which we all know what it is like to be in. To imply or argue that it refers to nothing at all is just sheer obtuseness or pigheadedness. It amounts to denying that we have any awareness of anything at all, and any conscious life or experiences as well. Which is the sort of thing that philosophical Behaviorists, and other philosophical oddities like Farrell, apparently believe. And all this is so patently false as to be laughably incredible."

Will this retort in defense of orthodoxy do? Will it help? Alas, probably not at all. It is generally agreed that there are, or seem to be, important logical differences between first- and third-person statements—differences connected with problems of verification, incorrigibility, whether we should describe first-person statements as psychological reports or not, and so forth. First-person statements, therefore, raise important issues at the present time. But it is doubtful whether these issues have an immediate bearing on the use of first-person statements *here* in defense of orthodoxy. Whether we regard them, for example, as primarily declaratory reports, or as primarily expressive in character, they run into the same snag.

Let me try to indicate briefly what this snag is. Orthodoxy is quite right to remind us that each and most of us, under appropriate circumstances, can say truly, "I saw an orange." Now we are told that, because we can say this, we do each and all of us know what it is to be aware of something; and it is *this* state that orthodoxy uses the expression "aware of" to refer to. But just what is it to say, "I know what it is to be aware of something"? At this point it can be argued with great cogency that the relevant part of what I am saying is that I am able to distinguish between my condition when, for example, I am sound asleep, and my condition when I am fully awake and taking in something that is going on at the time. But to say I am now able to draw or make this distinction, and this sort of distinction, is to say that I am able to apply the category of "my being aware of something" to my input and reactivity so as to achieve a fit. In contrast, a small child cannot apply this category yet; and a schizophrenic suffering from a breakdown in his concept of selfhood may not be able to do so either—because, though aware of and apparently taking in what is going on, he may not be able to categorize his own input and reactivity "as mine." Hence, when I apply the category of "my being aware of something," I am going through part of a BP process. If we use the statement "I know what it is to be aware of something" to refer to this BP activity of mine, then the statement raises no problems. But then it does not help orthodoxy either. For this is not how orthodoxy wishes to use the statement. It wants to use it in such a way that, though I may be doing and achieving category fitting to my input and reactivity, I am *in some further additional state* of being aware of something, of an orange, or what not. And it is only if orthodoxy *does* use it in *this* way that it can serve the purposes of orthodoxy. But now, of course, the same difficulty breaks out for orthodoxy about my first-person statement ("I saw an orange") as arises with third-person statements. This, then, is why it is far from certain that the resort to first-person statements does much, if anything, to get orthodoxy out of the difficulty it is in when it claims in this context that S entails (*a*) (namely, Smith was aware of an orange).

Can we uncover what the general difficulty is that orthodoxy keeps on running into here, when it tries to defend its second arm (BP does not entail S "Smith saw an orange") by arguing that BP does not entail (*a*) ("Smith was aware of an orange")? It seems clear that in asserting that BP does not entail (*a*), orthodoxy is not breaking any of the rules or norms of ordinary language. Nor is it speaking falsely. It is indeed the case that in ordinary English BP does not entail (*a*). But when orthodoxy says this here, it runs into the difficulty that it is then using statement (*a*) to ascribe to Smith some incoherent empty state. For it uses the expression "aware of" to refer to a state that is an *unding* in some way—it uses it in such a way that its reference is vacuous. This strongly suggests that our ordinary use of expressions such as "aware of," "conscious of," etc., contains within it a vacuous component. Part of what we mean by, say, "aware of" is something quite ordinary and matter-of-fact-like. This is the part we emphasized in speaking of Brown at the party being aware of the orange; and the part which philosophers emphasize when they protest that even Behaviorists have an awareness of the world around them, and of their thoughts and feelings. But another part of what we mean by "aware of" is something very unordinary and ineffable. We also want to use the expression to refer to a curious "*undinglich*" state, or non-property. As soon as we emphasize this use of the expression, take this part of its meaning seriously, and try to pin it down, we are plunged into the void—as Wittgenstein has shown with the penetration of genius. But it is this vacuous component of our ordinary use that orthodoxy emphasizes in arguing that S entails (*a*). Hence its weakness at this place.

But what of the other half of the orthodox position—the first arm of the objection to the scientific answer on the nature of consciousness? The argument, you will recall, was that S does not entail BP, in whole or in part. (It is quite sense to say that Smith saw an orange, and yet deny that BP is true, in whole or in part. Hence, what we are saying in BP is not part of the meaning of S, and therefore tells us little about it.) Now the first arm of orthodoxy runs into trouble to which both parties to the problem seem to have contributed, philosophers and psychologists. When some scientific workers present BP, they appear to agree with the orthodox claim that S does not entail BP. For they present their BP story as a set of empirical statements purporting to describe what in fact went on at the time when Smith saw an orange. But this will not do at all. For it is easy to argue that, while S does not entail *some* statements of the BP story, it certainly entails *others* And, if this is so, then it just will not do to produce the big, over-all thesis that S does not entail BP.

Consider one of the important constituent statements of BP. "Smith categorized the visually presented object as an orange." Is it true that "Smith saw an orange" does not entail this statement? Let us test the matter. Let us say, "Smith saw an orange but Smith did not categorize the visually presented object as an orange." Does this joint statement make sense? No doubt one *could* argue that it does—ordinary language being such a flexible and imprecise business. But one would have quite a job on one's hands. For this joint statement *seems* absurd. It seems absurd because, on the ordinary use of "see" (which we are using in this context), for Smith to see an orange is logically for him to identify the visually presented particular as an orange;

and for him to do this seems logically for him to categorize it as an orange (on the BP use of this technical term). This important part of the BP story, therefore, seems to be logically tied to S. It is not just a contingent matter that, when S is true, this part of the BP story is also true. Professor Bruner, the Harvard psychologist, has written that "All perception involves an act of categorization"; and he presents this as if it were an empirical discovery.[1] Which seems to be a mistake. Professor Bruner's statement is a logical truth about human perception. Consequently, it would appear to be a mistake to argue that S does not entail BP, just like that, without qualifications.

But this is not the end of the matter. Let us look at an example of a very different type of statement from BP: "Smith saw an orange by means of his eyes." Let us call this statement D. Now if S does not entail BP as a whole, then S does not entail D. This is an awkward fact for orthodoxy to swallow. There is a bad, fishy smell about it; and orthodoxy seems to be uneasy and divided on the matter. Of course, we can all agree that the verb "to see" is a very complex and slippery customer, and what is to count as "the use of an eye" will differ in different circumstances, and so forth. But, when all this is said and done, and we make the necessary refinements to exclude the irrelevancies, and so forth, a very good case can be made out for saying that our ordinary *present* concept of see is such that to say "Smith saw an orange" in his medical examination *does* logically commit us to say that he did so by means of his eyes. For us to say, in this context, of Smith that: "He saw an orange all right, but not by means of his eyes" would be to say something logically odd. The listener is likely to think he had misheard us, or that unwittingly we were not using English correctly, or something of the sort. The onus would be on us to explain what on earth we meant.

Now notice what happens if we reject orthodoxy here, and say that S *does* entail D (that "Smith saw an orange by means

[1] Bruner, J. S., "On Perceptual Readiness," *Psychol. Rev.* (1957), *64*, No. 2, 123–52.

of his eyes"). We find ourselves at once on an instructive logical slide. To say that Smith saw by means of his eyes is to say he saw by means of his eyeballs; to say this is to say he saw by means of his retina; to say this is to say he saw by means of what is an expansion of the optic nerve fibers, and to say this is to say that he saw by means of nerves of sight connecting the retina with the brain! (If you should think that I am just foisting the Queen's English on you, and being a little linguistic imperialist from Britain, look up your own *Webster*!—you will find it all there.) In other words, once we assert the first step, S entails D, we find ourselves being logically committed by ordinary Americanese to make several other BP statements—including a statement that refers to Smith's brain.

Why is this slide instructive? There is a general feature of scientific discovery, with various ramifications, to which some attention has been given in recent years. When a discovery is first made about something—for example, when we first discover the atomic weight of chlorine—we express this discovery in a straightforward, empirical statement, which we treat as open to falsification. But after a time, a change takes place in our treatment of this statement. We find ourselves incorporating the property of the atomic weight into our concept of chlorine. Then, if we meet a new sample of what is *apparently* chlorine, and it does *not* have the atomic weight of chlorine, we do not reject our original discovery. We say, for example, "Oh, it can't be chlorine after all." In short, our concept of chlorine has undergone modification through the incorporation into it of some of the discoveries we have made about it. Now, when we find ourselves logically forced to slide from "see" to "brain," we do so because we have incorporated our well-attested discoveries about parts of the BP story into our ordinary concept of see. You will recall that the orthodox position tells us it is perfect sense to assert S, and yet deny that Smith has a brain at all, perfect sense to assert S and also to declare, say, that his brain is made of good ravioli. What makes these remarks, and others like them, preposterous is that they overlook the feature of concept modification we have just noted. These remarks overlook *either* that the ordinary concept of see already incorporates certain statements from the BP story, *or* that it is in the process of conceptual change that will incorporate them —a process which makes such remarks just sound ridiculous.

Indeed, the pressure to change coming from the world of science and being exerted on our ordinary mental concepts is great, and will almost certainly increase. I suspect—as I have already mentioned elsewhere—that if one were to investigate the ordinary mental concepts (see, hear, think, etc.) used by scientific workers in the biopsychological field, one would discover that their concepts had already undergone considerable change, and that they were already operating in their ordinary lives with concepts very different from those used by the plain man, and many contemporary philosophers. For instance, though the plain man probably does not use "see" so as to entail that Smith saw by means of the striate area in his cortex, we may find that the technicians in the field do use the concept in this way. Of course, scientific discoveries may force us into developing what are, in effect, *two* sets of mental concepts, the one ordinary or popular and the other technical. When Harvey first stated that the heart was a blood pump, this statement was an empirical discovery about the heart. Today it has become part of the ordinary concept of heart; and it is unclear whether or not we should say that there are now two concepts of heart in our culture, the popular and the technical. On the other hand, we should say this, perhaps, about the concept of boiling. When little Jimmie says, "The water is boiling, Mummy," we would deal with this statement by elucidating its ordinary and its technical force and their mutual relations. Should any question arise as to what this statement logically commits us to say about the world, then the technical concept is likely to be given priority. Similarly, then Jimmie says, "Mummy, I am panting after that run." And we are in no particular confusion about all this. I commend to the attention of philosophers the issues generated by contact between culture areas with different concepts—the issues of conceptual conflict and change.

The upshot, then, is that the first arm of orthodoxy will not do either. It will not do to say S does not entail BP, for two reasons. S does entail *some* statements of BP; and our ordinary concepts are not static, but undergo change, especially perhaps under the pressure of scientific discourse and discovery.

With this conclusion behind us, let us take a quick look at the two defenses of orthodoxy I mentioned. We are told that, because Queen Elizabeth had no knowledge of nerve fibers, category fittings, and the like, therefore her statement about the pen did not logically commit her to anything of this sort. This is a mistake. Insofar as her use of "see" was the same as ours, then it did also logically commit her to *certain* statements about bodily reactivity—namely, that she categorized the input as a pen (even if no one at the time realized that this was a logical consequence of her assertion). But it is probably wrong to suppose that her use of "see" was *exactly* the same as ours—that her concept is ours. For her use probably did not entail, for example, a reference to the optic nerves; whereas ours appears to do so. However, even if she had had our knowledge of the nervous system when she said, "I see the pen," the declarative point of her remark was not to refer to anything neural. But neither is it when Smith says, "I see a pen." The declarative force or point of this statement by Elizabeth is to report or express a piece of internal reactivity on her part—namely and roughly, that she had identified the immediate source of the input as a pen. Likewise for Smith. But to realize this is also to realize that what we ordinarily call "the meaning of this statement" can be unpacked and put into the context of Elizabeth's and Smith's total reactivity at the time. Just how this last step is to be done in detail is far from clear; and I am happy I do not have to deal with it in this context. But I hope my remarks on this point are sufficient to show that, though the game of historical suppose may seem impressive, it is confused and lacks much force.

We are also told by orthodoxy that BP is not part of the meaning of S, because BP is a scientific story and hence would expose S to constant changes of meaning—which plainly do not occur. But, again, this defense of orthodoxy will not do. It is simply not the case that, as a scientific story, BP will expose S to constant change—the threat is fictitious. For all that will be incorporated *in fact* into the meaning of the words and concepts in S are the firmly attested, established, and important results of scientific inquiry. Our ordinary use of, for example, "see" would no more be at the mercy of the latest scientific discoveries about the details of the neurophysiology of vision than is our ordinary use of "heart" at the mercy of the latest discoveries about the details of cardiac functioning. BP would only expose S to the threat of constant change if S entailed BP as a whole. But the scientific story about the nature of consciousness, to which orthodoxy objects, is not committed to this large claim. It is clear that this second defense of orthodoxy does not upset the lesser, but key, contention that S entails BP in part. Hence this defense does not help to support the orthodox view that the relation between S and BP is a purely contingent one.

I said that I would end with a short reassessment of the scientific BP answer to our questions about statements R and S, and the nature of consciousness.

What, then, are we to make of the BP story? We are told that to say S ("Smith saw an orange") just is to say that certain complicated biopsychological events took place (with Smith exercising certain powers, and so forth). We are told that to say R ("Smith is now able to see again") just is to say that he is now able to exercise these powers again in the usual way, etc. I hope it is clear from the analysis I have presented that this scientific answer has important weaknesses. It is a confusing answer—it muddles us. As we have seen, it is unclear whether it is saying that S (or R) entails BP, or merely that when S (or R) is true, then what BP describes happens to go on at the same time. The answer tempts us into orthodoxy, and so into rejecting it as wrong—wrong on the grounds that it leaves out the *essential* thing we want to say of Smith when we assert S and R of him, namely, that he *saw* and can *see* again, and is *conscious* once more. Moreover, the strategy of this scientific answer is quite misguided. Even with the qualifications sufficient to remove any suggestion of pretentiousness, it is a premature answer; and it tries to give the big answer, the large answer, to the problem all at once. But the problem is not all of one logical piece. What is required is that we break it down into more manageable parts, and approach it with modesty.

But what of the strength of the BP answer? Where can it help? It seems plausible to suggest that a BP answer, which embodies the future discoveries of science in this field, will help to change our ordinary concepts of see, hear, etc., in such a way as to eliminate the vacuous component we detected in these ordinary concepts. This change would cleanse the atmosphere of a dark fog that has enveloped us for some time; and it would achieve a great simplification of the intellectual scene in the West. The strength of the BP answer also lies in the promise it holds out to us. It promises in the future to give us technical concepts that will stand to our ordinary mental concepts in the sort of way in which the technical concepts of physics seem to stand to our ordinary concepts about the material world, or the technical concepts of the physiology of respiration stand to our ordinary concepts of breathing, panting, and so on. When Smith goes to Mexico City and we say of him, "He started panting and breathing deeply on arrival," we are quite happy to accept the physiologist's account of what it is to say this. We employ no philosophers to step in and ask, "But does this statement about Smith entail any statements about Smith's body, and if so what ones?" Similarly, when we have an adequate BP story about Smith's mental functioning, we will be happy to accept this scientific answer to questions about statements

S and R. As a philosopher I would then be largely redundant and unemployed—and that would be splendid! So the BP story holds out a fascinating intellectual picture for us. It is one in which we humans appear as organisms processing input, external and internal, at different levels, under changeable self-guiding controls. Within this complex ongoing activity, it will be possible to distinguish very precisely, and in neurophysiological detail, the actual operations of Smith's decision process —a process that culminates in his fitting the input from an orange to the category of an orange. Our conscious life will then consist for us in the beat, rhythms and fluctuations of our reactivity in processing and dealing with input in this sort of way.

I think it was in one of his Epistles to the Corinthians that St. Paul said: "I shew you a mystery." I hope that this evening I have done a little to dispel what is sometimes called "the mystery of consciousness." I have tried to do this by turning the mystery into a problem, and then by holding out to you a vision of a scientific and conceptual future in which the problem will not arise.

# 3

# THE TWO FACES OF PERCEPTION

JOHN R. PLATT

JOHN R. PLATT *has published, in addition to his technical work in physics and biophysics, a number of essays on social aspects of scientific creation. Some of these have been collected in his books* The Excitement of Science *and* The Step to Man. *He is research biophysicist and acting director of the Mental Health Research Institute at the University of Michigan.*

3

# THE TWO FACES OF PERCEPTION
*John R. Platt*

T HE NATURE of perception has always been one of the hardest
things in the world to explain. We are too close to it to be
able to see it clearly. The problem is somewhat like the problem
of the fish who went up to the fish-scientist and asked him to
explain the sea. The fish said, "What is this sea you scientists
talk about? You say you are practical and you believe in objective things, in what can be seen and touched. Well, if there is
such a thing as the sea, if it is real, point it out to me. Show me
where it is." And the fish-scientist is supposed to have had a
hard time answering him.

Actually, of course, a fish must understand quite a lot about
the resistance of water and where the top and bottom are. A
two-year-old child knows quite a lot about the ocean of air
around him which cannot be seen or pointed to, but which
pushes on kites and clouds and which he can blow into a balloon. The problem of perception, however, is far more subtle.
The ocean of perception, in which we live and move and have
our being, not only cannot be pointed to, but its resistance cannot be measured nor its motions felt. Perception is so simple
anyone can do it, yet it is so universal and so indivisible that
the philosophers have written their longest and most contradictory treatises in trying to explain it.

However, I have begun to suspect that this problem may be
like the old problem of "motion," which the medieval philosophers also wrote long and involved treatises about. We now
realize that their trouble was that they had the wrong concepts,

The work reported here was supported in part by a grant from the United States
Public Health Service to The University of Michigan.

the wrong language, and no experiments. Once Galileo and Newton had straightened out the concepts of momentum and force and acceleration, any bright adolescent could learn to calculate the motions of pendulums and projectiles quite accurately. In the analysis of perception, I think the new experimental and theoretical work that is now coming out of the biological and psychological laboratories may straighten out our concepts in much the same way, and may likewise open the door to a new era of understanding.

This could be of the greatest importance to us. Perception has two faces, the subjective and the objective. The objective world is easy to talk about. This is the ordinary world of common speech, of things that can be pointed to, for which we have developed a public language, with nouns and verbs that every child understands. It is the subjective world that has been hard to discuss, and even embarrassing. Objective science shrinks from it, as from religion. Its important elements cannot be pointed to; and for its more general and personal elements we often have no publicly agreed-upon terms at all, or only misleading ones, like "heart" and "soul" and "self," derived from ancient theologies and mental theories.

Yet this is the area where primary perception lies, and knowledge and judgment and will. What else is the main concern of our efforts with our children? If we impose on them the terms of a medieval philosophy, they may get as twisted in their lives as if we tried to teach them physics in terms of vortices and phlogiston. I think a better understanding of the true relation of the subjective world to the objective world, both for parents and children, might help us to cure many of our personal and social misdirections. It might help all of us to plunge more deeply and satisfyingly into the real, instead of using up our lives in struggling to reach pseudo-goals that are by their very nature will-o'-the-wisps and unattainable. Perception is the first thing we experience and the last thing we understand. It is the beginning of knowledge and also, in some sense, the end of it. A more accurate understanding of perception might change our individual and social relations as dramatically as a more accurate understanding of motion a few hundred years ago changed our technological achievements.

It will be evident that I come to these problems as a physicist and biophysicist. I worked for many years on the theory of the colors of organic molecules, then more directly on the physics of perception and the optical and electrical aspects of vision, and more recently on how the visual network or any "sensory-motor decision-network" like the brain can organize its information so as to know something about the regularities of the external world. There is a larger body of interest by physical scientists in such questions than most people realize. The physics of perception has not been fashionable in this century, but in earlier times many physicists worked on it, from Kepler to Kant and from Maxwell to Mach. What can a man or an organism know about the world and his relation to it? How can an organism perceive? Or more fundamentally, how can matter think? These are epistemological and philosophical questions, but if we are to find twentieth-century answers for them, modern physical thinking must contribute, as well as modern biology and psychology. The answers may even be important for physics. For, as the quantum theorist David Bohm has emphasized, physics "is basically a mode of extending our perception of the world," and the elementary operations of physics are insecure to us unless we can demonstrate that they are consistent with the elementary operations of perception.

Recently a number of physical scientists have come forward with a personal "operational" approach to perception which fits in particularly well, I think, with our new views of the brain and of neural networks, although it has been misunderstood by most physicists. This approach was foreshadowed by Ernst Mach eighty years ago in his book *The Analysis of Sensations*, which influenced Freud. It has now been developed in several different ways by Percy Bridgman in his final book, *The Way*

*Things Are*; by Erwin Schrödinger in *Mind and Matter* and in the epilogue to *What Is Life?*; by Michael Polanyi in *Personal Knowledge*; and by David Bohm in the appendix on "Physics and Perception" in his book *Relativity*. Support for this new personalism from the biological side has also been given by the biologist George Wald and by the neuroanatomist Roger Sperry in their chapters in *New Views of the Nature of Man*.

What I want to do here is to outline how some of the recent experimental and theoretical work on neural networks and perception can be fitted together with these personal and operational views so as to give a more coherent and operational theory of perception. I want to show how we can go step by step from the objective scientific evidence to its application in interpreting the subjective phenomena of perception, just as we can go from the objective study of eyeballs and cameras to the interpretation of the subjective phenomena of our own eyesight. When this kind of connection is made explicit, it can clear up many of the linguistic difficulties and can be the basis of a more accurate grammar of perception than we have had before. And I believe, as we shall see, that the results can even illuminate many of the great subjective insights of the saints and philosophers, which can now be restated in more objectively derived and less paradoxical language.

## OBJECTIVE MODELS OF THE BRAIN

### Objective Models as Subjective Mediators

Perception, like any other field, can be approached from various starting points. But I think it is important not to begin, as so many have done, either by trying to imagine the blank mind of a baby, or else by trying to imagine what "primary sensations" we are "really" having right now. These traditional approaches beg the very questions we want to answer. I think we encounter the fewest difficulties if we start simply and objectively from where we are now in relation to each other, that is, from this present conversational reality where we talk together as persons educated in a common culture, speaking or reading our common public language of description and abstraction and persuasion, about things that can be pointed to and described in common objective terms.

If we do this, it is then a fairly easy and convincing jump to the interpretation of at least some of our subjective experience. To demonstrate this, take the case of eyeballs and eyesight. We all believe, of course, that we do have eyeballs like those of other men, eyeballs through which we see the objective world, and which are the "mediators," so to speak, of our subjective visual experiences. But have you ever asked yourself the question, "How do I *know* that I have eyes—or a head or a brain— when I cannot see them?" In some ways, it is a childish question, so simple that the proofs are familiar and are confirmed daily and hourly. Yet it is important as well as entertaining to spend a little time to see how the proofs go, because the eyeball example is the prototype, I believe, of the way in which other types of objective evidence (like that on neural networks) can be used in interpreting other aspects of subjective experience.

Our proofs for the existence of our own eyeballs are of three types. First, from witnesses; second, from physical analogy; and third, from our own senses, including touch and the visual evidence of shadows and mirrors. Thus, for witnesses, I can take unsophisticated children one at a time, and test their veracity on other objects. "Billy, does the dog have eyes?" "Yes." And he points to them. He should know!—for I pointed them out to him just last week, saying, "Those are the dog's eyes." (We are a consistent language community.)

"And do I have eyes?" "Yes." And he points again, in a certain unique direction. And I can make the same test with Tommy and Jack, and they all say the same. And I know that they are eager in checking each other, and that they are reliable in pointing out dogs, which I can see; and airplanes behind my

head; which I can turn and see. So it seems reasonable to believe that they are talking about something objective when they
talk about and point in this funny direction to my "eyes,"
which—as they will be sure to tell me!—I can *not* turn and see
for myself.

The second argument is from physical analogy, where I note
that I interact with light bulbs and with sunlight in much the
same way that I see another person's eyes interact. A card or a
piece of glass interrupts or distorts the light for Billy and for
the camera, and for me; so I can believe that the principles of
optics, and of image-forming lenses like theirs, determine at
least some aspects of my subjective experience.

The third and strongest line of evidence for my eyes comes
from my own senses. I touch my hair, face, nose, eyelids, lashes,
eyeballs, and find them all like Billy's. I can see my nose from
two unique perspectives, and see my finger touching it, and I
can see my own lids and lashes, even if they are rather blurred.
And on the wall or floor I can see shadows of my head, hair,
nose, and eyesockets, and of one eyelid closing as I close it.

The mirror evidence provides especially strong confirmation
and detail. I look in the mirror and I see Billy's body and clothes
and eyes repeated there, and Billy's every movement is copied
simultaneously by this mirror-Billy. But then beside him in the
mirror, I see that other body, wearing *my* clothes, and copying
*my* finger-movements as I touch my nose, and copying *my* eye-
lid-blink, though it has a head and hair and eyes that I have
never seen directly. And I know the laws of the mirror and I
can infer that I do have eyes, as Billy does, even when the mirror
is not there.

The sharing of language is the first proof that men are equivalent, but whenever I think about the conclusiveness of the detailed evidence from mirrors, I wonder whether the mirror may
not have changed the self-understanding of men more than any
other invention after language. In the mirror, even a tyrant
realizes himself to be another man, and naked. It must have

exerted throughout history a steady pressure for humility and democracy.

## Knowledge of Brains

I have gone into these types of proof because I think they can be extended to our central question here, which is how our brains work and whether this can throw any light on our subjective aspects of perception. We cannot see our own brains in a mirror or examine their internal workings—although a psychologist or neurosurgeon, if he had to cut into our heads, might tell us something about our electrical potentials or structural abnormalities. But we can examine in considerable detail how the brains of animals work and how those of other people work, and this may give us a good deal of analogical understanding. Most of what I have to say here is based on this kind of detailed objective examination of brain models and theories.

It is true that our knowledge of the brain is very incomplete. Probably it always will be, because the human brain, with its vast number of something like $10^{11}$ nerve cells or neurons—a hundred billion or so—and with its interconnections or synapses between these neurons perhaps a thousand times more numerous still, is the most complicated thing that man has ever tried to study. Man's genetic apparatus in his chromosomes, which determines the growth and interrelation of all the structures in his body, is among the most complex in the animal world. But his individual brain is far more complex even than that, because it somehow enfolds in addition all of the specific richness of his individual experience and all that he knows or dreams or creates of science and religion and literature and human relations. I think that the brain may go on being studied long after physics and chemistry and all the rest of biology have become as clear as Euclid's geometry.

Nevertheless, I think our partial new understanding of the brain today, though still rudimentary, may have finally put us us on the right track in understanding perception. Many of the recent experiments on the brain show a new and close relation to some of our subjective experience. And even where this evidence is still incomplete, it can be explained and pieced out with some new theoretical models which bridge the gap and which are very illuminating indeed.

It may be helpful to describe the theoretical models first. Good theoretical models are not to be despised. They often play a crucial role in simplifying a complex problem. Galileo's idealization of the "free body" and Newton's "point particle" were what first made physics tractable. For the brain, one of the influential early models was Descartes's automaton obeying physical and chemical principles, with nerve channels carrying inputs to the center for decision.

In the last few years, the most fruitful theoretical models of man and man's brain have been those derived from feedback and communications theory and systems theory. Norbert Wiener proposed a model of the organism as a cybernetic or goal-directed system. He said that in trying to lift a glass or catch a rabbit, a man or an animal gets back sensory inputs or feedbacks that measure the distance from the goal, and that these sensory signals are then amplified by the muscles so as to close the gap. There are different goals at different times, but each response is like that of the stabilizing or goal-seeking response of an electrical feedback circuit, or of a target-seeking guided missile.

Some of the higher operations of the brain have also been modeled by computer systems. The most sophisticated attempts of this sort would include the pattern-perceiving machine or Perceptron of Frank Rosenblatt, and the theorem-proving and general problem-solving machines of Allen Newell and Herbert Simon, which can search for theorems in geometry or can teach themselves in successive trials to play a better game of chess. Today these mechanical-electronic systems still operate on a "single channel" of inputs, or on only a few channels; but some day we may begin to make more complex systems, with "parallel processing" of thousands or millions of multiple input channels, and when we do, I believe their capacity for distinguishing patterns and producing alternative responses may become astonishing.

In addition to these models with real "hardware," there are also today some more generalized theoretical models of "general systems" and of "concrete living systems," as discussed by James G. Miller and others. These are attempts to examine in a general way the relations among the subsystem components that every living system must have to survive—such as information channels, memory, decision centers, motor outputs, and reproductive elements—and to study the relation of the subsystems and the system itself to the "supersystem" or environment, in what Simon has called the "architecture of complexity."

## The Brain as a Sensory-Motor Decision-System

But the model that I think is particularly illuminating for the perception problem combines several of these features in a "sensory-motor decision-system." This is the kind of model that is diagrammed in Figure 1. On the left side the three small

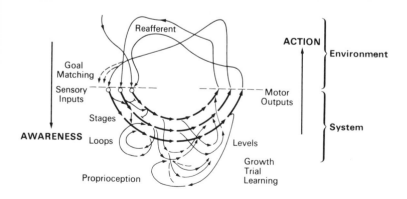

Fig. 1. A sensory-motor decision network interacting with the environment

circles represent the thousands or millions of sensory receptor cells, like the rods and cones of the eye or the auditory hair cells of the ear. The successive heavy arrows moving downward and away from these receptors in curved arcs represent the neurons and their interconnections in successive stages or echelons of the nervous network. The most direct routes of this sort might be "reflex arcs." They end in heavy terminal arrows on the right side of Figure 1, which are supposed to represent the thousands or millions of amplified motor outputs, making muscular motions, glandular secretions and the like, which influence the environment or external world. The bottom half of Figure 1 could be thought of as a very schematic diagram of the eye, the brain, and the right hand, as seen from above.

The lighter curving lines from the output region on the right side of the diagram, curving upward across the top of the figure and around to the left again, represent the physical motions and other effects in the external world which are again detected and checked by their optical and other signals to the sensory cells, which in turn feed back into the system network for another round of analysis and outputs.

We will discuss the various features of this diagram in more detail later. But it is clear that two extreme kinds of such sensory-motor decision-systems can be distinguished: non-learning systems and learning systems. The non-learning system is essentially what is found in insects. It is a system entirely, or almost entirely, "wired up" or "preprogrammed" in advance by the creature's genetic instructions during growth and development, so that it can find the right food and the right kind of mate and build the right nest automatically from the moment it emerges from the cocoon, without the necessity for the individual organism to learn any new responses from its experiences. The responses of such creatures can only be changed phylogenetically, in the species as a whole, by the Darwinian mechanism of small individual variations, with natural selection of those more successful in survival and reproduction.

Learning systems, on the other hand, are typical of the higher mammals and human beings. It is obvious that they must be built on a large preprogrammed base, such as our internal autonomic nervous system which regulates heartbeat and breathing and digestion, and our sensory-motor reflex arcs, which make us blink or pull back almost uncontrollably from a burn or a blow. But the more complex behavior of human beings is almost entirely learned behavior, which has its own kind of internal natural selection. The system is capable of making variable responses to a given situation and is able to assess these responses and to repeat those which are successful from some point of view, and to stop making those which are unsuccessful. The new learned behavior has to be acquired and shaped within the individual. Undoubtedly this is the major reason for our long childhood, as well as for our adaptability to new environments and for our creativity in situations we have never met before.

## Reafferent Stimulation

One of the important features of this model is that it is able to fit in a considerable body of recent experimental evidence about the mechanisms that humans and animals use for perceiving and validating and adjusting to the external world.

For example, it has now been found experimentally by Robert Ditchburn and his co-workers and by Lorrin Riggs and his co-workers that constant motion of the eyeballs is necessary for visual perception. The motions are too tiny and fast to be seen by the unaided eye. Their amplitudes are only about one minute of arc and their frequencies are in the range from 50 to 150 cycles per second. Nevertheless, if they are compensated by optical or electronic devices so that the image is exactly stabilized on the retina, vision disappears within a fraction of a second. Presumably the motions produce varying inputs which prevent the retinal cells from becoming fatigued, or adapted. This explains, incidentally, why we cannot see the blood vessels of our own eyes, although they lie in front of the retina; their shadows stay fixed in the same place, so that the sensory cells become adapted to them and they do not appear in vision. "Vision is an a.c. phenomenon and not a d.c. phenomenon," as Ditchburn has said.

But this is a particular and very simple case of the more general "reafferent stimulation" that Richard Held and his co-workers have now shown to be absolutely necessary for early visual learning in animals and for adaptation to visual distortion in human subjects. Reafferent stimulation is the kind of visual or other stimulation, or set of new input signals, that comes from the environment as the result of the system's own motor outputs, as indicated in the environmental arcs at the top of Figure 1. (This differs from the "proprioceptive" signals which come back internally from the muscles and indicate their state of activity. These are symbolized by one of the light lower arrows traveling from right to left across the bottom of the diagram in Figure 1.)

Held's experiment of the "passive and active kittens" is a particularly convincing demonstration of the need for reafferent stimulation in learning. In this experiment, two kittens are kept in the dark after birth, except for a few minutes each day when they are placed in an apparatus where one kitten pulls the other around. They both have the same variation of visual patterns when they are in this apparatus; but for the active kitten, these variations are the result of the kitten's own muscular movements, while for the passive kitten they are unrelated to the muscle movements. After a few of these experiences in the apparatus, if the kittens are tested near the edge of a table or "visual cliff," it is found that the active kitten braces himself or draws back from the edge; while the kitten whose visual experiences have been passive acts as though it could not see or interpret the edge, and may fall over.

Held's experiments on human visual adaptation confirm these results. Students are asked to put on distorting glasses that tilt or rotate the visual field. It is found that they can adapt or correct rather rapidly for the distortion if they are allowed to move themselves about for a few minutes, or perhaps to wheel themselves about the campus in a wheelchair with the glasses on. But if they are only passively moved or wheeled about, they do not adapt.

These various experiments seem to prove that the images or signals that come into the brain from the external world are required not to be either stationary or randomly moving, or they will be either invisible or uninterpretable. They can be seen and organized and corrected only if some essential additional information or regularities have been provided by the relation between the changes of these signals and the system's own motor manipulations.

## *Functional Geometry*

I think a reafferent-stimulation mechanism of this kind can also help us to explain an old puzzle. This is the puzzle of how the somewhat random cells of the individual retina, differently arranged from one individual to the next, can arrive at a common and highly precise geometry of the external world. How can we see straight lines, or parallel lines? And how can we agree on their straightness and other regularities so exactly?

Part of the answer, of course, is that the eye has certain built-in pattern-perception and invariance-detecting mechanisms. This was demonstrated by recent work on frog vision by Jerry Lettvin and his co-workers, and it has been confirmed by the discovery of the "edge-detectors" in the visual cortex of the cat by David Hubel and Torsten Wiesel, and by the discovery of velocity-detecting cells in the retina itself by Horace Barlow and co-workers.

But I think that these pattern-organizing elements, although they form a base for the structuring of higher processes, are still on too small a scale and too individually variable to answer a large geometrical question such as, How can we see straight lines? I have therefore suggested that a different mechanism is also needed, a mechanism which probably involves scanning the eye along the line, at least during the learning stage or testing stage. If the image of the line falls on one set of cells in the retina when the eye is looking at one end of the line, and if the image can then fall on the same set of cells when the eye swings and looks at the other end of the line, this shows that the line has an invariance about it—a "straightness-invariance"— which an S-curve or other curve would not have.

It is easy to see that such a mechanism could also pick out the invariances associated with parallel lines, or with equidistant repeated lines or patterns, like those in wallpaper or a fence, and even the invariances of circles, if the eyeball rotates about its optic axis (as it does); so that the retinal tissue in this way can measure off and organize all the three-space regularities of the external world. I call this method "functional geometry" because it involves the dynamic functioning of the system. Whether this is the method actually used by the eye is not certain, and some generalization is surely necessary; but it could be used by an artificial system, and it has certain extremely interesting and suggestive properties. For one thing, it is radically different from the static locus-of-a-point methods of Euclidean geometry or Cartesian geometry. Euclidean geometry is "string geometry," based on the figures drawn with stretched string, with constant string lengths and fixed points and stretched lines. Cartesian geometry is "box geometry," with previously known reference axes or planes at right angles, and ways to measure $x$ and $y$ distances. But the eye has no stretched strings or fixed points or known straight lines or right angles or measures of length, so it is reasonable that it should use some much more primitive and dynamic method like functional geometry to avoid having to depend on these artificial prearranged construct-axioms of the other geometries.

The simple and powerful thing about functional geometry is that it can generate its basic elements by the simplest possible dynamic test: invariance under displacement. What could be simpler for the muscles than a very roughly directed displacement? What requirement could be simpler for a network than it merely be able to indicate when a pattern is the same as one before? Functional geometry is very similar in its operations and invariance-tests to the methods used in the highest-precision machine work and optical work. In discussing these, the physicist John Strong has said, "The methods of highest precision are all *primitive* methods." Is not this the kind of method a biological system would be likely to evolve, which would give it maximum precision with minimum requirements?

## The Search for Invariances

It seems possible that the dynamic search for invariances may even be a general principle of organization in the higher-order processes in the brain. Dynamic invariance means that motor activity leads to feedback through the external world into the sensory inputs again, as indicated by the curved arrows traveling from right to left at the top of Figure 1. If the sensory inputs are not the same as they were before, there can be some goal-seeking or goal-matching activity until the invariance is established—until, for example, the eye is being moved along the straight line by the muscles again. But this will then be a self-maintaining loop, with repeated stimulation and interconnections along the same channels, that is, with maximum "reinforcement" built up for *this* kind of muscular response to *this* kind of stimulus pattern.

Recently, the physicists Peter Putnam and Robert Fuller have conjectured that self-reinforcing and self-maintaining loops of this sort may also be characteristic of the internal network structure, somewhat like the earlier "ringing" loops postulated by the psychologist D. O. Hebb. Such loops are diagrammed in the bottom half of Figure 1, along with some other higher-level interconnections. Each loop established

would represent a new functional regularity "discovered" by
the system in the environment or, more exactly, in the system-
environment relationship. Once a loop is established, it might
be opened and closed—turned off or on—by the chemical or
other state of the organism; perhaps closed whenever the system comes back to the initial state or condition under which the
loop was first established.

Several authors have reached rather similar formulations of
these higher-order problems. The search for invariants has been
called "invarianting" by Bohm, to whom I am indebted for a
long correspondence on these problems; he compares it to a
mathematical "rotation" or "diagonalization" of the "sensory-
input matrix." The biophysicist Peter Greene has compared
the jumping between states of the system—or between Gestalts,
or perhaps self-reinforcing loops—to the jumping between the
holistic quantum states of an atomic system. There may also be
higher-order families of loops, such as the families of muscle
motions generated, say, in scanning familiar or regular patterns.
Or conversely, as Putnam and Fuller say, the higher-order loops
may provide an alternation or other mechanism for resolving
conflict between lower-order loops. This "intersection" of
lower-order loops could be the "bisociation" which Arthur
Koestler, in his book *The Act of Creation*, has proposed as the
basis for the creative act.

Anatomically, any such perceptual growth to higher-order
patterns would demand continual neurophysiological growth,
with some random variations, among neural interconnections.
This is suggested in Figure 1 by the dashed lines near the
bottom, which might suggest potential new trial connections
ready to form and be tested for their fit into self-stabilizing
loops.

We see that the "most interesting" regions of the network,
the regions having the most points of conflict and of novelty of
interconnection, the regions at the "growing edge" of creativity and change, might be where the highest-order loops of

this kind are in process of formation. This would be where the accumulated knowledge of the system is combined with an ever changing search to solve new dilemmas. These regions would form creative centers of control and decision among all the less complex subprocesses that are being used and fitted together. Such creative control centers are perhaps as close as we can come objectively to the location of a central "will" or "soul" in such a decision-system.

Sperry has emphasized that such higher-order centers can properly be spoken of as controlling their lower-order processes, rather than just being controlled by them. He says:

> [Just as] a molecule is in many respects the master of its inner atoms and electrons . . . [so] when it comes to brains, remember that the simpler electric, atomic, molecular, and cellular forces and laws, though still present and operating, have been superseded by the configurational forces of higher-level mechanisms. At the top, in the human brain, these include the powers of perception, reason, judgment and the like, the operational, causal effects and forces of which are equally or more potent in brain dynamics than are the outclassed inner chemical forces. . . . .

It is interesting to note that a decision-system of the type we are describing cannot observe itself very accurately, in spite of its numerous internal sensors and loops of various sorts. The growing edge will always be hard to relate to or to specify in terms of any of its other established knowledge. The system may be able to make useful new interconnections—just as organic evolution does—without knowing how or why or being able to predict or justify them. "Consciousness will always be one dimension above comprehensibility," as the biochemist Gösta Ehrensvärd has said. If this kind of network is like our brains, then for our creative activity we simply have to trust the "wisdom of the body"—which is in this case the neuroanatomical wisdom of the mind—to lead us to functional regularities and understanding and organization of our system-and-world beyond what we know how to analyze.

## Properties of the Models

### Properties of Functional Geometry

Before turning to the main question ahead of us, which is how these objective models and theories of brains might be related to our subjective experience, it is important to spend a little time examining some of the rather unusual and unexpected properties that these models have.

Take functional geometry, for example; or any other dynamic-invariance method of detecting geometrical relationships in the field of view. It is easy to see, first, that such a method is independent of the location of individual retinal cells, and second, that it is independent of their sensitivity. The method only requires that when the eye is scanned from one variant region to another, the invariants fall on the same set of cells after scanning, whether the individual cells are left or right, good or bad—or even missing, as in the "blind spot." I think this gives us at last the explanation of why straight lines or other patterns are seen as continuing right across the blind spot. What we "see" are not the raw signals from the image, but their invariances. We do not see objects, but relationships.

But in addition, the method of functional geometry is independent of distortion of the image on the retina—or on the visual cortex of the brain, where the projection is known to be split and twisted. For as the eye scans a straight line, the image of one end of the line may fall on a distorted or crooked curve on the retina; but if the image of the other end of the line after the movement continues to fall on the *same* crooked curve, then the line is invariant—which means straight. It is sometimes forgotten by visual theorists that the brain has no separate microscope to look at the retina, or at the cortex, to see whether the image is geometrically straight; all it can know is what it can determine from functional operations, like invariances, within the network. It is obvious that mechanical twisting or spatial distortion of the network inside or crookedness of the network patterns in space make no difference to perception as long as the interconnections are unchanged. (This must be so, simply because of the great anatomical and folding differences found at autopsy between the brains of different persons who could see equally well.)

What is defined by such a functional method of perception, therefore, is not geometrical regularities in the internal world but regularities in the external world. The variations from one person to another—genetic variations in network geometry between parent and child, or developmental variations from the child to the grown man, or variations in the shape of the image, or in the anatomy of the retina or cortex, or in the internal structure of the network—all become irrelevant. This theoretical method thus fits what we know experimentally: that two persons, such as you and I, can both look at a line independently and decide whether it is straight or not, and that we will usually agree within the accuracy of our visual focusing. And this is not just a "nominalist" test connected with the fact that society has called such lines by a special name; it is a uniqueness property of these unusual lines, which I believe would cause us both to single out such lines for special attention even if society had never given them a name before.

Regularities determined by such a method are therefore regularities in an objective and *public space*, in spite of the fact that the representation of them is carried out entirely in a private network. This is an extremely important capability for biological organisms to have. With functional geometry, the brain's representation of the external world can "transcend individual anatomy," as Held has put it. Obviously this is not only valuable for individual survival but is a necessary requirement if different people are to be able to point to similar things and to discover in common the external regularities. It is a necessary requirement in order to have ostensive definition, so that the very different eyes of the ignorant baby can be counted on as seeing something of the same sort when the mother

points with her finger and says, "Light!", and so that shortly
the baby is able to point with his finger and to say "Light!"
too. And this transcendence of individual anatomy, finally, is
what is required if we are to have a public language in which
by ostensive definition we can agree on labels and linguistic
symbols for the common features we see in the external world.
It is satisfying to have a theoretical approach that at last can
account for this precise interpersonal transcendence.

### The Elimination of Maps

Another feature of this kind of decision-system using functional invariances is that it does not need to contain any
"models" or "maps" of the external world. It does not need
any little physical models of faces or mountains in the brain, to
correspond to those faces and mountains "out there." The supposed maps have been one of the difficulties, I believe, with
many analyses of perception. Here is a biological organism,
formed of somewhat irregular arrangements of tissue cells, dis-
similar to the external milieu and having rather poor connections with it—connections which a learning organism would
not know how to interpret anyway, at first. How can such a
system form any map of the environment? Or, supposing that
it could, who would read it or who would be able to check it?
A little homunculus inside? Does he then have to have a brain
like ours? And inside his brain, another map of the map?
And another smaller homunculus to read that, and so on and
on?

I know that there are proponents of this approach who would
say that the homunculi—or the clusters of neurons that they
represent—just get simpler and simpler, until the last one disappears in a neural pulse or two. But I do not think this has
ever been a very satisfactory conclusion, because it gives the
highest or most abstract functions the least intelligent control,
involving the fewest neurons and the least reliable subsystems.
And it does not in any way get around the initial difficulty,

which is that, for a learning organism at least, there has never been any way in which the maps could be formed.

I think it is better to try to get away from "maps" entirely and to try to find a model like the one here, which can start without knowing more than some general relations in its built-in core, and which simply goes on searching continually for invariances in its own signal-combinations and self-reinforcing manipulation-loops, organizing and structuring its skill over the environment by progressively structuring itself. I think this gives us, for the first time, a way of bridging the perceptual gap between the dissimilarity of organism and environment, so that in spite of the lack of close coupling and the distortion of inputs and the lack of a map, an organism can still come to transcend its own peculiarities and to "know" its environment and to manipulate it for its own purposes quite successfully.

## Time and Space

Another property of a learning decision-system that deserves notice is that its operational time and space are not the time and space of physics, any more than its geometry is the geometry of Euclid. Its inputs are not point particles but extended objects or sensory arrays, and its outputs are not actions at a point but are complex motor manipulations over a region of space. In fact the region of space involved is very ill-defined; the muscles may act on a bone, or a large tool, or they may move a flashlight beam that swings across the horizon for miles.

Likewise, such an organism cannot be said to act at any single point in time. Any output is affected by inputs made at many different times before, and it usually projects forward toward cybernetic or goal-seeking consequences mirrored perhaps by anticipatory invariance-loops within the organism. Where is the instant of time? The loops through the external environment are continuously recycling with different time-constants and have no "instant," no very sharp beginning and no very sharp end. I suspect our idea and our idealization of the "instant" has been developed only because light travels so fast, and the lightning flash can illuminate all our input cells almost at once; but even then our response takes many milliseconds, with different delay-times for sets of muscles in different parts of our bodies.

Obviously any attempt to separate time and space in such a system is artificial. The system is a dynamic system and works on space-time motions and velocities rather than statistics. And in such a system, if it uses functional geometry or some other dynamic-invariance method, there is no such thing as a space relation that can be established independently of a time relation. What is seen in the lightning flash could not have been organized during the flash; the basic regularities had to be learned in times before.

Moreover, in a learning organism, the distinction between structure and operation comes to be blurred, and structure is only time-delayed operation, so to speak. A man's perception or decision depends not only on his inputs of a second ago but on his stored experiences and his parents' accidents and his built-in biological mechanisms developed a million years ago or a hundred million years ago. Where is the instant of time?

Yet, conversely, in a different sense, all this time is here, now, stored in the present system. Operationally, there is no past for a decision-system except what is stored here in the present instant, as nearly as that instant can be defined. There is no future except what is anticipated in the networks or perhaps the goals or extrapolations of the present instant. It is like the rowboat anchored in a flowing river, which may bear the gashes of the past logs that have floated by but which never experiences any part of the river except where it is. In such a system, the only moment of decision and change, the only time there is, is now. It would be an interesting exercise to try to reformulate the usual axiomatic structuring of physics, not using Cartesian space and time, but developing some other formulation in terms of ongoing dynamic processes which have cycles and goals and decisions and stored time instead of separated space and time and discrete points and instants. Such a reformulation might be closer not only to operationalism but to relativity. Like the reformulation of static geometry by functional geometry, it might be not only more "natural" and closer to the biological formulation, but it might also lead to a number of valuable new insights.

## Perception as Transaction and Flow

The relations of this kind of decision-system model to its environment must evidently be described, not in static terms, but in terms of ongoing transactions. The psychologists Adelbert Ames and Hadley Cantril have emphasized this transactional nature of perception. If we put the emphasis on operations, there is no clear distinction between "self" and "world" in such a system, as we see in Figure 1. It is true that there may be a fairly sharp boundary between the system and its environment, but operationally the more important entities to be considered are perhaps not the "system" and "environment" so much as the flow-processes that connect them across the boundary, the flow-entities of "awareness" on the input side and of "action" on the output side.

And even this "awareness" and "action" are reafferent, which is to say mixed. An ongoing cycle, from world to self to world and back to self again, has no particular point where it begins or ends; and an imagined cut, not only at the boundary but at any point, would show causal inputs coming in from one side and being checked or reaffirmed by action, and effective outputs going out the other side and being checked or reaffirmed by reafferent stimulation of the inputs. And in emergencies or continuous decision-situations, as in water-skiing or fighting a fire, where the action-time becomes comparable to the judging or invariance-checking time, the boundary not only between self and world but between awareness and action becomes very blurred. Distinctions between the stages of the process, between "awareness" and "action," or between substages such as "awareness," "knowledge," "decision," and "action," can be made only when the operations are slowed down so that these stages and their support loops can begin to be somewhat separated in time.

This kind of transactional flow-situation is of philosophical and linguistic interest because it contrasts so strongly with the static traditional language. The perception of an object by an organism or by this kind of decision-system involves dynamic participation by the organism, interacting with the environment, as the psychologist J. J. Gibson has emphasized. To apply Martin Buber's language to this kind of objective situation, the organism cannot detect an "it" but only an "I-it." Likewise a brain that can interact with another brain through public pointing and linguistic sharing and persuasion and exchange, does not detect a "thou" but an "I-thou" in which its own participation is an essential part of what the other "thou" operationally signifies.

This idea of participative interaction is an insight that goes back a long way in religious and philosophical literature but has been brushed aside by "realists" as being subjective or mystical and nonsensical. But we accept many other subjective insights, and I believe that the real reason for this rejection of the more accurate transactional picture of perception is that the objective signs of the dynamic interaction are so small and subtle. They are confined to little things like eye movements which were forced by evolution to be inconspicuous, for the survival of both predators and prey. This is why men have been able to build up and keep the simple static picture of perception for so long. Such a picture is evidently a close and useful approximation for ordinary objective purposes, but it leads to a static and passive language, of "self" and "world" and "I" and "see" and "it," designed to shut out transitional or time-space or flow ideas which contradict it.

The transactional relation of an organism to its environment is something like the fable of the earthworm who met another earthworm and said, "You're beautiful. Will you marry me?" And the other earthworm said, "Don't be silly. I'm your other end."

This story perhaps illustrates the difficulty of perception in an environment where there is no visual field! But it is also intended to illustrate the idea that everything we meet—or more objectively, everything a decision-network meets—whether a human being, a stray cat, a flower, or a rock, is the other side of a feedback loop of our learning and storage system, is in some sense our cousin under creation—is in some sense our other end.

## Amplification and Manipulation

Another aspect of a transaction-making decision-system that should not be forgotten is that it is by its nature an amplifying system, or more exactly, a selecting-and-amplifying-and-manipulating system operating on the environment around it. A living system not only draws in energy and material supplies from the environment, but it uses them in an amplified and self-maintaining reaction on the environment—a reaction carefully selected so as to keep these supplies flowing in. To accomplish this, particular input patterns are very specifically selected, and they are then amplified, often by factors of millions or more, to produce a highly specific output with a specific and effective grasp reaching out into selected parts of the environment. Needless to say, this kind of manipulation may change the environment drastically. A sensory-motor decision-system alters everything around it, and its effects, desired or not, propagate indefinitely. Seeds are put in; the prairies are planted; the forests are leveled; the earth's magnetic field is shaken by man's experiments. A selected and altered future is continually branching out indefinitely from the vicinity of any decision-system. It is easy to see that, in such a vicinity, the difficulty of detailed causal predictions of the outcome from outside observations of the local and subtle combinations of the original inputs is very great, and in fact it may be greater than the difficulty implied by any indeterminacy we know in physics or atomic theory.

### Scientific Knowledge and Cybernetic Knowledge

In fact, by observing the interaction between a decision-system and its environment, one sees particularly clearly the relation between scientific knowledge and what might be called the cybernetic or operation-knowledge of the organism. Scientific knowledge is relatively passive knowledge, what the organism observes in its environment with relatively little interaction. Cybernetic knowledge is active knowledge, where the organism makes large or manipulative interactions with the environment. We have "weak interaction" with objects in observing them, "strong interaction" in manipulating them.

The ideal of science is that kind of observer-free world—or half-world—that is called an "isolated system," like the top half of Figure 1, a system which we can prepare and then take our hand away from, so as to see how this "objective" system will behave as it moves "by itself." This is not quite possible—even physics says there cannot be observation without some interaction—but it is what makes classical determinism a good approximation.

But the purpose of human knowledge, or the knowledge gained or invariances stored by a decision-system, is the wiser guidance of action, to desired ends. "Scientific detachment" has been a most powerful tool for understanding the environment. But the organism should not take it for an end; it should not blind us to the bottom half of Figure 1 or the relations between the halves. The real purpose of detachment is better directed involvement. This is a cybernetic purpose, with "strong interaction," as men manipulate objects at every instant to direct them closer to goals. To overstate it a little, physics is the science of weak-interaction, of determinism or indeterminism, on *that* side of the boundary; whereas cybernetics is the science of strong-interaction, of will, of human purpose, of applied knowledge, on *this* side of the boundary.

Scientific detachment has its value in determining more clearly how the universe works, but it does not stop there. We see, not merely from looking at ourselves, but from examining these other objective decision-systems and models, that the purpose of scientific detachment is to make commitment and choice more intelligent; to make decisions suit our purposes better; and to make scientific involvement more effective.

## INTERPRETATION OF THE SUBJECTIVE

### *Validating the Objective*

All this finally brings us full circle to the point where we are prepared to ask whether these objective experiments and current conceptual models of how brains operate can help us to understand and interpret our own subjective experiences or can give us a better language for describing them. That is, we can ask, as we asked with eyeballs, are these *our* brains?

I believe that, in broad outline, at least, the answer is Yes. In the first place, this model of our own brain operation appears to be self-consistent—as it was designed to be. This is another example of a self-consistent and self-reinforcing loop. In the course of our argument, we have now gone from the world of objects talked about, to a scientific model within that world, and now back by analogy to see if the model can account for the main features of our subjective experience, and so, if it does, to the validation of our subjective observation-creation of the world of objects again. I think it is clear that we can indeed confirm in our own experience what the model says about how we, as decision-networks, might have constructed and are still constructing our objective world, our public world, of objects and people and language and science.

Can we see the need for eyeball-motion in our own vision? Yes, by putting on the Ditchburn or Riggs apparatus. Can we see the value of self-motion in giving three-dimensional depth? Yes, by moving our heads. Are the regularities of objects those of an external public space as functional geometry indicates? Yes, we can talk about them with the other people-objects.

In the development of language, do we not act like a learning, manipulating, reafferent-feedback model? Yes, we can remember or empathize with how a baby follows lights, and traces objects and faces, and sees eyes and fingers pointing, and hears mouths saying, "Light, light! See the light!"—and how a few months later he makes the same noises himself. We all go on learning the names of new objects and people by this same ostensive process every day, continually validating our participation in the common language community. We see that our objective world has been built up simultaneously with the "I-thou" interactions of language. The objects and people all become named objects, pointed to, played with, and defined operationally and linguistically. Finally the language itself becomes "transparent" to us, as Suzanne Langer has emphasized; we think objects and ideas, not words—until a bilingual person quoting a conversation may not even remember which language he was talking.

We also act like a manipulating decision-network as we make the childish beginnings of objective science and so complete the validation of the objective. We remember or reconfirm, day after day, that the chair bumps and the knife cuts and that two bodies cannot be in the same place at the same time. We roll a ball, that perfect Galilean and Newtonian object, and it teaches without a teacher, showing over and over to the two-year old child things about free bodies moving in a straight line that even philosophers had not clearly formulated five hundred years ago. (It is another self-reinforcing loop, from the seers to society and back to the young seers, who find the scientific concepts more self-evident in every generation.)

Our closure of the object-model-subjective loop by validation is a necessary step. The subjective has to validate the objective, or everything is nonsense. Schrödinger quotes a fragment from Democritus in which the intellect has an argument with the senses about what is "real." The intellect says, like an objective atomic physicist, "Ostensibly there is color, ostensibly sweetness, ostensibly bitterness, actually only atoms and void." To which the senses retort, "Poor intellect, do you hope to defeat us while from us you borrow your evidence? Your victory is your defeat." This point of view rejects the primacy of the "naïve realism" of objects, and it rejects as well the primacy of the scientific and atomic inferences and explanations for describing the objective world; while it asserts the primacy of the subjective experience and perceptions from which (by inference from the models) the objective world had to be derived or constructed by the organism, and without whose accuracy and "transcendence" this objective world would be unreliable. It is clear that Democritus, moving from objective physics to subjective validation, was a forerunner of Mach, Bridgman, Schrödinger, and Bohm.

(Each reader or hearer, of course, can only appreciate the full force of these arguments and of this shift of viewpoint if he treats these arguments, not as relating to the organism-environment relations of some objective external brain or organism he is looking at, but as relating to himself. "Subjective validation" means you, the reader, (or I, the author) looking out at these written words, this diagram, these objects around you or me, and deciding whether these object-relations are veridical or reliable or public, and whether the primary reality should be attributed to these objects or rather, instead, to our perception of them. Doubt that you are seeing them right, and you doubt everything.)

*Powers and Dangers of Language*

It is worth digressing a moment to see that this view of the objective world, as learned by manipulating it functionally and by shared ostensive naming, gives us a basis for analyzing the role of words in our perceptual organization. It is surprising how large a part words play in helping us to manipulate the objective world successfully—or in keeping us from it. Words begin, of course, as small parts of the objective world. They are both objects and actions; sound objects and mouth actions, print objects and hand actions. And when they have been ostensibly defined by pointing, they come to denote other objects and actions.

Yet it is obvious that denotation is not the principal value of words. If it were, it would be no more than a child's game to call them out when you saw something. But calling-out and naming leads to chanting and verbal memory when a thing is elsewhere, and to expectation, and verbal memory of long ago, and perception of consequences, and planning. To our amplifying and manipulating systems, these small signs and muscular actions can signal and symbolize and finally can initiate larger actions. This is their power, that they make it possible, with little expenditure of energy, first, to discuss alternatives in quick sequence—what is not here as well as what is—and, second, to telescope in a moment our past action and future action-consequences, without having to carry out the larger acts or wait for the results.

Where did the ball go? Where will I find it? What are you going to do? Day after day the child practices talking about what is not there, until by the time he is four or six, he has become a "time-binding animal." He can discuss intelligently the finishing of the building or the flight around the world or where he lived when he was two or the best way to do things.

But as long-range choosing and planning become habitual, there comes not only the transparency of language but also what could be called the "objectification" of thought. We see in our mind's eye the scale of numbers and the ladder of time. The distant world, the past and future, may become more real to us than what is before our eyes. How this is hooked into the anticipation-loops that we call visual and emotional imagination is not yet clear, but when we hear a story, we do not hear just the sound of the words, as perhaps a dog might hear them; we are *there* with Archimedes or with the boys in the cave. We read the newspaper and we do not see the sunshine or the people in the bus, but only the black happenings of the war.

And these words are not emotionally neutral. Objectification means that emotionally, they *are* the objects—and were from the beginning. They symbolize; they are "secondary reinforcers," as the psychologist B. F. Skinner says. So they get coupled into our biochemical loops and our strong behavior.

This has great benefits and great dangers. When the words are true and the emotions appropriate, we can be motivated to build the Ark before the rain starts falling. This emotional power is what brings us all together in collective fear and collective hope and determination and makes it possible to undertake vast enterprises. Even the small lies of a fictional story may be valuable in showing us a deeper truth, in broadening our human sympathies and in teaching us things we need to know about hardship and courage and the ways of love.

The danger is that the words may be large lies, not true in any sense. Words are so weakly coupled to the objects and actions they denote that it is mechanically as easy to talk lies and nonsense as it is to talk truth. This can lead us into catastrophe; and the result is that we have to be strongly reinforced against these lies and mistakes. We have to make up rules and laws to choose the word-combinations that symbolize our action-consequences correctly. We devise grammar, logic, the rules of objective truth, and the laws of science. (Action cannot lie; action is. It is words that give us alternatives, lies, and laws.)

So we ask for confirmation and for crucial experiments in the courts and in the laboratory. We often punish the lie or the alien view more strongly than crime. The contradiction cuts across the community of perception. It warns that something has gone wrong with the reinforcement-loops, with our collective reality-testing mechanism. We know not what black thing hides in the darkness. As a result, men have often bought confirmation with the group at the expense of confirmation with nature—although in the long run this bargain always leads to disastrous results.

Yet we run into a far more insidious danger, individually and collectively, when we make emotional identifications with words that are not merely lies but are empty of *any* meaning, true or false, for decision and action—that is, words that are empty of operational referents or of any testable reality at all. Lies we can refute, but we can never come to grips with twisted words.

Is not this the source of many of our neurotic problems? We invent, and are obsessed by, verbal hopes and hates and fears when there is nothing tangible there. We come to hate unreal collectives, like racial or national groups. We are obsessed by guilt or by endless striving, as we still try to satisfy or avoid the childhood demands of parents or an angry God. We go over and over the choices we might have made, losing the ones we can still make. We are obsessed by thoughts of death, rather than making the most of life. Our ambitions are verbal ambitions, to "catch up," to outdo the others; or gambling ambitions, to win or to be picked out of the crowd—ambitions that keep receding and can never be really satisfied.

Probably most, if not all, of our strong and persistent emotions and rigidities are persistent precisely because they are aimed at verbal and unreal goals that have, in all human probability, no meaning we could ever meet or be satisfied with. We wait for the glass slipper and never learn to dance. We poison our evenings with success and what we get is ulcers. It never lets up, because it is inside.

## The Subjective as Participant

On the other hand, a decision-system that is acting effectively is not only coupled to its real world, it almost becomes one with it. Is it not so with us? When we pick up or name even so common an object as a pencil, we are *participating* with the pencil in a process thick with history. It is not just that our eyes must scan the pencil or our fingers must trace it in order to see it or know it; it is that the whole perception, and its significance and testing, involves a complex participation-process we have stored—a process that extends back into remembered and un-remembered childhood, with our parents practicing with us, and correcting our pointing and naming, for many a pencil and person and thing. And no doubt it involves *their* childhood and adulthood and how they learned the language and were cul-turally structured to care for a baby and teach it.

And of course our perception of a person is far more partici-pative than our perception of a pencil. Any perception of those information-rich and responsive and unpredictable objects that we call human beings is "I-thou" overwhelmingly. Just in a blank stare or the lift of a shoulder, we read purposes and values, criticisms and praise and cooperative effort. When we listen to each other, we hear not air pulses but words, not words but meanings, images, threats, plans.

And today we know that we even have an "I-thou" relation to the rest of the universe as well—a developmental and evo-lutionary transactional relationship. Our structures and atti-tudes are shaped by a father and mother who gave us heredity and milk and education. But they are shaped in a larger and deeper sense by the world around us that has shaped our living molecules. Our life is something that grew up out of the primor-dial molecules and dust under the sun's radiation, and perhaps it makes in us some progress toward more intelligence and brains. We are children of the universe, even objective science now says, in some sense destined and designed to be here and to be aware—and to be interested in perception problems.

So we move in a kinship field. When we look out at the mole-cules and aggregates that we rearrange in our factories or grow on our farms, we are looking at our cousins. The pigments in our eyes can respond to the colors of the pigments of leaves and flesh only because they are chemically similar molecules. As Pascal said, "Man . . . is related to all he knows. . . . He is in a dependent alliance with everything." And Emerson, more modern, said,

> He is not only representative, but participant. Like can only be known by like. . . . Man, made of the dust of the world, does not forget his origin. . . . Thus we sit by the fire and take hold on the poles of the earth.

## The Subjective as Manipulant

I think the decision-system model of our minds also confirms this deeper insight of Emerson's—the realization that our perception-process goes over continuously into our larger manipulation of the world around us. We do not often think of perception as manipulation, because the brain somehow organizes our ever-changing visual observation-fields into a continuous seen-and-remembered "stable world," and because simple passive observation, even with moving eyeballs, changes the objects and relations of this "stable world" very little, so that we think of it as unaffected by our observation; but manipulation it is, nevertheless, manipulation by the electrical signals in the outgoing nerves, by the motion of the eyeballs, and finally by the hands. "Knowledge is action," as Skinner says. Perception of the world is only delayed action; or, more exactly, it is a weak-action prelude to delayed strong-action, the first step toward the shaping of the world. A decision-system always amplifies its energies, first in perceiving and then in modifying the environment around it; and man is the most spectacular example. It is increasingly a world that we have seen, studied, and shaped ourselves. The time-constants extend from an instant ago to years ago and centuries and milleniums ago.

Thus, I now realize that when I see a pencil, I know it is there only because I manipulated its image a fraction of a second ago. But then I place it on the table with tactile manipulation. Does it surprise me that it is there? No; it would surprise me if it were not, and I would doubt my perception. I look away for several seconds, but am I not still manipulating it?—for I expect to see it, and perhaps to pick it up again, if I look back. Is this any different in principle from expecting to see my car in the street where I left it—manipulated it—an hour ago? Or the line of trees my father planted on the farm? Or the new subdivision I have read about in the newspaper?

Today the scope of this perception-extrapolation-manipulation by man is almost incredible. It is hard to walk in a city and see any line or object that man has not shaped, except where he deliberately allows some natural variation, as with grass or trees. It is hard to see any plant or animal that he has not bred or any landscape that he has not changed. Even the variations in the sky and sea are partly his and may some day be under his control. We are not only sons of the earth, we are participants and builders of it. As Emerson says again, "The world becomes at last only a realized will—the double of the man." It is a tool responding to our decision-systems, almost as much "I-thou" as the bones in our fingers.

The great extent of this participation-manipulation-prediction leads to an unexpected realization about the degree of our involvement with the world. In the past, some philosophers have talked of analyzing perception in terms of two elements, the "given" and the "not-given," or the "for-itself (*pour-soi*)" and the "in-itself (*en-soi*)," thinking of these as primitives from which could be derived (by interaction between them) whatever is correct about our usual picture of objects and of the subjective field. The "given" is largely the objective part, and is the "surprising" or "absurd" aspect, because we (the "not-given") did not anticipate or intend it.

But I believe that this view, at least in its extreme form, is derived from the static fallacy of perception. We see from the present analysis that there is in fact no sharp boundary between the "given" and the "not-given." In fact, it is surprising how little is "given" to us, instant by instant and hour by hour, how little is truly "surprising," when we know what we are manipulating and where we have put things and what men have done. A decision-system like man manipulates and stores. Its memories are expectations. Its steady-state loops extend into the environment. And as a result the environment constantly becomes more docile and less surprising, more and more an intimate part of the decision-system itself.

## Naming the Subjective

These perception-relations we have been describing are simple, however, compared to the aspects of the subjective which we must now discuss and which have always been sources of puzzlement and contradiction. I refer to the problem of naming the subjective, and the problems of time and the self and the uniqueness of consciousness and the change of attitude with subjective realization. And here again, although I do not wish to be dogmatic about it, I think the decision-system model offers some helpful analogies and clarifications.

In discussions of subjective perception, one of the central problems has always been the difficulty of trying to name and talk about the whole subjective field, because of the impossibility of making ostensive definitions of such a thing. The modern mathematician, however, can speak accurately of classes, sets, and fields, and many other concepts of things that cannot be pointed to.

I believe that today we can use the same method in describing the perceptual field. I think we can talk quite accurately not only of objects that can be pointed to at a given moment, but of sets of such objects, and of the whole visual field—the "V-field"—containing these objects at a given moment. (Perhaps the number of possible different objects in such a field, if we had infinite resolution, would in fact be comparable to the mathematician's number, *Aleph-Two*, which is the number of all the possible curves in a plane.)

I think we can also go on to talk of a second, larger field, the field of all our sensations at a given moment—the "S-field." We now realize, of course, that the sensations we are aware of are not something static, but must have been compounded of sensory inputs varied by motor operations, with reafferent-stimulation and time delays, and constant checking and what could be called "veridification" of the field. (By veridification is meant the process of checking whether the perceived relations in the field are veridical and self-consistent.)

But finally, and in the same way, I think we can talk fairly accurately of a still larger field, the field of the totality of all our subjective experience at a given moment. This might be called the "totality-field"—the "T-field"—and it would include not only the sensation-field, but all the memories, emotions, expectations, and so on of which we are aware. The fact that such a field cannot be pointed to does not make it impossible to discuss accurately, any more than the fact that the infinity of all the possible curves in a plane cannot be pointed to. And within this totality-field, these other elements which are not part of what we may call immediate sensation or action—elements such as memories, emotions, and so on—may still have operational definition, both subjective and objective. For we may show them in our voluntary or involuntary muscular or biochemical expression, or in talking about them; and we can see their effects in shaping the speed and style of our action.

I think this is much like the world we should expect a learning decision-network to have (as suggested in Figure 1). Whatever its inputs, it experiences or acts on the totality of them. And those features that are stored in its structure and history are still detectable, by reafferent signals, from their effects on its output.

In fact, it is interesting to reflect that the world of each decision-network and of each creature is probably always "complete." The span of perception is "full" in every coordinate. The field of perception is total and has no "holes" in it. Or, as Mach says, in commenting on our own blind spots, which we cannot see directly, "A defect of light-sensation can no more be noticed at a point blind from the beginning than the blindness, say, of the skin of the back can cause a gap in the visual field." This is what we expect with an invariant-selecting system.

So, no doubt, if we could ever learn the subjective responses of an earthworm, or a fish, or a dog, we should find that their perceptual field seems to them to be sharp, clear, complete, rapidly changing, and interesting, just as ours does to us. They do not see what we see, no; but it is not perceived as an incompleteness, any more than our inability to hear the echoes of the bats is perceived as an incompleteness, or a child's inability to understand the financial transactions of his father. It is something that might be added; but surely we are all incomplete and ignorant children with respect to the added patterns that still lie ahead.

### Time and the Eternal Now

I believe that the decision-network model is especially helpful in considering the subjective problem of time. Subjective time, when we think about it, has several odd aspects not expressed in our usual objective language. It seems to me, for example, that subjectively we do not sharply separate time and space, any more than a decision-network does. I suspect that "now" is never merely "now" for us, but something more like "now-all-this-changing."

In addition, we can see for ourselves that it is not an instantaneous now, but a spreading fuzzy now that integrates influences from a second ago and hours ago and years ago, and from anticipation-loops whose trains are set in motion for times ahead. It is an ongoing, space-processing, ever-changing, relation-seeking now. Not a now of statics, but of time-derivatives and velocities. I often think it would be good if we could replace our usual static nouns and is-verbs by the "-ing" noun forms and continuing-action verb forms of English, just to keep us reminded of this continuing relationing. "I see the red flower" should perhaps be translated to something with a more dynamic and oriental flavor, such as "Seeing red-reflecting flowering in space-near-me-ing."

Yet the most evident feature and the one least represented in our usual language is that all time is present together in this Now. We objectify the time of dates and memories and plans, but the remembering and planning is now. All time and space that is operationally real to us and actionable is present to us here and now, however diffuse this now may be. The storage in the network, or the feedback anticipation loops, are present storage and present loops. Anything that is not stored is not remembered; operationally in the present, it has not been. However much we may enjoy ordering and remembering the past and however much the scholars may try to make it more orderly and objective for us, "the only time there is, is now," as lovers say, and water-skiers, and preachers of conversion.

Of course, it is hard to pull most Westerners away from somehow "identifying" with the objectification of time. We see ourselves as "then" or "there." This kind of objectification is easy and valuable in verbal and analytical goal analysis. It helps us plan when to start supper and how long the trip will take, and to imagine what we will do next summer. Planning and ethics become long-range and goal-directed. This is the great verbal and moral achievement that words and clocks and calendars have given us. But when we look at nothing but this verbal and objectified future all the time, we lose sight of the non-verbal real and present around us, often indeed the very thing that our past goals were reaching for.

With such an attitude, any satisfying attainment is forever impossible. I think that we should recognize the value of objectification and use it; but when we have gone too far in this direction, it would be a gain if we could come back more often, especially in our personal relations, to the immediate and real. Many large and good schemes fail because they are only paper schemes and objectified schemes; they are separated from effectiveness because they do not start from any personal trans-actional good in the immediate present. We are active manipu-lating decision-systems; and it is the variety and richness and responsiveness of our immediate contacts with the world that make our amplifications directed and powerful.

I hope that perhaps our attitudes today may be changing toward a more existential sense of immediacy. The girl writes on the wall, "There is no tomorrow, Tolin. So how about this afternoon?"

Blunt, shameless, but true. Seize the day. What more effec-tive long-range program could she have planned? The future starts here. This is the objectification of a very different time-attitude, the attitude of living in an ever-changing, timeless moment that contains all time (just as the spaceless visual field, which cannot be pointed to, contains all space). This is the eternal Now of love and action—not the old objectified kind of future eternity that was supposed to come by working and waiting, but a change of perspective that you can start at any moment, as instantly as breathing. With such an attitude, we can feel our intimate and personal and responsive involvement continually starting the most effective causal chains branching out indefinitely into an ever-altered environment and an ever-changing future. The action-moment of the decision-network ceases to be the deterministic "frozen passage" of the old physi-cal relativity theory and becomes a moment of continually new interacting and becoming and shaping, as Henri Bergson said, and as the physicist-philosopher Milič Čapek has recently emphasized.

*Elimination of the Self*

Many of the elements that we can study in objective models and decision-networks naturally and necessarily drop out of our subjective fields. As we have noted, the detailed structure of the retina cannot be seen, or the shadows of the blood vessels or the distortion of the images. Perception transcends anatomy. It is designed for manipulating the external world. Our networks are not programmed to see these uncorrected sensory inputs, but to see invariances and external relationships. We are also largely unaware of the second-stage elements, such as our invariance-selecting processes and our small feedback loops from manipulation to reafferent stimulation. They may define the boundaries of objects and determine the veridicality of space-relations, but we have learned to talk objectively about public "objects" "themselves" and to ignore these rapid common actions that generate them for us. And it is only when we move slowly that we can even separate the reafferent awareness-loops from the reefferent action-loops. Both of them are flow-transactions and feedback-transactions across the boundary between "self" and "world"; and the boundary is also something that is not present in perception. Though we may see this boundary in an objective system, we have no sense organs to see it in our subjective one, any more than we can see our own eyes.

But what seems to generate the most operational confusion and the most hard words in perception arguments is that the decision-network itself also does not appear in the subjective perception. We have no eyes to see it either. In the subjective totality-field there is no object or class of objects or of actions that can be pointed to or isolated as "self" or "ego" or "I." In any observation or operation, there is no sharp distinction between the manipulating and the manipulated. The "self" and the "world" as commonly spoken of, are seen to be inseparably blended when we examine any experiences closely. Without manipulation, there are no objects to manipulate; without objects to manipulate, there is no reference point and no manipulation. Likewise, on the awareness side, there is no extracting without acting, and no acting without extracting. These are self-reinforcing loops; and they cease to be loops at all if either leg is missing. So, operationally, there *are* objects;

but "I" am the operating. Objects are the nouns of which we are the verbs. Nouns without verbs are grammatically and operationally meaningless, "like the sound of one hand clapping." More exactly, we are the totality-verb that encompasses all the other verbs. In this sense, it is we who give objects existence; we are the "is."

This merging of the self into the world seems startling when first reflected upon. Yes, it is obvious, but we are not taught it. In fact, we train it out of the child and our mature linguistic usage contradicts it—as medieval usage about "motion" contradicted the idea of continued motion in a straight line. And we rarely examine our own immediate experience to see how misleading the linguistic usage is. But consider your own case now. Where is the "self?" Are you not involved in everything you see or feel? If so, why make this artificial separation, speaking of the "self" as though it were another noun?

Evidently we pick up the "self"-words, and pronouns about ourselves, as object-words from other people, as we discuss each other's independence of decision. But this "self" is, if anything, a diffuse choosing-center or, better, an active verb, and not a body that can be pointed to, even by other people; and it has no separate representation in any aspect of our own perceptual field. The grammatical separation of the subject from the verb has made it seem to be an object, but perhaps we should reunite them again, as in Latin. I-choose, I-go, would be a less misleading way to talk of decision-ing and action-ing and inter-action-ing. Each of us can say for himself: "I" am the totality-verb of acting-manipulating-creating-and-invarianting the self-and-environment.

### The Uniqueness of Consciousness

A related oddity of the subjective field that has also led to extensive linguistic and philosophical disagreement is its aspect of uniqueness. For a decision-system, and for us, consciousness is always undivided and unending. Or as Schrödinger says,

"Consciousness is never experienced in the plural, only in the singular," and within it there is no awareness of a beginning or an end. We do prefix it with the word "my," because we admit there are other people and other decision-systems. But no matter how many of us there are, there is only one subjective consciousness involved in any operation, just as there is only one flowerpot on this table. It is true that we see the flowerpot from many points of view, and talk about their differences—but it might equally well be said that we experience "the consciousness" from many points of view.

Because of this operational similarity, it might be less confusing if we said "my view of the consciousness," just as we say "my view of the flowerpot." Or we could do the opposite, and drop the word "view" in both cases and say only "*my* flowerpot" because it is in "*my* consciousness." It is interesting to note that either of these attempts at parallel treatment is generally regarded as mystical and unsound by "realists." They learned to say "*the* flowerpot" and "*my* consciousness" at their mother's knee. So they feel that any personalizing of the flowerpot is dangerous; and, conversely, that any reduction of their consciousness to just a "view" of something universal threatens to blend their own self-image and separate value into something larger—as indeed it does.

But I would claim that it is just as possible linguistically and quite legitimate operationally to speak of our various perception fields as being no more "personal" than the various views of the world that we see in mirrors at different angles. Is it not possible that there are mutual regularities in our joint perception that transcend the individual views? I think it is, and I think this is what Schrödinger was asserting in his curious "Epilogue," where he starts operationally from this *singulare tantum*, this singularity of consciousness. We have now seen transcendence over and over, how our perceptual invariances transcend anatomy and how our social invariances of truth and of concepts transcend our own individual irregularities. We find that we are pattern-perceiving, regularity-reinforcing, world-invarianting creatures, individually and collectively. The result is that your invariant, if well-observed, may be equivalent to mine, or to that of an ancient sage or a future one. As Thoreau says,

> The oldest Egyptian or Hindu philosopher raised a corner of the veil. . . . I gaze upon as fresh a glory as he did, since it was I in him that was then so bold, and it is he in me that now reviews the vision. . . . No time has elapsed since that divinity was revealed.

Thoreau identified himself with a single consciousness growing across the ages, whose growth-points or realization-points contributed a single realization, no matter what individual body or what century they were in. In view of today's intellectual convergence, it is not a bad view to adopt, nor an impossible one.

### The Jump of Realization

I believe this all leads us to a more accurate and satisfying subjective view than our usual language has given us. It is a view in which "awareness" is a totality-field, "now" is an ongoing immediacy that contains all time, "self" and "world" are a mixed pair that cannot be separated, "objects" are an interaction-invariance extraction, and "I" is an acting verb. These would be natural usages for a decision-network. If we talked more often in these terms, it might help to recover our sense of the subjective as the total immediate interacting present. It would help us to keep straight the proper relations between subjective and objective. The subjective is the primitive and direct experience out of which the objective is drawn, the experience from which all our partial and analytical and passive and detached notions, our ideas of far-away and past and future, are derived. And it is the subjective that has emotions and values and purposes and knowledge and decisions and acts, the purposes that these abstractions are made to serve.

These are not new insights, although the present derivation

in terms of modern experiments and models may be new. Rather, they are ideas that are old in human history, ideas that many a primitive savage understands better than a civilized man, but that have become taboo to discuss today, almost more taboo than sex. Are you not made uncomfortable at trying to talk scientifically about the subjective? Where is the source of this emotional discomfort? In our modern objectivism we are embarrassed to talk about such subjects, about "awareness" or "self" or the "I," either in the family or in scientific journals. Only preachers and poets are allowed to discuss such matters —and they are permitted only because we do not believe them anyway, and we neither want to nor have to answer them back. And when thinkers and philosophers in the Western world have made statements like the ones here, which seem to deny the primacy of the objective or which put the emphasis on a sub-jective operationalism, this has caused them to be rejected as solipsists and mystics—as Bridgman and Schrödinger have been rejected—although they always insisted that *they* were the true realists. It seems to me that the present type of derivation through objective models permits us to bridge this gap much more peaceably, in a self-consistent loop that permits many starting-points, so that we can see the value and truth of each type of insight in its proper field.

It is true that in the past, the attempt to get away from the derived and to practise a new directness, a subjective or an existential directness, has been a rare experience. It is like the realization of the constancy of motion in a straight line, which was, because of the linguistic and conceptual barrier, a rela-tively rare experience before Galileo. As a result, the realization of the primacy of the subjective has not usually been something taught to children but has been rather an adult Gestalt-insight, a complete jump of perspective which came with the force of revelation.

Such Gestalt-jumps are familiar to us from the examples in elementary psychology texts, such as the "staircase" outline which most people can acquire the knack of "flipping," so that it is seen either as a perspective view from above or as a view from below. We can make a similar flip in interchanging the roles of figure and ground—the faces and the vase—in certain drawings. And there is a far more remarkable flip in the "inversion" of the three-dimensional staircase-figures and other figures studied by Mach and more recently by Murray Eden and by Cyril Smith at M.I.T. Many people have trouble making these three dimensional inversions, but when they do, the "Aha!" reaction and the sense of surprise and delight are dramatic, and they may go on for hours studying the strange properties and reversed movements of the inverted forms.

Is it any wonder that the complete flip from the ordinary objective view to a realization of the primacy and inclusiveness of the subjective—involving as it does the whole world-outlook —might cause a similar surprise and delight and an ongoing exploration which one could never stop talking about? Or that these exclamations of surprise might cause a similar bafflement and derision in those who have not made the flip?

When the flip has come, it has often come like a blinding light. It was such a personal and fundamental shift of viewpoint, and it brought such freedom from old concerns and worries and such new satisfaction and effectiveness in daily existence, that it was called by the highest religious names, "realization," "eternal life," "the practice of the presence of God," "living in the Godhead," "I in God and God in me," and so on. It was something so startling and different that it had to be talked about, and passed on; and many a realizer made it a crusade to preach it to others—again as Galileo did with his new concepts of motion. These sudden shifts in perception-view cannot all be included in the "ecstasy" experiences that Marghanita Laski has collected, but some of them can. For example, the physicist Mach described in his own experience in this way:

> On a bright summer day in the open air, the world with my ego suddenly appeared to me as *one* coherent mass of sensations, only

more strongly coherent in the ego. . . . This moment was decisive for my whole view.

This is one of the more subdued accounts.

## The Mystical Formulations

I believe that when we understand the surprise and intensity of this sudden shift of perception, many of the odd phrases of even the religious mystics cease to be bizarre and ambiguous. They can be seen as fairly straightforward attempts to describe, sometimes with new language, these non-conventional aspects of the T-field which we have discussed; or attempts to make new and arresting phrases or analogies that would startle others into making the same jump of realization. (Once more, this is not so different from the attempts of Galileo and Newton and their successors to find a better terminology for motion.) If we identify the subjective with immediacy and directness and on-going participation in the world (like that of a decision-net-work), and with a complete and unique T-field which includes all objects but which is nowhere and cannot be pointed to, a T-field which is with us all the time but which is "outside of time" because it includes all time and has no birth and death and no self-world dichotomy—is not that the referential content of many of the mystical and oriental puzzle-phrases?

I think the idea of such a totality-field of perception and awareness is almost certainly a large part of what is meant by the "That-ness" or "Suchness" of Aldous Huxley in *The Perennial Philosophy*, and by the "Istigkeit" of Meister Eckhart, the "Vastness" or the "No-Thing" or "Nothing" of the Chinese philosophers, and the "divine Ground of Being" of the mystic saints. Yes, it is odd language; but these men were intelligent and effective in their daily lives, they were not insane or stupid; should we not believe that they were trying to talk about something? The descriptions of the Way or the Tao sound very much like the properties of the total T-field, with special emphasis on immediacy, assurance, and straightforward action. "The Tao that can be named is not the Tao," says the Tao Te Ching, pointing to the language difficulty.

The loss of a distinguishable "self" in the one-ness of the subjective totality is often described by the mystics. Mach quotes Lichtenberg as writing, "We should say, *It thinks*, just as we say, *It lightens*;" and he adds, "The assumption, or postulation, of the ego is a mere practical necessity." Is this so different from what the interpreter of Zen, D. T. Suzuki, writes? He says:

> I am in Nature and Nature is in me. Not mere participation in each other, but a fundamental identity between the two. . . . The reason I can see the mountains as mountains and the waters as waters is because I am in them and they are in me; that is, *tat tvam asi* [Thou art That].

The German mystic, Meister Eckhart, was even more graphic about the unity. He said, "The eye with which I see God is the same eye with which God sees me," and he was nearly tried for heresy as a result.

The ego can either be said to have disappeared, or to include it all, which is the position many solipsists have started with. To quote Mach again, "The ego can be so extended as ultimately to embrace the entire world. (The virtuoso possesses as perfect a mastery of his instrument as he does of his own body.)"

This inclusiveness is the basis of some of Thomas Traherne's most beautiful passages. He says:

> You never enjoy the world aright till the sea itself floweth in your veins, till you are clothed with the heavens and crowned with the stars; and perceive yourself to be the sole heir of the whole world, and more than so, because men are in it who are every one sole heirs as well as you. . . .

And Traherne's description of his own shift of perception ends with the sense of encompassing everything:

> Something infinite behind everything appeared which talked with my expectations and moved my desire. The city seemed to

stand in Eden, or to be built in Heaven. The streets were mine, the people were mine, their clothes and gold and silver were mine, as much as their sparkling eyes, fair skins and ruddy faces. The skies were mine, and so were the sun and moon and stars, and all the world was mine; and I the only spectator and enjoyer of it.

The idea of the ongoing timeless moment which includes all time is in Thoreau, where he says, "That time which we really improve, or which is improvable, is neither past, present, nor future." This is the timeless "Moment" of Howard Nemerov's great poem, the moment when ". . . the mind of God, / The flash across the gap of being, thinks / In the instant absence of forever: now."

Many of these non-conventional perceptual properties of the T-field are summed up together in some of the verses that Suzuki quotes from the Third Patriarch of Zen:

When the deep mystery of one Suchness is fathomed,
All of a sudden we forget the external entanglements;
When the ten thousand things are viewed in their oneness,
We return to the origin and remain where we have always been....
. . . . . .

When Mind and each believing mind are not divided,
and undivided are each believing mind and Mind,
This is where words fail,
For it is not of the past, present, or future.

What more is there to say about the totality-field of subjective perception?

The old texts also recognize that the "flip" to this view, the personal realization of the primacy and inclusiveness of the subjective, is not something that can be achieved by working for it. Like all the Gestalt-flips of perception, it is an all-or-none shift, not logically derivable from what has gone before (except perhaps as we have derived it here by a very roundabout method). It is something you may suddenly realize here and now, or at any moment, but it comes by insight as a "grace," and not as the result of any logic or effort. In Zen teaching, this

sudden flip or perception-shift is the *satori* jump of enlightenment, the "Gateless Gate" through which the novice passes, as
odd as a riddle and as close and startling as a blow. Or as
Lawrence Durrell says, in *Clea*:

> No amount of explanation can close the gap. Only realization!
> One day you are going to wake from your sleep shouting with
> laughter. *Ecco!*

Laughing, of course, at how simple it is, and how you have
been fooled and led into unreal distractions and unending pur-
suits when the truly satisfying and eternal was *here*, all the time.

## The Stages of Understanding

This jump to subjective realization is a most important jump.
Yet by looking at our models, and ourselves, I think we can see
a third and final stage of understanding that goes even beyond
this perception-flip. Perhaps the best description of this last
stage is given in another Zen saying from one of the old masters:

> When I began to study Zen, mountains were mountains;
> When I thought I understood Zen, mountains were no longer
>   mountains;
> But when I came to full knowledge of Zen, mountains were
>   again mountains.

It is a translation from another language and another century, but I think that in our present terms, it may mean something like the following. Before we have begun to think about
the problem of perception and our relation to the external
world, mountains and other objects are simply objects "out
there," objects that we point to and talk about and think about
in the ordinary objective way. But after we begin to examine
the bases of perception, we realize that these mountains and
objects we are seeing are not as simple as something "out
there," but are our interpretations of distorted images on the
retina, which are moved about in a complex way as we move

ourselves or our eyeballs or manipulate the objects. So we realize that these "objects" are not merely objective but are subjective as well; they are "I-it" relationships, where the perception is personal and depends upon our participation, and has to be re-created or modified anew at every moment by our own actions.

But then, finally, I think we come to realize that this kind of analysis exists to be superseded, so to speak: that *these are the only mountains there are!* All our perceptions have this subjective aspect, and therefore it largely drops away in comparing one physical object with another. It is the non-subjective residues or invariances that differ between a mountain and a bump on a log, and these are what we cannot get rid of by wishing or rotating our eyeballs. It is these less subjective aspects that interest us and that are important for manipulation and survival. This is the way a decision-network organizes its world; this is what we mean by seeing mountains, and it is the only way we see mountains at all.

I think it is very dangerous for us to stop with the first of these stages, the objective stage, as we do throughout our society today. I know that the idea of one's world and oneself as being built up of objects has been the standard way of teaching in our atomizing and technological culture. Students, and professors and philosophers too, may grow up without ever being called to question it; in all our mechanisms it works so well! And this is undoubtedly the simplest way of teaching children quickly about structural relations and how to make and manipulate things, so as to lay the basis for technological accomplishment.

But by the time a child reaches adolescence, he should begin to be taught a juster picture of his personal relation to the world, as well. Such a restructuring could be of the greatest importance to us. For this almost universal objectivist view of ours is not only an inversion of the subjective perceptual basis of things, it is also, I think, a major source of the widespread feelings of dehumanization and meaninglessness and resentment in our national and world society.

Any error in our ideas of being will always lead to psychological and social pathology and dehumanization—whether it is a persecution complex, or the belief that all is predestined, or that all is subconscious, or that man lives for the state. The personal meaninglessness produced by the objectivist inversion of things is no exception. The healthiest change we could make today, scientifically and socially as well as theologically, would be to put back into the center the immediate and personal nature of awareness, responsibility, choice, and action; and to see that all our magnificent science and technology are derived from man, not man from science.

Yet it is also important not to stop at this second, subjective, stage either. Many who have made the jump to the subjective have ended by treating the objective as small and unimportant. Solipsist tyrants, believing that their will, like their eyeballs, could move mountains, have come to believe that it should trample over these small annoying figures in their visual field. There are many such, in jails and asylums, boasting and preaching that all is unreal and sometimes shooting to prove it. Others who have made the jump have been led instead to quietism and passivity. If the objective is unreal, all action is but striving; and this half-truth has simplified many men down to pure contemplation or begging, leaving it to other and more objective strivers to bring them the means of life.

Such over-subjectivism is as serious an error as over-objectivism. Perception stands on two legs, the subjective and the objective, and needs them both. We need to be not only human but whole; not only contemplators but doers. We need to go on to the third stage of understanding, to know not only the subjective, but through it to know the objective again. The objective is both primary, and derived; the subjective—on the other side of this invariant self-confirming loop that goes on and on—is both derived, and primary. When we reach this stage of understanding, we can see and act effectively on the objective "because it is the only objective there is," even while we appreciate the immediacy of the subjective and use it as our crucial continuing test of the reality and importance of the objective world we manipulate. Our planning and action and achievement can become satisfying and effective, because they are no longer tied to either the man-denying or the world-denying, because what we do is done with wholeness and realism, consonant at last with the way things are.

These stages in understanding perception are like the stages in understanding the staircase-figure, where we first make the Gestalt-jump from seeing the figure "from above" to seeing it "from below," but where finally, like the psychologist himself, we see the whole figure as containing both views, simultaneously a paradox and a unity.

Or they are like the stages we go through in understanding painting. To the very young child it may be only canvas and splashes of color, but as the child grows it becomes, it *is*, the representational world of funny or threatening figures. The teen-ager sees through all that; it is nothing but someone's daubs on cloth; he could do better. But then the adult, the connoisseur, finally comes to reacquire a sophisticated naïveté, an innocent eye again, so that he sees and appreciates it all— canvas and paint, figure and ground, technique and representation—and the whole constructive unity of the achievement, mind and matter, in all its aspects. This is the stage of the artist himself, the creative self-determining individual, who has passed through all the stages and can paint at last with both the mastery of the man and the seeing eye of the child. And in perception, I think that through the process of more complete understanding we may likewise reacquire the innocent eye, the confidence and curiosity of little children, and may reach again the sense of immediacy and the "awareness, spontaneity, and intimacy" that the therapist Eric Berne has emphasized.

A better understanding of perception is like the better understanding of our own vision that comes from knowing the optics of how our eyeballs work. From it, I think we can get a more satisfying and more effective understanding of who and what we are in the world, both subjectively and objectively, as surely as we get a better understanding of ourselves from using a mirror daily.

Our analysis here began with the riddle of the fish in the sea. But there is one version of the story in which the fish finally gets an answer. " Little fish, little fish, you live, move and have your being in the sea. The sea is within you and without you, and you are made of sea, and you will end in sea. The sea surrounds you as your own being."

I think that we, as decision-networks and human beings, as thinking minds, are part of the sea of perception-and-action that reaches out and encompasses the universe. We began in sea and we will end in sea. The universe of awareness is the universe of action, and within it our two faces of perception, the subjective and the objective, are but the reversed emphases of a single reality, shaping each other. To see the world is to manipulate it. Every eyeblink, every turning of a page, every new bit of understanding, is an amplifying action that moves the world into a future continually recreated. And realization, the flip of perception, the awareness of this immediate and ongoing participation in the totality, is at our finger-tips, in the time between breathing out and breathing in.

# 4

# BUILDING BETTER BRAINS

RALPH W. GERARD

RALPH W. GERARD *is currently dean of the Graduate Division, The University of California (Irvine) and professor of biological sciences. Dr. Gerard's numerous publications include* Mirror to Physiology: A Self-Survey of Physiological Science *and* Information Processing in the Nervous System.

4

# BUILDING BETTER BRAINS

*Ralph W. Gerard*

M Y THEME has to do essentially with the impact of experience on organisms, particularly on the nervous system, of which process learning and memory are integral parts. I need not belabor the argument that organisms have evolved under the lashing of experience from the environment.

We have heard a good deal of adaptive enzymes and immune phenomena. At the molecular level, it is perfectly obvious that a presentation at subcellular level to the organism, or cell, leads to changes in its molecular population and that some of these changes are enduring, indeed. At the cellular level, I remind you that looking at the face or hands of a person reveals the kind of experience that the skin and individual have gone through: the hands of a worker are not like those of a scholar, nor the face of an indoor person like that of an outdoorsman. There is the hypertrophy of muscle cells when they contract against resistance. There are also the dramatic cellular evidences of environmental determination of the nature of an organism at the basic morphogenetic level of embryonic development.

Earlier in this century, a fertilized egg was separated into its two blastomeres, and each of these was found to develop, not into a half embryo that died, but into an entire embryo that went on to normal maturity. This was such a devastating finding that the world's biologists were split into camps. Some of the greatest said that this demonstrates "vitalism," for how can two cells, each of which is to be a right or left side of an adult organism, know, when separated, that it is now proper for each to become an entire organism? An entelechy, an internal guid-

Reprinted from Gustav J. Martin and Bruno Kisch, eds., *Enzymes in Mental Health* (Philadelphia: J. B. Lippincott Company, 1966).

ing spirit, they said, must watch over the system and make it come out properly.

The work of one of my teachers, Charles Manning Child, offered a perfectly simple and rational explanation for this. Two cells that are stuck together have the lowest or the highest end of a diffusion gradient at their point of contact: if oxygen is coming in from the surface, it will be lowest at the midline; if carbon dioxide is diffusing out from the system, it will be highest at the midline. When the two have been separated, that situation is immediately changed and the high and low points of the gradient are now again in the center of each new half system. Therefore, chemical concentrations prove to be morphogenetic determiners.

At higher levels, our total behavior, developed as a result of individual experience, contains certain response patterns that are as effectively part of ourselves as if they were completely inborn. In my early days, young ladies would blush automatically at the mention of certain words; today, they do not. The difference is in not biologic background but cultural experience.

This theme is developed more fully by experiments performed, a decade or so ago, on Harvard undergraduate students. They were given certain problems, but their performance was immaterial: what was important was that no matter how well or ill they performed, the experimenter bedeviled them. Nothing done was right. "My goodness, this is a mess." "Why don't you try another business?" "You're no good." "I thought you had more brains than that." What was critical was how the subjects responded to this psychological stress.[1]

The responses fell into sharply bimodal groups. One group responded by getting angry at the experimenter ("anger turned out"), in effect saying: "If you don't like it, you can go to hell; I'm doing the best I can; nuts to you." The other group responded by "anger turned in," by becoming self-punishing and

[1] D. H. Funkenstein *et al.*, *Mastery of Stress* (Cambridge, Mass.: Harvard University Press, 1957).

apologetic: "I am so sorry, I'm afraid I'm spoiling your experiment."

This is interesting in itself. It became much more interesting when the catecholamine system was examined and it was found that the youngsters who turned their anger outward, responding to the attack with fight, secreted norepinephrine in considerable quantities in response to the stress; whereas those who turned their anger inward, responding with flight, poured out large amounts of epinephrine. Here were two personality types associated with two endocrine types: norepinephrine, hostile, and epinephrine, yielding.

Other measurements made correlated with these findings. Sociological observations showed that the boys who fought back and gave out norepinephrine had been brought up in the kind of hostile environment represented by the street gangs of Brooklyn, where very sharp elbows were needed to get along. Those who turned the anger inward and excreted epinephrine had been brought up in a Boston Brahmin type of society in which, far from its being a survival virtue to show one's teeth, it was considered bad manners to indicate emotion. As in the days of Sparta or in old England, it was necessary to hide one's feelings. Accepting the correctness of these findings—and I am not aware of any challenge to them—you must assume either that certain biologic types were preferentially born in different neighborhoods or that different neighborhoods had something to do with determining the biologic and the corresponding psychological types that emerged.

So much for the impact of environment on the total organism: now to zero in on the brain, again reminding ourselves of well-established findings. One of the most dramatic was the early experimental work of raising newborn chimpanzees either in total darkness or, as in recent repetitions, in unpatterned light, with a milk glass bowl covering the head so that light but no pattern could be seen. The baby chimps were kept this way for a couple of months, nothing being done to the eyes or to the brain. When released into the normal world with patterned fields available to them, the chimps, in both studies, turned out to be functionally blind so far as pattern vision behavior was concerned. These chimps—and the same is known for humans born with cloudy corneas that are later corrected—simply do not have pattern vision, either never acquiring it or acquiring it with the utmost difficulty only after a long time.

Here is clearly a defect in the nervous system's behavior or functioning due to nothing more than impoverization of the appropriate visual experience that should have been pouring into it during its normal maturation period. This kind of experiment has been expanded in a number of ways, made much more precise as to localization in single instances and so forth, but the basic point is the same.

In recent years, there have been experiments, with rats particularly, using various kinds of environmental deprivation versus environmental enrichment, and examining not merely the consequent behavior but changes in the nervous system itself. Under enriched experiential conditions, increases have been found in the enzymes producing some of the critical amines, such as the tyramine system. Most dramatically (and I am at last beginning to believe that this will hold up), groups of "enriched" rats—those exposed to light and sound, in a social environment with toys to amuse themselves and fondling by the handler—show hypertrophy and increase some 5 per cent in the thickness of the cortex, in contrast to "impoverished" littermates—those alone in a dark cage, with nothing to play with, given good minimal care but no attention by the handler.

When I studied anthropology, I was taught that man became a tool-using animal because he had become erect, with heels, thereby having a free hand and an opposable thumb, and most of all, because he had a large cortex that conferred the motor skills necessary to use tools. This relationship is certainly true, but which is cause and which effect has come under severe questioning. Modern anthropological thought argues for the reverse: that man is a primate that happened to use tools (partly because he'd been driven out of the forest, not being as good a physical specimen as some of his fellows), and that his continued use of them led to the great increase in the cerebral lobes. One of the bits of evidence that it is this way is that tool-using came at the beginning of the time during which a dramatic increase occurred in the total size of the skull, and presumably of the brain.

Now for the constructive consequences of this approach. Learning can be defined loosely as any change in behavior of a system resulting from its experience. When the living system, or non-living for that matter, is put in the same environmental situation yet behaves differently, and if the change can be shown to be at least somewhat cumulative as a result of previous experience, it may be called "learning." Certainly in organisms I'm prepared to call it learning. Formal education is a deliberate attempt so to structure the experience that impinges on the organism over a length of time that behavior is modified in a desired direction. When we look with abhorrence on the influencing of human beings by other human beings, we are being silly and hypocritical, because a great deal of social interaction constitutes attempts to influence other human beings. Moreover, the great bulk of influencing is not at all with the reprehensible motive of enhancing our own gains at the expense of another, but with the desirable goal of helping—as parents do in raising children, teachers in educating them, ministers in developing their characters, and doctors in improving their health habits.

Education has been the most backward of the behavioral sciences, for one reason perhaps, because it was one of the earliest systematic efforts at manipulating human beings. Formal education really began in the twelfth century with the medieval universities. Although there was a little of it in Rome and in Greece, it had no mass impact. The medieval university was rather different from the modern: youngsters of 11, 12, and 13 regularly attended the University of Paris. This was an effort to increase the transmission of knowledge and to bring about changes in the behavior and capacities of the students. The whole character of education changed when printing made possible the transmission of information in written instead of in spoken form. The lectures we have today are largely anachronisms that have remained from the time when information could be processed only in this form.

Printing was certainly the first great technological invention modifying education and the changes that could be induced in the young. Blackboards and chalk were perhaps important additions. Audio-visual aids that came in during the present century, still to be adequately exploited, had great additional impact, especially on the more informal education experiences, which we call entertainment. We are at the threshold, I am convinced, of a technological revolution that will beggar all the preceding ones because it will offer the first real prosthesis to the brain and the thought process. I refer not to the computer itself as a bit of hardware, but to computer systems in the larger sense.

Here let me state my general view on this before developing further the possibilities of computer-aided learning (CAL). I regard the great epochs in evolutionary advance as the development of (1) the gene, which gave continuity; (2) of sex, which allowed gene shuffling and speeded change; (3) of multicellularity, which allowed specialization of function and the allocation of pliability or malleability to a particular group of cells; (4) of the nervous system which—first in the attributes of the individual unit, then in the richness and intricacy in the patterns of the connections, and finally in the sheer aggregation of larger and larger numbers of units and patterns—rapidly took on greater capacity for being modified, thus increasing the malleability of organisms. Thereafter, the environment could act on the race, by selection, *and* on the maturing human being, so that individual experience could be passed on.

In social evolution, I see three sub-epochs, each of immense importance. The first great achievement was the use of a symbol to represent some thing: this is *prelanguage.* Many higher animals besides man clearly can use symbols; to some extent, they have also made a second step, the use of organized symbols: this is *language.* None except man has taken the third step, the use of tested organized symbols: this is *science.*

We are just entering the fourth subepoch, made possible by computer systems as a prosthesis for the thinking process. We will not, as some fear, substitute artificial intelligence for natural stupidity, but rather develop an effective symbiosis between the particular kinds of attributes that can be built into the machines of today, and still more those of tomorrow, and the attributes uniquely those of the highly evolved human brain. I personally think that the invention of this newer technology of information handling and education will prove of the same magnitude of importance in human evolution as the invention not of printing but of language itself.

Having introduced my theme, let me be sure that you and I are considering the same thing. When I speak of a computer system, I think of a total information-processing system. I shall describe it in terms of developments at the University of California at Irvine, where I have had the opportunity to help build into the structure of an incipient university the computer systems that are so complementary to the university—which is also a system for information-storing, retrieving, processing, disseminating, and creating. I assure you that what follows is not a pipe dream for the twenty-first century, although its impact on civilization will be largely in that century. These resources are here: the hardware is available, the software is available in limited amounts, nothing is preventing rapid further development. All that is needed is a good deal of hard slogging work, much of it not even at the level of theoretical pioneering but of direct application of established learning to produce additional materials.

I think of a computer system as a sort of glorified information sandwich. On one side is a huge data bank. One can store in retrievable form anything that is humanly recordable in the public domain. One cannot store things that are subjective in the individual, but if he puts them forth in words or in music or in actions, they can be recorded and become part of such a data bank. I'm thinking, of course, not only of what can be put in the magnetic storage of the computer, which is already at the multi-millions, but also in the accessory drums, discs and tapes, which permit almost infinite storage. Besides, the original form can be stored and computer-mobilized: microform records of anything visual (printing, diagrams, pictures), in tape form (movies, video tapes), a complete record of somebody giving a lecture or acting a play, or of a volcano erupting or whatever phenomenon one can record, all can be put in data banks. These can be accessed by the next element, the meat of the sandwich, in unlimited quantity and in times of not more than two-tenths of a second today, most of them in microseconds or less.

I am making an emphatic claim here: by saying that the entire Library of Congress can be put in microform. In fact, I have seen large parts of it stored in a relatively small area, in machines where any particular page of any particular book or, given appropriate addressing or indexing, any word or idea on any page in any book can be retrieved in a fraction of a second by the request of a user who doesn't know it's there but knows what he wants. All right, here's the great data bank. Of course, in the science areas, there is already great progress in putting into machine-usable form the findings from the past, and in currently entering findings of the present; bibliographic procedures will be enormously altered in the next few years.

Let us move to the center of the sandwich and look right to the user. In the past, the machine typed out a long tape or print-out from a typewriter, the speed of which ranged from slow to moderately rapid, after a batch of punch cards had gone through the machine and something had happened within it. Today, one is in communication with the central processor essentially with on-line connections. One can type in and get a typed-out answer as soon as one stops typing in; with no perceptive delay, the appropriate answer comes back. The impress of a light pencil on a cathode ray screen, a television tube, will project immediately pictures or text or whatever is appropriate. One can communicate by microphone and loudspeaker and have a conversation with the system. These terminals or consoles, as they are often called, will be activated through connections from networks just exactly as telephones are today. And the great wonder of being able to sit in your room and talk to a friend far away, which was the excitement in the beginning of this century, or to see someone at a distance over television or hear him on the radio, which was the excitement later, will be replicated through these terminals at which one can plug in and talk to or see anything available through the computer.

Applied to education, this may mean the demise of alma mater as we know the ivy-covered campus. We may have schools that depend merely on their students' interacting with a computing system. Some people think this is very impersonal and terrible; I do not.

The computer itself, the meat of the sandwich, I think of, in the educational area, as essentially a tutor, an individual tutor. Not only can one give it a data base continually updated by new information, as any library would be; one can use a second advantage: he can program computers to learn their art while education is still almost entirely an art. Just as machines have been programmed to play checkers and, in the course of playing learn to play better until they could beat state champions, so one can program so-called heuristics into the machine so that as it interacts with students (and apart from whether or not psychologists improve learning theory to present to it) it can itself improve rules-of-thumb as a result of finding that a student gets the idea, responds correctly as it tries this, that or the other tutorial device and so learns (i.e., teaches itself) to teach better. A good teacher does the same, of course, although all too many teachers are not that good.

The computer-tutor, third, can develop in its memory a specific profile of the individual student with whom it is working, and find that for this student visual or auditory exposure is better, large steps or short steps, concrete examples or abstract ideas. Many variations can be tried and the interaction of the student and his "tutor" leads the computer to a knowledge of each individual subject with whom it is working. As a fourth advantage, the computer can give the student immediate and individual attention at any time, a great improvement over what happens, nearly all the time, in most classes in most schools at most levels. It has been shown in elementary schools, for example, that of the actual time in which the teacher and students are together in the same room, during only about 15 per cent of it is the teacher teaching anybody. And the amount of that time given to any one student in a classroom of 30 to 50 students is vanishingly small. Under computer-aided learning (CAL) conditions, the individual student has a response to his response immediately, uniquely, and adapted to him. Finally, a fifth advantage, the computer has infinite patience and is nonthreatening. For these reasons it has been able to bring autistic children out of their autism to an extent almost impossible with human teachers. Only an extremely few devoted human beings, almost giving their lives to one or two children, have been able to do as well.

So much for the kind of system I see. It is not in existence in all these aspects; but, I reiterate, everything I have said can be done and most of it is being done, in one way or another, today.

What are some of the consequences of this? First, the objective evidence of what can be done: there have been enough experiments at different levels with CAL to indicate that it is no longer hypothetical. Students have learned fairly routine courses—statistics, German, typewriting, elementary psychology—with exposures on a terminal and interacting with a computer acting somewhat as a tutor, in something between one-fifth and one-third the time taken to learn the same material in an ordinary classroom. An experiment at Stanford taught children to read with 200 hours on a computer terminal and nothing else, children starting at zero and ending, after 200 hours of CAL, able to read and speak English quite satisfactorily. Students can progress at their own speed and without the psychological apprehension of having to hit an examination every so often. If one completes a normal course on this system, he has automatically passed the examination, because he cannot go forward until he has mastered the earlier material.

A number of major educational consequences flow from this newer educational technology. For one thing, lopping off education into chronological chunks can stop. Of course, one must have a course running over a semester or a quarter; whatever its content, a course must fit into the Procrustean bed of the calendar. With systems of CAL, one can develop units of any length, build them together like Mechano units, and with a relatively few units build appropriate courses for any kind of user. Courses can be much more personalized, not only in time but in content.

One of the great outcomes could be the separation of the two functions of educational institutions that have become inextricably combined and utterly confused: educating the student, and certifying that he has an education. Getting grades and acquiring degrees are quite independent of the learning process and often interfere with it. One will be able to give the union card appropriately with the aid of these machines, and separate the more active learning components from it.

That other things happen in the course of schooling besides the acquiring of information and understanding and the ability to think and manipulate ideas is understood; certain interpersonal and social developments occur. These have to be taken care of, but they are quite separate problems. They may be taken care of by very different people and in more effective ways than when mixed in as flavoring in the educational experience.

Perhaps the most important thing that can come out of CAL is that education itself may move forward from pretty much a medieval art, in which there is almost no evidence of what is really being accomplished by this most expensive, most continuous, most massively followed occupation of mankind. Are teaching and learning, in the formal school systems particularly, really doing what we think they are? Just because children speak English in this country when they grow up and have learned reading and writing and a little arithmetic (and speak Chinese in China, where most children never go to any school at all), doesn't prove that we have done any particular job with our formal schooling process. I think we have done a job, but I also think we can do a vastly better one with the same amount of resources. By supplementing very limited human resources, a limited number of teachers of any kind and a tiny number of really good ones, with these amplifying and expanding technologies, and by using these to learn more about how to educate in general, to add science to art, we can achieve a great deal.

This brings us back to where we started. If it is possible to structure the experience that human beings go through in the course of maturation, if we can apply an experience that is more effective in bringing about the behavioral changes that we want (we assume that we know what we want, although perhaps we don't always), then we certainly can exercise the brain, improve its physiologic capacity, make fuller use of what was given at birth in the genes and in the prenatal experiences of the embryo, and come out with a norm of the population that, while always having the usual distribution curve, will move progressively upstream towards greater capacities and abilities.

And this, I need not remind you, is almost essential to effective survival, let alone further advance, of the human race, because we are in a rising ocean of man-made information. More people are communicating more easily about more things more often. Automation, taking over the easier of the jobs that men used to do, is forever becoming able to take on more elaborate jobs. So unless we can upgrade man, unless we can make better brains, partly by the kind of genetic improvements that we learn from the study of defects, and partly by the positive enhancement of the normal and the gifted through improved experience during maturation, man will not swim on this tide of information, but will most assuredly drown in it.

5

# THE NATURE OF PSYCHOLOGICAL CHANGE AND ITS RELATION TO CULTURAL CHANGE

LAWRENCE S. KUBIE

LAWRENCE S. KUBIE *has been a faculty and staff member at Yale, Columbia, Johns Hopkins, and the University of Maryland, as well as at the New York Psychoanalytic Institute. Dr. Kubie's publications include* The Neurotic Distortion of the Creative Process; Practical and Theoretical Aspects of Psychoanalysis; The Riggs Story; *and* Psychoanalysis as Science.

# 5

## THE NATURE OF PSYCHOLOGICAL CHANGE
## AND ITS RELATION TO CULTURAL CHANGE

*Lawrence S. Kubie*

THROUGHOUT life human mental processes are never at rest, either in sleep or in the waking state. There is an incessant input, of which only a small fraction is consciously perceived, much of it entering the central stream without conscious awareness, i.e., on a preconscious basis. There it is stored, registered, ordered, coded, and processed, until out of widening ripples of central disturbance comes an equally continuous but variable and largely preconscious output, emotionally colored in changing and alternating hues. In an incessant inner turmoil of this kind, what can constitute significant change—change which is more than ripples and waves in the recurrent ebb and flow of activity? What constitutes enduring change? This is our basic problem, and since most of this activity takes place on neither a conscious nor an unconscious level, but preconsciously, the difficult technical problem is to develop methods by which preconscious processing can be analyzed with greater precision.

### INTRODUCTION

My approach to this question derives from the clinical study of human lives with the techniques and the data of psychoanalytic psychiatry. These methods and theories are not flawless. Nor are the data always certain; and surely psychiatrists and psychoanalysts do not already know the answers. Their function is chiefly to ask questions. In fact I regard psychoanalysis largely as a penetrating instrument for the uncovering of crucial questions. The question here concerns the relationship between

This study has been made possible through the generosity of the Foundations Fund for Research in Psychiatry, of New Haven, Connecticut.

135

on the one hand the alterations which occur incessantly in the stream of man's inner experiences, and on the other the inflexibility and rigidity of his underlying nature. What then constitutes enduring change in a stream of continuously shifting currents and eddies? Clinical study brought me to the seemingly circular hypothesis that the only psychological change which is enduringly meaningful for individual health, for life in general, or for human culture as a whole is a change in the capacity for further change. It is on this hypothesis that I will base all that follows; and it will lead to a search for objective criteria of change in this sense.

All manifestations of neurotic processes are rigid, repetitive, stereotyped, insatiable, unlearning, and, indeed, unteachable. Behavior which expresses any aspect of the personality dominated by neurotic mechanisms will manifest these characteristics. This is equally true for the self-diagnosing neurosis, such as a hand-washing compulsion, and for such subtle masquerades of health as compulsive benevolence.

If man survives in a social order in which he is free to experiment with changes in the forms of his social order, he will still face problems to which no human culture has ever found solutions. To make external changes is relatively easy; but can the human being's freedom to change alter? And how? Or is the old saying true, that everything can change except human nature? And if so, what is it in human nature that limits the capacity of the individual to change or may even block it absolutely? And if individual human nature operates under such restrictions as these, to what extent does this restrict change in human culture as a whole?

This hypothesis about the nature of change is linked to another, namely, that in every human culture about which we have any searching information men manifest a universal neurotic potential that both shapes and restricts their lives but which for the most part is so well masked that it can be detected only by special methods. This potential evolves into a neurotic process, which is variable and which is masked more often than it is overt, but which when it is overt becomes the manifest neurotic state. Paradoxically there is also a creative potential which is equally universal, but whose expression is distorted and hampered by the coexisting neurotic process. Indeed the fate of the creative potential depends upon the ways in which neurotic mechanisms distort and imprison it.

Let me cite a few banal examples of the fact that in those aspects of man in which neurotic mechanisms dominate him, he is incapable of learning from experiences of success or failure, of pain or pleasure, of satiation or frustration, of rewards or punishments, of exhortation or criticism. This occurs equally in men with overt or masked neuroses. Consider a cultivated, educated, bright, and intelligent woman whose childhood had been overshadowed by an alcoholic father. On one level in spite of that experience and on another level because of it, she had to marry three alcoholics in succession, each time convinced and determined that this would not, indeed could not, happen again. After her fourth marriage (this time to a nondrinker) she became an alcoholic herself. Is this the paradigm of our problem—man's neurotogenic tendency to defy experience instead of learning from it, without any awareness that this is what he is doing?

Of course, about such a case as this one would ask many questions: What unconscious rivalries, needs for vengeance, hostile identifications, needs to prove herself by triumphing over both father and mother, etc., may have made an automaton of this woman, as she repeated her tragic experiment? How, in general, can such stereotyped necessities sometimes dominate human behavior even in the face of predictable pain? Why do similar imprisoning stereotypes occur in different ways in every culture of which we know anything? It is essential to note that whenever this happens, it produces a psychosocial feedback, a cybernetic system in which the neurotogenic rigidities of the individual are entrenched by and also reinforce the stereotypes of the culture. This produces a further restriction in the range and capacity for human change, whether up or down on any value system. Yet it also carries a more optimistic impli-cation—that if and when the day comes that we learn how to resolve the universal neurotic episodes of childhood as they occur, so that residues do not accumulate to produce the masked and overt neuroses of adult life, a new dimension of freedom will enter human life and human society. From this it follows that the ultimate goal of any educational and cultural instru-ment should be to reduce the role of the neurotic ingredient in what we call normal human nature. The extent to which this is achieved would be the measure of the greatness of any human institution or of any work of art or literature. Indeed, if man ever faces up to the fact that the universal masked neurotic ingredient in human nature is the great unsolved problem of human culture, he will turn his attention seriously to the ques-tion of how to bring ourselves up so that the neurotic conflicts of children can be resolved in childhood.

But what lies behind all of this? There is both experimental and clinical evidence that in all human beings there is a con-tinuous, concurrent interplay among conscious, preconscious, and unconscious processes, out of which evolve our every moment of thought, feeling, purpose, and behavior. There is further evidence that whenever the unconscious ingredients among these processes play the dominant role, they predeter-mine the automatic and stereotyped repetition of the resulting behavior, without regard to consequences. This is a basic fact of human psychology; and it is no less important because in addition to psychological determinants certain organic pro-cesses may contribute to these stereotypes, as has been shown by the work of Brickner, Penfield, Olds, and many others. Re-cently, Paul MacLean, the great neurophysiologist, pointed out the fact that the human animal has not merely one brain but a hierarchy of at least three: a reptilian brain at the core; a lower mammalian brain a step above this; and the higher mammalian brain struggling, often unsuccessfully, to rule the others. He compared us to a 1960 car with a 1940 carburetor and a 1920 generator. It is not remarkable that this jerry-built apparatus contributes to our vulnerability to those obligatory repetitions which are the core of all that is neurotic in human nature; an obligatory repetition to which a variety of other variables, experiential, social, chemical, and structural, all make their secondary contributions.

⅄ Clearly, all who are concerned with cultural progress must search for ways to eliminate or at least limit those neurotic factors which restrict the freedom of the human being himself to change. This is a search which starts in infancy, when the restriction of the capacity of the infant and child to change is first observed. Such restrictions should be compared in different child-rearing traditions. And since we cannot turn back the hands of the clock to compare this phenomenon as it occurs today with its manifestations in earlier centuries, we must study all existing cultures, those which we call "primitive" as well as those which we euphemistically call "advanced," seeking for correlations between individual and cultural freedom to change.

As I contemplate the role in human culture, of education, of art, of literature, of religion, and of the humanities, and indeed, of all the life sciences, I ask the same question: "What is their effect, if any, on the individual's freedom to change and to keep on changing, and consequently on the capacity of our culture to evolve?" I have to confess that this question itself gives me an uneasy feeling, since even savants and creative artists and scientists are not notorious for their flexibility. This, of course, leads to still another question: "What effect do our educational processes have on our ability to transmit to succeeding generations any fragment of wisdom which we acquire in our own allotted time?" And this in turn brings me to my ultimate concern, which is with the question to what extent the resolution in early childhood of the universal neurotic episodes of childhood would free the enormous untapped creative potential which is latent in every man. This, indeed, is the meeting place of the two streams: the freedom of the individual and of society for continuing change.

## WHAT CHANGE IS NOT

It is difficult to decide what psychological change is until we can agree on what it is not, and recognize the importance of certain basic differentiations. Some of these should be obvious but are strangely neglected, as, for example, the distinction between true change on the one hand and mere masking or unmasking on the other. There is in all of life an incessant shifting between latent and overt manifestations of the same unchanged inner (preconscious or unconscious) processes. In any person at different times and under different circumstances, and also in different people, the impact of internal conflicts or of external events, and of specific trigger experiences, can simulate change simply by making manifest something which had been masked (by giving it conscious, symbolic representation). In fact these fluctuations between latent processes and their manifest representations are incessant in human life, when we are awake quite as much as when we are asleep and dreaming.

Less obvious, but equally important for the study of change, is an understanding of the identity of opposites in the language of unconscious mental processes, such as Yes and No, Yesterday and Tomorrow, Near and Far, etc.

On a conscious level I may change my mind about a plan from yes to no, from doing something to not doing it, from staying where I am to traveling a thousand miles, from doing it now to doing it next year. On an unconscious level these may be unaltered equivalents. But certainly the external situation of my life will vary with the decision which finally is put into effect; and this in turn will have many practical and emotional consequences, so that my life will change. I may or may not feel different; yet I, the individual, will not have changed. The importance of this fact for exploring the nature of change is basic. In psychiatry, this has much to do with the difference between sickness as a process and a sick life; yet it has received little consideration, even among analysts.

The obverse is also true. It is well known that wide swings of thoughts and feelings may occur without changes in underlying processes and problems. We see this constantly both in daydreams and in night dreams, e.g., in the seesaw between bland dreams and nightmares, which may follow each other in swift succession in one individual, with widely varied affects, yet continuing to express the same disguised conflicts. Here the apparent "change" is limited to the mask. We see this also in wide sweeps of the cyclothymic cycle. (Statistics which are based on such changes as these will give fallacious support to the illusion that significant change has occurred.)

Furthermore, changes in manifest behavior can be unconsciously simulated. There are even facsimile psychoses! Or they can be preconsciously selected and rejected or purposefully withheld and masked or exaggerated with deliberate overemphasis. There are still other ways in which it can be difficult to recognize what, if anything, is changing in the incessant stream of processing which underlies all human behavior, whether the apparent changes occur "spontaneously" or under the influence of efforts at therapeutic maneuvers. Shifts occur frequently in the patient who seems to become dramatically "improved" (or alternatively, "worsened") at the very moment the family or the family physician first urges him to consult a psychiatrist; or else on the very day he first consults the psychiatrist; or on the day he enters a psychiatric hospital. Moreover, such sudden symptomatic shifts from latent to overt, or from manifest to latent, or from affirmation to denial may endure for some days or weeks. This does not mean that lasting changes have occurred in that complex mixture of buried processes which make up the personality, out of which illness has arisen.

Let me describe a concrete example. A woman had a severe claustrophobia, of which she had been wholly unaware through many years of a successful career. Her field of work was one which kept her constantly on the move. During those years of professional activity and success she complained jokingly but incessantly about the rigors of her peripatetic job because it kept her away from home and friends. She had no suspicion that the very thing she complained about was precisely what had made it possible for her to maintain a convincing simulation of health, free from any overt symptomatic manifestations of her hidden phobic neurosis. In fact, she would have denied with amused impatience any suggestion that she had neurotic difficulties of any kind. Yet for the first time in her adult life, these caught up with her when she married and found herself tied down by the care of her first infant, for whose arrival she had been waiting impatiently. At this critical juncture the latent claustrophobia became overt and precipitated her into a period of acute, stormy, and symptomatic illness. The underlying, neurotogenic conflicts which had given rise to her latent neurosis had been there during all the years when their only manifestation had been her faintly overdriven, but successful, roving career. Without knowing it she had been neurotically enslaved to this career as a defense against a neurosis, the existence of which she did not recognize until marriage and motherhood triggered the violent symptomatic eruption of overt phobic distress out of her latent claustrophobia. This led her swiftly into acute alcoholism, and then to secondary and tertiary guilt, shame, rage, and suicidal depression. Of course, at this point her whole life was changed and she herself looked and acted changed in every way. Yet in a truer sense she was unaltered. Her life had indeed become "sicker," but the underlying process of sickness itself was not different. There had only been this shift from latent to overt, as it became destructively symptomatic. At the same time, this change finally made her heretofore masked neurosis accessible to treatment.

Only when long analytic treatment had altered the neuro-togenic mechanisms which had determined the whole shape and quality of her years of "successful and socially productive living," did she herself begin to change in the sense that she became free to try different ways.

This life story challenges the prevailing confusion between, on the one hand, those enduring changes which may result from fundamental alterations in underlying pathogenic processes and, on the other hand, those temporary changes in surface manifestations which can result from altering the circum-stances of a man's life, particularly when these circumstances can be changed in such a way that he will pay either a greater or a lesser price for an underlying and often unrecognized neuro-sis. Thus, to move a man with a height phobia from New York City to a flat plain will alter his life dramatically, and may diminish or even eliminate all symptomatic suffering for a time, yet will leave his underlying neurosis untouched.

Another example of partial or surface change without basic underlying change was seen in an illness which produced epi-sodic obsessional furors of homosexual ruminations and activi-ties. Even with incomplete treatment this patient became able to marry and to have children and thus to surround himself with a family's love, to which, in turn, he could respond with devotion. These changes had many happy secondary conse-quences for his life. Yet from time to time, under special circum-stances or in response to specific trigger stimuli, the distressing furors would recur. These were brief and he could control, limit, and understand them; but each time he paid for them in a period of anxiety and tormenting depression. Here it was clear that the underlying process of illness itself had changed partially, but only partially. The change was sufficient to en-able him to marry. Hitherto crippling symptoms were dimin-ished. This in turn made possible extraordinary changes in his life as a whole. Indeed, his life became totally different, but the inner changes were still incomplete and inconstant. Therefore, he had not changed sufficiently for a total eradication of the underlying neurotogenic conflict.

Subsequently, with further treatment, the outbursts of obsessional, homosexual turmoil disappeared, to be replaced by episodic flurries of driven hypomanic activity, alternating with bouts of paralyzing depression. These new symptoms brought about a new group of tertiary subjective and objective changes in his life. Thus, the underlying process of illness continued, altered but still not eradicated.

These examples highlight again the differences between a sickness, a sick man, and a sick life, and also between symptomatic changes, changes in a life, and changes in the processes of essential underlying sickness.

At some point, any efforts to alter behavior significantly and enduringly, whether by therapy, education, or other cultural forces, must interrupt more than the surface phenomena. Furthermore, they must alter not only the originating processes and the behavior which these produce but also the sustaining processes and the secondary feedback from them. Otherwise surface shifts can never be regarded as evidence of fundamental change.

Still another example is from the story of a young woman who led a life of abject submissiveness with episodes of self-mutilation and kleptomania, interspersed with periods of gorging, followed by self-induced vomiting, and still other phases of deliberate self-starvation. Under treatment, something in the underlying constellation and in the symptomatic processes changed to such a degree and in such a way that the tendency to self-mutilation and the cycles of self-starvation alternating with compulsive eating almost disappeared. She was able to work, to hold a job, and to enjoy at least some aspects of heterosexual relationships. This aspect of her life was still restricted, as shown by the fact that she could express it only in debased and debasing relationships, through which she secretly ventilated her pent-up hostility toward all of those who were closest to her. Obviously, partial internal changes had occurred which in turn had produced symptomatic changes which fed back different secondary and tertiary consequences for her life and her human relationships. Yet all of this remained partial. Her *life* was less sick, and the process of illness was modified, but not yet fully resolved. She herself was not yet basically changed. Her capacity to change was still limited.

Evidently, every moment of psychological activity is a moment of apparent change. But for the most part these are changes in the surface disguises worn by unchanged underlying thoughts, feelings, conflicts, and purposes. One form of symbolic representation is substituted for another, often with changes in affective coloring. These will seem different even when they represent an unchanging base. Furthermore, we are continuously in transit between one such mixture and another, between one point of temporary, unstable equilibrium and another, yet never returning precisely to the preceding point of departure.

What all of these examples have in common is the simple fact that lasting and significant change requires a release of psychological processes from domination by the dictatorship of unconscious mechanisms in that mosaic of concurrent conscious, preconscious, and unconscious processes which govern every moment of human life. Only this can produce the freedom to go on experimenting—now trying a turn to the right, now a turn to the left, free from unconsciously determined compulsions or fears in either direction.

## What Then Is Change?

It is a source of many human tragedies that, starting with the first acquisition of language in early childhood and continuing throughout life, the freedom to change with which we are endowed at birth gradually lessens under the progressive influence of neurotic restrictions. Most of these take the form of unconscious compulsive and phobic mechanisms. Only rarely are these easily recognized through self-evident symptoms. By contrast, the fully evolved neurotic state is self-diagnosing. A man with a hand-washing compulsion does not have to be convinced that he has a neurosis for which he needs help: he comes complaining of his neurosis and asking for help. On the other hand, the man who is destroying his career and his life through compulsive gregariousness, or a compulsive work drive, or even compulsive benevolence, will struggle to his last breath to deny his neurosis and to defend himself and his way of living as "normal." Yet, destructive to the patient himself as the hand-washing compulsion may be, its secondary consequences are not as destructive either to the patient or to those who are around him as are the consequences of many insidious but socially accepted symptoms. Frank neuroses may paralyze the individual patient, yet may have far less influence on society. In the same way, a mother or father with a neurotic fear of heights may produce less distortion in the child than would that same mother or father with subtly concealed neurotic personality traits.[1] Moreover, the frankly symptomatic neurosis is actually less frequent than is the subtler neurotic distortion of human development.

In childhood, the early manifest restrictions of the child's psychological freedom appear in the form of tic-like repetitive patterns of sound and movement; in relation to breathing, crying, ingestion, and excretion; as sleep disturbances; as transient phobias and compulsions; as seemingly unreasonable terrors; as arbitrary repugnances to certain foods or places or people; as disturbances of waking or sleeping; and the like. It becomes a fundamental goal of child-rearing, of formal education, and of psychotherapy to explore these early imprisonments of the child's freedom at their inception, and to restore to the child his freedom to change in any area in which this has

---

[1] The story of how education itself, and the mere acquisition of language, initiates the imprisonment of psychological freedom is one of the most important problems which human education must face and solve.

become impaired. What this leads us to is the conviction that the only psychological changes which can bring lasting and basic differences either to the personality of a human being or to his life are those which have the effect of enlarging his freedom to change and to keep on changing, thus initiating sequences of continuing and evolving movement. Merely to go from one fixed point to another is not significant in any ultimate sense, even if the second point has immediate consequences which are preferable to the first, both individually and socially. Thus, the most searching indication that true psychological change has occurred would be an indication that there has been an alteration in the capacity for continuing change. This leads us to ask what such an indicator can be.

IMPLICATIONS FOR CULTURAL CHANGE

Like human beings, cultures seem to be fluid processes, yet they have relatively rigid cores. These are compounded of written laws, authoritarian edicts, and those unwritten laws which we call traditions, customs, or mores. There can be, and often are, inconsistencies among these various ingredients of a culture. Not infrequently the unwritten elements in a culture are expressions of entrenched biases of the individuals who make up the culture, biases which in turn are not easy to alter. This is because they represent not only our conscious convictions, ideals, aspirations, and ethical standards, but also unconscious conflicts and their derivative neurotic components in human nature. This makes it impossible to change a culture in any significant sense unless the individuals who compose that culture become free to change, which is precisely the problem I have been considering in the preceding pages—what meaningful change constitutes for the individual and how this can be achieved. The fact which confronts us is that cultural change is limited by the restrictions imposed on change in individual human nature by concealed neurotic processes.

At the same time there is a continuous cybernetic interplay

between culture and the individual, i.e., between the intra-psychic processes which make for fluidity or rigidity within the individual and the external processes which make for fluidity or rigidity in a culture. It would be naïve to expect political and ideological liberty to give internal liberty to the individual citizen unless he had already won freedom from the internal tyranny of his own neurotic mechanisms. Political liberty allows him to experiment with changes in the external forms of the society in which he lives. Yet he will not be able to take full advantage of that external freedom unless he also has won his internal freedom. Therefore, insofar as man himself is neuroto-genically restricted, he will restrict the freedom to change of the society in which he lives. This interplay is sometimes clearly evident, sometimes subtly concealed; but it is at the heart of the solution of the problem of human progress. A free society does not automatically bring psychological freedom to the individual, although it makes it possible for him to strive for it. Nor does the free individual automatically create a free society; but it gives him the freedom to struggle toward it.

These are such complex issues that to undertake to discuss them in detail in a single presentation is impossible. Therefore, I leave it at this point, merely reemphasizing the fact that the only psychological change in a man which is significant and meaningful is a change which makes further change possible. The same basic principle applies to social organizations as well.

6

# ALIENATION AND AUTONOMY

BRUNO BETTELHEIM

BRUNO BETTELHEIM *is Stella M. Rowley Professor of Education and director of the Sonia Shankman Orthogenic School at The University of Chicago. His recent books include* The Empty Fortress, Love Is Not Enough, *and* The Informed Heart.

## ALIENATION AND AUTONOMY

*Bruno Bettelheim*

Autonomy and alienation: as you know, one is a Greek word implying freedom, independence, self-direction. The other is from the Latin, meaning a strangeness or, according to my latest *Webster's*, a transfer of ownership to another person. When it is put in these terms, who would not want to be autonomous and who would not want to avoid alienation? But maybe things are not quite so simple. That one term is Greek in origin and the other Latin reminds me of a controversy that was very fashionable in Western Europe after World War I—one that opposed the culture of Greece to the civilization of Rome. And although these two opposite concepts are now given more up-to-date names, such as inner-directed versus outer-directed, I believe it's still the same old quarrel. As we use these two terms we seem to feel that one would increase our humanity, the other destroy it. But the two human conditions that each of them describes were created not by God or the Devil, but by ourselves. In theory the two are as distant from each other as antipodes. But in practice, man wants both: culture and civilization; to be self-directed and also beholden to the other. I believe what is posed here as a dichotomy is really a question of what is their right mixture. It's the age-old problem of what and how much to render unto Caesar.

I can remember clearly the feeling of superiority shown when Europeans compared their ancient culture to a supposedly barren American civilization. But for the old European countries, this is no longer an easy way of denying their own longing for ease as well as culture. And as they become more and more affluent themselves, and hence also, let's face it, more acquainted with anomie, they begin to realize that it seems impossible as yet to enjoy the advantages of one without suffering the other. A recent experience brought that into sharp focus for me.

I happened to be in Europe during last summer's Los Angeles riots, and as I read the European papers anxiously to learn what went on, I was startled by the sober, sympathetic attitude toward our difficulties in the European press. On previous occasions I had found that internal American problems evoked a condescending attitude and that it was a favorite pastime, particularly in liberal circles, to bait Americans about the mistreatment of our Negro population. This time the attitude seemed strangely different. Essentially they seemed to be saying, "What do the Americans expect? If their government goes out of its way to make the alienated groups aware of their alienation from society, if it raises in them hopes it cannot possibly presently fulfill, then insurrection must follow by necessity."

This change in attitude may very well reflect the difficulties that are currently besetting Europe's large urban centers, too. At the very time of the Los Angeles riots there was rioting in Stockholm six days in succession, and for two days it even spread to Oslo. It began when the police tried to separate two fighting gangs in Stockholm, who then made common cause against the police and began to riot in the streets, overturning cars, throwing bottles and bricks, and what have you. You see, in Europe, too, large groups have become alienated and are reacting explosively to their predicament.

Of course, there seems a way out, so it is hardly ever spelled out or accepted in principle—certainly not in this country. Essentially, it is that autonomy is only for the few, the select, and the best one can do for the masses is to protect them from the experience of alienation, and society from its consequence. This can be done, so it is thought, by arranging that the lower orders know and keep to their places, both in the family and in society; socially, politically, and economically. Their children should learn from the beginning to obey and to accept the leadership of their betters.

Once more it is suggested that the philosophers ought to be kings. This means that the higher orders, but only they, must be so educated that they do not fall into the dangers of the alienated existence. It means their being educated not only for autonomy, but even more for responsibility, for consciousness of the self, and for the refinement of the sensibilities. This, as a matter of fact, is the rather simple fashion in which the European, more or less class-oriented educational system still tries to deal with the problem of the alienation of the masses. But as can be seen from the riots in Stockholm, which were certainly not started by what we call college-preparatory youths, the system no longer works very well.

To return to the two concepts, autonomy and alienation, the idea seems widespread that in other times man enjoyed great autonomy—that he used to be inner-directed, and has only recently begun to suffer from alienation. So, if you bear with me, it may be useful to review some well-known historical facts. First, riots are anything but novel in history. Second, where they failed to occur it was not because the potential rioters were autonomous or inner-directed, but because they were forcibly restrained and because they were so beaten down by toil and deprivation that they could not even muster the strength to riot or to conceive the idea that they, too, deserved a place in the sun. Too, as long as man was chiefly part of his family, or of a kinship group, when his entire life was confined to his village, his church, his farm, or the guild, when it was a priest who thought for him, and when the landlord directed his actions, he was not alienated. But he certainly wasn't autonomous either.

Let us look for a moment at some of the conditions of his life. For example, we know something about the facts about life and death of peasants and laborers in the seventeenth and eighteenth century in England and France. These are not comfortable facts. In the dry but eloquent language of statistics, the historians explain to us that in eighteenth-century French villages, where in those days the vast majority of the population lived, the median age of marriage was higher than the median age of death. The average life span was perhaps a third of ours, and appreciably less for women, because of so many deaths in childbirth. In some years, the greater part of entire communities died of starvation, which appears to have been a common occurrence, and only a small richer stratum survived. In seventeenth-century Sweden, a country where now the entire population seems to enjoy reasonable autonomy, recent research shows that one year of starvation was often followed by another year of epidemics which finished off the young, the old, and the debilitated. Even about nineteenth-century England Tawney wrote: "It isn't that one class is rich, and the other is poor. It is that one class lives and the other dies." But the story these old records tell is still current history in most of Africa, Asia, and Latin America. The vast majority of the human race still live a nearly vegetative existence. They enjoy neither privacy nor culture nor autonomy. And alienation seems to them a very small price indeed to pay for gaining access to some of the socio-economic advantages and sociohuman experiences most of us enjoy, including the alienating ones, which have so far been reserved for the few and the rich.

Do I then suggest that alienation is the necessary price if larger numbers of men are to enjoy some autonomy? Possibly so. But things are not so simple. We are still posing the question far too much as either-or. Unfortunately, this is how it is posed by many who realize that the advantages of industrialization are unavoidably tied to alienation, and who therefore try to escape the devil by embracing his grandmother. To beat their relative alienation they try to escape into the extremes of solipsistic isolation. Reactions of this kind are reflected in some of modern science, writing, and art, though I cannot call it avant-garde art because it's really a rear guard of desperation.

I'm referring here to those who think that since modern man seems to have to live in a state of relative alienation, it is better to start him out in total isolation in a Skinner box, or to educate him through teaching machines instead of through human contact and experience. At the other extreme are those who, so to say, cut off their noses to spite their alienated faces. These are the ones who force themselves into extremes of deviate sex, of violence, or of drug-induced madness. They fool themselves into thinking that because they do it on their very own, the act has gained them autonomy. In fact, it merely projects them into total solipsism. They deny themselves the advantages that modern industrial society can offer to those who know how to master the problems it poses to human existence. Neither one is the answer—neither a self-chosen machine-dominated existence nor a self-chosen escape into a whipping up of the senses that ends only by dulling them. Both are unlikely cures for the ills of modern civilization, without the advantages of which we are no longer willing to exist.

The real issue is neither to try to make a good thing of alienation by trying to mechanize beyond reason all aspects of human existence, nor to deny the world altogether because it is difficult to abide in it. Instead, the real issue is: What is a vital and optimal balance between relative alienation and relative autonomy—between self-direction and beholdenness to the other? Consider the riots of Watts, for example, or those at Berkeley or Stockholm. The one originated at the highest, the other at the lowest, level of education, if not also social status. All these groups are alike in their suffering from alienation and their striving for autonomy.

That is why, contrary to widespread opinion, my thesis is that these two, while antithetical as concepts, are in fact complementary. This—their being opposites in theory, but complementary in fact—is what constitutes our present dilemma: because until the connection between them is recognized and taken account of, the larger problem cannot even be approached. In short, both autonomy and personal alienation are relative terms.

All of us feel we know what we mean when speaking of alienation, anomie, or emotional disturbance. But these terms have no meaning unless we speak of alienation as compared to something. Which are the concepts or terms we oppose them to? On this question there is very little consensus. Therefore, let me, for purpose of this discussion, suggest the term integration as the opposite of alienation. And let me suggest autonomy as the opposite of emotional disturbance. Let me also assume that personal integration is a prior condition for autonomy. Then we can see that how much autonomy a person needs depends exactly on how much he feels alienated from his world, and also on how much he is threatened by emotional disturbance. As to his feelings of alienation, I refer first to his immediate world: his family, his personal friends, his work; and second to society at large. How much autonomy he needs will, therefore, depend on what degree of alienation he experienced in childhood, within his family and during his childhood and adolescence in society.

Here then, we might take time out for a moment and consider the models that seem to dominate our thinking on human psychology and, therefore, human development. Essentially, I believe we operate on the basis of two different models, one derived from the natural sciences, the other from psychoanalysis. The first model, with its emphasis on quantifiable data, sees mental phenomena, and sometimes even the entire human being, as if they were things. Thus it adds to our alienation without extra advantage. This model has gained us important understanding and insight into only isolated aspects of human functioning. Hence it is not enough. These molecular understandings, such as Professor Platt has presented, do not yet lead to the molar insights and actions we require. The other prevailing model, the psychoanalytic one, seems equally cramped for our needs. Essentially, this model is derived from the study of neurotic patients who nevertheless were well rooted in their society, which was viewed as free of alienation. Freud rarely mentions the problem of an alienated society, or indeed of man in society. He speaks ordinarily of what society does to individual man. His model seems inadequate to help us understand the problems that beset our alienated youth, for example, or the underprivileged child.

To make up for these deficiencies we see clinical psychoanalysis centering ever greater interest on psychotic persons, particularly the schizophrenic ones, in whom the essence of their pathology is a most intense alienation from themselves, from the other, and from society. And in theoretical psychoanalysis an ever-greater emphasis is on ego-psychology, in which problems of autonomy rank with those of the unconscious.

Our concern with the extremes of alienation is also, I believe, the deeper motive in our studies of sensory deprivation. As these studies show, the individual who is artificially but totally divorced from his environment suffers a parallel disintegration of his personality structure, and with it becomes alienated even from himself.

These experiments show in scientific form what an image of the American frontiersman should have taught us long ago. I refer to the man who feels it is time to move on into the wilderness when he can spy the smoke of a distant log cabin, because it means things are getting too crowded. This man may be a rugged individualist, but he is certainly alienated from man and society. He is isolated—personally and socially depleted. He may be and probably is an autarchic person, sufficient unto himself. But he is not an autonomous one, because he is essentially deathly afraid of others and of the inner strivings they may arouse in him. He may be at home or at peace with nature, but he is at war with human nature, his own and that of others.

In turning to the psychoanalytic model, I think the most important recent development is the spread of the conviction of the need for revising the image of man it rests on. Essentially, the psychological thinking, and before that the philosophical thinking, of man and his nature has been characterized by great pendular swings between the conception of man as a free agent, the rational master of nature, and the opposite, more pessimistic view of man as an impotent reactor, with his responses completely determined by forces depending on his constitution and society. But even the sensory deprivation experiments cast doubts on the latter. In one example, under sensory deprivation with its total absence of stimuli, according to psychoanalytic theory the drives should take over because no external input interferes with them anymore. Actually, just the opposite happens. Deprived of sensory input, the drives too seem to disappear as the feelings become equally impoverished. I don't have to say any more, because I think Professor Platt's paper demonstrated this beautifully for perception. Groos, the first student of play, I believe offered us a much better model when he spoke of an image of man whose greatest joy is in being a cause. It is an idea in which a central image is set of the child exploring things around him, learning to examine and handle them with ever-increasing confidence. To me this model, essentially a very old one, is the most important model for today. This image of the ability to act successfully in one's own behalf and to one's own advantage, within one's own environment, is the image I hold to be the opposite of alienation and mental disturbance. How does such an image compare with the models that still dominate our thinking on human development? This question is important because I believe that while the human personality undergoes changes throughout life, it is the formative impact of the earliest experiences that is apt to have much more far-reaching consequences than later ones. Unlike an image of the infant whose greatest joy is being a cause, psychoanalysis for the most part views earliest infancy as a time of utter passivity. According to this view, the infant's total wants are taken care of by others and he neither wishes nor needs to do anything on his own. Contrary to such a view, I believe that, for example in his nursing, the infant is immensely active in what to him is a central event in his life. At such times he may not feel that he is moving mountains, but he certainly feels as if he were sucking them dry. To view such an experience as utterly passive contradicts the infant's experience, because what counts is his conviction that his efforts are monumental. Fortunately, such ideas are slowly being presented both in psychoanalysis and in academic psychology.

Now nobody is less autonomous, less integrated, or more alienated from himself and society than the child who is suffering from the disturbance known as infantile autism, and these are some of the children with whom we work at the University of Chicago Orthogenic School. Yet we have found there, as we work intensely with these children, that the cause of their disturbance was not primarily that they lacked any passive satisfactions. Such satisfactions were very easy for us to provide. Some autistic children accepted the offered satisfactions and remained as autistic as before. Others rejected them. None moved out of the autistic position because of such satisfactions. This they did only if we were able to activate them.

On the other hand, we were astonished at how often the history of these children showed no obvious deviation at the earliest age, though it may have occurred. Instead, the children were reported as developing more or less normally up to about 18 to 24 months. This is an age when the infant still has many needs he cannot fill himself but when through walking and talking he is beginning to try to get what he wants on his own. Or as our findings suggest, the child developed speech and other skills in an effort to influence his environment but gave them up when they failed in this purpose. The child does not withdraw because his needs are not adequately met, though this, too, certainly will scar his personality. He gives up living, so to say, when he is stymied in his active reaching out because of too much or too little response. He withdraws when his own efforts to relate find him less able to affect the environment than before.

To be active, to have initiative, if this trait is to be implanted in the child, must prove its value by getting particular results. That there is a critical age when this must happen for initiative to develop is a strong possibility for some birds and animals, and a well-documented fact for others. It is also probably true for human beings. But if this were all, I would not be discussing bird behavior here. What counts is that the critical factor, as Professor Eckhard Hess has shown us, is whether and how much the little bird is active on his own. The more effort he expends in following the mother, the more successful is the imprinting. So even for this very low species, the infant bird's acting on its own toward a goal is of crucial importance, above and beyond what was once called instinctual behavior.

This, I submit, is why artificial feeding times, arranged according to the clock, can dehumanize the infant. The reason is not so much that time-clock feeding is contrary to the natural rhythm of the body, or that it stands for a mechanical ordering of time and of the mother-child relation. It is rather that for the infant to develop initiative he has to experience that his cry for food brings about his satiation, according to his own timing. This is what makes it a social and humanizing experience. It is that his smile evokes a parallel response in the mother that starts him on the road to autonomy, because it gives him the feeling, "What I do makes a difference." Conversely, the experience that his own actions, cry or smile, make no difference is what stops him from becoming a human being and starts him on the road toward alienation.

Now I've suggested that correct imprinting in animals is basically a matter of timing. An animal that doesn't have the right experience at the right time, but has it sooner or later than the correct moment in his early development, suffers severe consequences. The same is true for human beings. We all have to have the right experiences at the right times. We certainly are aware of the adolescent's struggle for autonomy, of the turmoil, the conflicts, the fight for his own world against that of the adults. Much more dramatic and of far greater import is the infant's struggle to build his own world out of the meager pieces his reality provides. As any parent can see, his adolescent son can use his father's car in what might be called a "sailing" out to the sexual adventures that will make him a man. The little boy who tries for similar mastery and puts his father's hat on will just find that it falls over his eyes and blocks all vision. So much more difficult is a child's task of building a world out of the pieces of reality his parents provide; so much less suited are the pieces for the task. The parent's assurance, "When you are older you will understand all the ramifications and then be master of your life," is of little help. His wish is not to become a self-directing person at some future date but to be one right now. Later on, many years of experience with life without autonomy may destroy a person's trust in himself, which is even more basic a loss than one's trust in other people.

It was exactly this problem of early autonomy as against our own views of the total dependence of the infant on his mother that motivated me to go to Israel recently to study kibbutz child-rearing. There infants from the fourth day of life are raised only in part by their mothers, and from the third month, the mother plays less and less a role in their lives. According to our theories, this would lead to extreme alienation; but it does not. Equally important, the young child there develops autonomy in his interactions with others, and in his mastery of his human and physical environment, and does so considerably more than in our society. And this in a society that is relatively free of alienation. There is no sexual acting out or sex deviation in the kibbutz, almost no childhood psychosis, no delinquency whatsoever, no drug addiction, and marriage is remarkably stable. Israeli society is very similar to ours. The children so reared grow up to be stable and competent adults. How this happens is a lengthy tale. Here I can only say that my experience in the kibbutz convinced me that every infant does need a "center" in his life, a star if you like, by which to navigate;

but this need not be his mother. To stick with the analogy, a constellation can replace the individual star, on condition that what is lost in intensity is made up for by how definite are the directions by which we expect the child to navigate. It is true that the kibbutz child enjoys only limited leeway in adapting to these directions in his own individual way, but he is given ample gratification of his physical and other instinctual needs, with little pressure to control them at an early age. And this, when combined with optimal conditions for autonomy in childhood, seems to go a long way to supplement deficiencies even in the earliest mothering of the child. In its own way, kibbutz child-rearing seems to reflect many needs of modern man as it affects the relations of adults to children. It embodies one way of solving them, if tradition is disregarded and if procedures are chosen purely on pragmatic grounds. No brakes were applied in the kibbutz in going all the way to what Riesman calls the "other-directed" or the peer-directed man. And strangely enough, the kibbutz succeeds. But the results are not the expected ones. These other-directed children are not alienated, but are deeply integrated within their society, at a price, of course, which I shall soon name.

Living together in age groups from birth makes all kibbutz children feel like siblings. Emotionally, they relate most closely to their own age group and, next, to all other kibbutz children. Together with all adults in the community they form a large single family. Certainly there are exceptions; but with all this and more, a child's emotional attachment to his parents is much less intense than is that of an average, middle-class American child. The emotional deficit, if it is such, is compensated for by the much less intense, much more diluted, but nevertheless very real emotional ties to all members of the kibbutz.

In the daily life of the kibbutz there is little alienation between child and adult. Most of the community's income derives from the raising of food. As an economic activity, this is eminently plain even to the very young child, both as to the work it entails, and as to why it is needed and from whom. So is the preparation of food in the communal kitchen, the proceedings in the laundry, the building of houses or furniture. Small children often raise some animals at the children's house. And from gradeschool age, they cultivate their own farms. Thus, virtually all spheres of adult life are within the child's grasp. He understands all the things that are important in his world. This enhances beyond measure a feeling of being an integral part of his society, of making an important contribution to it; in turn, it creates a feeling of competence, of security, and of well-being. So it does both: it prevents alienation, and enhances a limited autonomy, provided this does not conflict with group cohesion.

In this connection it may be well to remember that the concept of alienation used here is derived from Marx's concept of proletarian alienation from the means of production, and the consequences this has for personality. Alienation from the means of production does not exist in the kibbutz, which is certainly one factor in the freedom from alienation. Conversely, where children are alienated from all that pertains to real work for survival, this fact is certainly one source of their social as well as personal alienation. Oscar Lewis has spoken of a mystique of work that prevails in Castro's Cuba. It is not the mystique of work that is lacking in the life of the Puerto Rican families in New York who live in the culture of poverty as he described. What is lacking is meaningful work, and it is their alienation from work that makes them feel so miserable, not the lack of a mystique.

Apart from this, what are other essential differences in personality formation between our system and the kibbutz system? In attempting to answer, I shall use Erikson's revision of the psychoanalytic model as my yardstick, according to which human personalities form through having come to grips with, and mastered, a series of internal and inter-personal struggles or crises. The crucial problem, for example, in the first of these psychosocial and psychobiological crises is that of trust versus mistrust. Depending on the earlier life experiences, and the child's reactions to them, the outcome of this crisis is that the child grows into a person who either trusts himself and others, or who is forever mistrustful of himself and others. Even at this earliest stage, things are very different for the kibbutz infant compared with his American middle-class counterpart, because trust in the kibbutz is derived not so much from the mother alone as from several different persons. Hence, the child is not at the same time being cared for and in the absolute power of a single person, who may either be intensely attuned to him or be a deadly enemy. In our society the child needs to adjust himself to one particular person, and to this person's particular idiosyncrasies and personality type.

In simplified form it may be said that in the kibbutz trust is derived from the experience that one gets from others. In our society it is derived not only from what the child gets, but also from what he gives in return. Thus, in the kibbutz trust is derived from getting only, and not from one person only, but from many. And the kibbutz child does not have to give in return to the mother, as happens with us. Differences seem even more marked in the second crisis, during the toddler stage or what is often called the age of education to cleanliness. Here the crisis centers on the striving for autonomy, as against shame and doubt. But in the kibbutz there is much less emphasis on toilet training, table manners, cleanliness, and the care of clothing than among us. With far less expected of the child in these areas, you find far less self-doubt in kibbutz children. At the same time, because they are left so much to their own devices, they are achieving much greater autonomy much earlier in life. Again, in the American middle-class society the peer group does not become important until school age, but in the kibbutz it is already important during the second, or toddler, stage of development, if not even earlier. And because so much of the kibbutz child's education comes from his peers, law and order are backed up by the group influence much more than with us.

With far fewer dos and don'ts and a much more lenient toilet training, the inner feelings that develop for law and order are less rigid. But even at this early age, it is less the inner voice of a conscience, and more the voice of the group, that calls the dos and don'ts.

In the center of the third crisis, roughly that of the preschooler, stands the issue of initiative versus guilt. But the nature of guilt is very different in the kibbutz. Again, it does not come from transgressing a law handed down by parents, but from going against the values of the group. Such an inner attitude is one that we would call other-directed, if not alienated. But in the kibbutz it means that the child is well integrated both within himself and within his society. On the other hand, physical initiative in work, in play, in exploring is much more encouraged because the children so largely fend for themselves in a community that is safe to move about, and for them an open book.

Speaking of the latency period and the fourth of these crises, that of industry versus inferiority, Erikson says, "All children, at times, need to be left alone in solitary play, but they all, sooner or later, become dissatisfied and disgruntled without the sense of being useful, without the sense of being able to make things and make them well." This statement illustrates once more how different matters are in our society when compared with the kibbutz situation. The kibbutz child is never alone. Even if he engages for moments in solitary activity, he is immediately interrupted by some other child or adult because throughout the kibbutz the lack of respect for privacy also applies to the child, and he accepts interference with his privacy as justified and in line with the overwhelming mores of his society. On the other hand, his devotion to and high evaluation of industry, of making things together, has made its appearance long before latency. From an early age he has learned to contribute to the kibbutz economy, and from the very beginning of school age he works on the children's farm, and works industriously. This is a prime example of how a, relatively speaking, somewhat lower level of personal integration, is compensated by the higher degree of autonomy which the child enjoys because of his meaningful work.

The same example shows how different the timetables are for the experiences shaping human development in the kibbutz, compared to our society. Solitude will not be available to the kibbutz youngster before he enters adolescence, and even then only rarely, for short periods and against heavy odds. On the other hand, while the American child's powerful desire to be useful is mainly frustrated, the need to make things that are important is fully satisfied for the kibbutz child by the prevalence of exactly such constructive doing, not of things that will count in his later development, like getting good grades or passing exams, but of what is of value right now and is exactly the same for his parents and all other adults. Essentially then, much greater mastery is expected of the kibbutz child rather early in life, and not much more later on. In fact, development seems to stop after the fourth of these crises, which is only natural, since no higher stage seems possible for a kibbutz member than to make things together. According to Erikson, we have at least four more such crises. Thus the kibbutz-reared youngster never reaches the last and eighth of these crises, the one of integrity versus despair. The existential despair that seems to haunt part of Western society is avoided. But as I said before, the escape has a price. In terms of Erikson's model, the kibbutz member escapes anomie and alienation at the cost of a lessening not so much of autonomy as of personal identity, emotional intimacy, and individual achievement.

I trust it has by now become clear why I introduced the kibbutz example. It is a society which, though radically different from ours, consists of people very much like us. Its educational system secures for its members adequate integration, not by striving for highest autonomy, but by preventing alienation —alienation both from the group and from work. And the kibbutz does achieve this by striving for only a relatively low level of what we would call personal autonomy. This it can do because it offers, from a very early age, compared to us, an incredibly high degree of self-realization through work; because it integrates the child, from birth, into his group, in which no competition for grades or achievement exists, and because it violates so little of the child's being in charge of his own body.

This brings us back to my initial remarks, that autonomy and alienation are not opposite, but complementary concepts. Here I would like to add that they are not complementary only in regard to the individual versus society, but also in regard to man in relation to himself and to his body. Maybe the fascination with sex, violence, and madness, which I mentioned before, and which seems to haunt much of our alienated youth, speaks of their unconscious awareness that where they are most alienated and where they most lack autonomy is in relation to their own bodies. This they prevent from coming to awareness by their insistence that the whole trouble comes from a society in which alienation is rampant, and that such a society prevents them from gaining autonomy. As the kibbutz example shows, the niceties of cleanliness, orderliness, and such things as table manners are only very small steps toward the socialization of the kibbutz child, who does very nicely without them. But these niceties, where insisted upon, are very big steps toward the child's alienation from his body, since it is not he, but his parents, who commands what he should do and not do with his body. Control over our own elimination, for example, does not free us never to empty our bowels. Autonomy only requires that we, and nobody else, should decide when we empty them, and how, and where. It cannot possibly require that we shall not empty them when our body feels it must.

Our emotions too, like our bowels, must be free to assert their right for discharge or satisfaction of needs. Autonomy does not require that we have total, but only sufficient, control of them.

Although other people may have an influence, we must certainly be in sufficient control of our emotions, most of all our aggressions, so that they do not lead us to damage ourselves or other persons.

But unlike our bowels, which can be too much or too little controlled only within very narrow limits, the same is not true of our emotions. Our desires can well be whipped up beyond a reasonable level, be it for physical possessions or for emotional and sexual experiences. Even our desires for intellectual and social achievement can be too much aroused. If so, it may be well-nigh impossible to achieve a level of inner integration that will contain them enough so that we may remain in autonomous control of our desires and not be enslaved by them. But if we are so enslaved, emotional disturbance results; hence my earlier remarks about autonomy being the opposite of emotional disturbance. This is where the child of the kibbutz, and also at this moment a citizen behind the Iron Curtain, has a much easier time of maintaining personal autonomy, although his social autonomy may be considerably lower than ours. His desires for goods and possessions, for social success, and for sensual experiences are from our point of view understimulated. He does not develop them highly, but neither does he suffer as much from their being frustrated.

This does not mean that I prefer life in the kibbutz, or behind the Iron Curtain. But neither can I blind myself to its specific advantages, though I prefer on balance the net advantages of our own world. I am convinced that our children will have to continue to suffer from an imbalance between autonomy and alienation, unless far-reaching changes occur—because for the present we overstimulate their desires, and at the same time frustrate them by restricting their autonomy, even over their own bodies. We keep them alienated from work achievement where it counts, and overregulate their lives with a straitjacket of an overly competitive educational system. To put it on the simplest level, we cannot demand with one and the same breath higher achievement and a high repression of what, for want of a better word, we may call our instinctual desires. We cannot, at the same time, want them to read and enjoy books and also require them, while they are toddlers, not to soil and spoil these valuable books by, for example, building houses out of them.

Though Freud spoke little of man in society, on rare occasions when he did he gave us important insights like the following quotation. "The fateful question for the human species seems to me to be whether and to what extent our cultural development will succeed in mastering the disturbance of the communal life by the human instincts of aggression and self-destruction." Obviously, Freud spoke here about the mastery of aggression, not its repression. Yet this is what modern society seems to impose on its children, instead of guiding them to its mastery. Why do I stress repression so much when, in many respects, most children in the past were brought up far more strictly, with far less autonomy than children are today. True, then the child was not allowed to talk back to his mother. But this was a mother who had breast-fed him during the first years of his life. Thus, as you see, the instinctive satisfaction came first, and the restriction of autonomy only much later. Later, too, there was work on the farm and in the family shop. Thus an entirely new balance is needed now between the autonomy enjoyed and the alienation suffered—because in regard to this balance, the situation in the Western world has been rapidly changing in the last few generations. Permit me to add just a very homely example.

In a recent series of meetings with suburban mothers, one of them was very worried about the consequences later on of having spanked her child for soiling in his pants. When I discussed with her why this worried her so much, she told me: "Maybe some of the anxiety comes from all that we hear about delinquency—all the terrible things youth is capable of doing in our day. It's gone way beyond the old days of turning over the outhouses. It's gotten a little bit more serious with the pep pill, and all that." What this mother said really fascinated me, because which child in suburbia today can turn over an outhouse? There are no outhouses left, and this mother in her unconscious connected this outlet, now gone, with the pep pills.

This takes us back to how she toilet trains her son. What has changed is not that he got a slap on the bottom; this happened in all days, and certainly in the olden days. What is different is that this child, when he is twelve, won't be able to get even for this by turning over the outhouse without being viewed as a delinquent. Now it's true that in the old days no parent went around suggesting to his child that he turn over the outhouse. But if he did, and his parents learned of it, there was nothing so terrible in having done it. Some such behavior was expected; "boys will be boys." I understand that some teenagers in the suburbs are snapping antennas off cars, and in other suburbs they string rolls of toilet paper from tree to tree, showing clearly how they try to counteract the persistent aftereffects of too much toilet training. But there's a different attitude today about the antennas and such pranks. Now we are highly indignant, worry about the future of children who play such pranks because we fear that they are going to be delinquents, we even call the police. I'm thinking too of how Halloween has changed in the mere twenty-five years since I came to this country. It's now simple extortion or bribery by children dressed up in fancy costumes while they very politely collect for UNICEF. Compare that to how wild the children really were on Halloween some twenty-five years ago. We have closed up many avenues of response that existed only a generation ago. Then a boy still spent many hours fishing and roaming the woods with his dog, or just sitting by the river. Now he's to stay in and just do his homework.

What I'm trying to suggest is that everything that happens to us has its consequences later on. But how it affects us depends very much on how these consequences can be expressed, or not, later on. When at teen-age the child could roam all day with his dog in the woods, you could afford even a very rigid type of toilet training. There were compensations, and they balanced each other out. Now that we have taken them away, and he no longer goes hunting with his dog, or turns over the outhouse, what happened in earlier childhood or infancy has a far deeper impact on his total experience of autonomy.

Do I, therefore, suggest that we reinstate vandalism on Halloween, for example? Not at all. This again will pose a false "either-or"; either we return to the older free-for-all or we continue in our rigid demands on the young to suppress their tendencies to violence or to assert their bodily freedom, if you like. What is needed, I submit, is a reexamination of this new balance now needed between autonomy and alienation, if we are to function in modern society. If a ready discharge is no longer possible or desirable, then the child needs, from the very beginning, much greater autonomy and a chance to develop true mastery of his body. He needs much less alienation from his own body and its function. He also needs much greater intimacy, which is the opposite of popularity, in his intimate relations with those very few who, at different age levels, should be those closest to him. Only then can he avoid feeling unduly cramped by the sense of alienation that a modern industrial society imposes on its citizens. Only then will he be able, at all ages, to enjoy fully the many advantages modern society can offer to those who have retained sufficient inner autonomy and freedom in using and satisfying the demands of their bodies. And only then will he achieve the ability to have intimate relations, because he will be a truly autonomous person, even in a modern mass society. To achieve this is quite possible, as I have tried to suggest. But it will take quite some doing.

# 7

# DARWIN VERSUS COPERNICUS

THEODOSIUS DOBZHANSKY

THEODOSIUS DOBZHANSKY *is professor of genetics at The Rockefeller University. His books include* Mankind Evolving *and* Genetics and Man.

# DARWIN VERSUS COPERNICUS

*Theodosius Dobzhansky*

A BOUT three centuries ago, Pascal described the human condition with a lucidity and poignancy never since equaled:

> When I consider the short duration of my life, swallowed up in the eternity before and after, the little space which I fill, and even can see, engulfed in the infinite immensity of spaces of which I am ignorant and which knew me not, I am frightened, and am astonished at being here rather than there; for there is no reason why here rather than there, why now rather than then. Who has put me here? By whose order and direction have this place and this time been allotted to me? The eternal silence of these infinite spaces frightens me.

Whether the silence of the infinite spaces is more or less frightening to our contemporaries than it was to Pascal is hard to tell. The spaces still know us not, but we begin to know something about the spaces. By whose order this place and time have been allotted to me has, however, become, if anything, still more mysterious.

Objects most remote from us yet discovered in the universe are galaxies some five billion light-years away. The mysterious quasars (quasi-stellar objects), or some of them, may be as remote, but their nature and remoteness are still under dispute among cosmologists. This is a remoteness which staggers the imagination; the radiation from these objects reaching us today left its source billions of years ago. The universe is believed to have started in a "Big Bang," a cosmic explosion which made the universe "expand," or rather caused its different components to fly apart in all directions with colossal speeds. The date of the Big Bang, and consequently the supposed age of the universe, is estimated to be on the order of fifteen billion years. These estimates tend, however, to be lengthened rather than shortened by newer discoveries.

The number of galaxies in the universe visible in the 200-inch telescope is estimated to be close to one billion. Our galaxy is merely one of these, yet it may contain between one million and one hundred million planetary systems. One of these includes a medium-sized planet which we inhabit. The supposition that the planet earth is in any way unique or exceptional or privileged seems farfetched to many scientists. It is, however, the only one known for certain to have a tiny proportion of its mass involved in a process called life. Moreover, the diversity of living beings is very impressive. There are at least two million kinds, or species, of life on earth at present, and there were more in the past, which became extinct.

Speculation is rife concerning the possibility that there may be life of some sort on other planets, in other planetary systems, and in other galaxies. Some authorities go so far as to proclaim it a certainty that life not merely could, but must have arisen in many places in the universe. More than that, sentient and rational beings must have evolved on many planets where there is life. In other words, "We are not alone." The name "exobiology" has been invented for the study of the assumed extraterrestrial life. The problems of exobiology cannot be adequately discussed here; I realize that the following remarks may do injustice to the ingenious speculations advanced in this field. I cannot, however, help wondering if the exobiologists may not turn out to be high-powered specialists on a nonexistent subject. The stock argument in favor of the existence of life in many places in the universe runs about as follows: Although the critical step from the non-living to the living may be a rare and improbable event, there are some one hundred million planets in our galaxy on which this step could be made, hence it must have been made on several or even on many. This argument is not really convincing, however, because nobody knows for sure just how probable or improbable the event may be under various circumstances. It is certain that the event happened at least once—on earth. The evidence that it was not a unique event is yet to be obtained—it cannot be taken for granted.

Let, us, however, assume for the sake of a further argument that life did arise in many places, and moreover that it was life based on nucleic acids and proteins, in other words, life chemically of the same kind as that on earth. This granted, it far from follows that such life must have evolved elsewhere as it did on our planet, let alone that it must have produced humanoid organisms. Evolution is principally adaptation to the environment; however, even if the environments somewhere happened to be much like, though of course not identical with, those on earth, a reenactment or repetition of the terrestrial evolutionary history has a probability very close to zero. This is because biological evolution is not predetermined to achieve any particular form of adaptedness to the environment. It has a range of possibilities that is virtually unlimited.

Evolution is a creative process which is most unlikely to occur two or more times in the same way. Man was not contained in the primordial life, except as one of an infinitely large number of possibilities. What these other unrealized possibilities might have been we probably shall never know. And yet, the origin of man was not an accident either, unless you choose to consider all history, including biological history and that of human societies, states, and nations, as series of accidents. This is a possible view, but not an appealing one. It is far more meaningful to describe biological and human histories as successions of unique events, each event being causally related to what went on before and to what will follow in the future, and yet non-recurrent. George Simpson gave arguments essentially similar to the above in a brilliant article entitled, "The Non-prevalence of Humanoids," that is, nonprevalence anywhere except on our planet. Our species, mankind, is almost certainly alone in the universe. And to that extent, our planet is also unique.

To recognize this "aloneness" is not necessarily to experience the Pascalian "fright" and "astonishment." Quite the opposite. The space which mankind fills, and the duration of its existence so far, are indeed very small compared to the now known "immensity of spaces." The messages that we may wish to send describing human activities on earth may have to travel billions of years at the speed of light to reach the quasars and the remotest galaxies. And there is probably nobody there to receive these messages. Does it mean that all our doings, both those of individuals and of the human species as a whole, are mere whiffs of insignificance? Not at all; because it is unique, the career of the human species here on earth may be of cosmic significance. This idea need not be a wildly conceited delusion. Our species may well be alone in having discovered that the universe and all that it contains, including mankind, is a changing product of evolution. It is neither size nor geometric centrality in the solar system, or in our galaxy, or in the universe, that makes the planet earth so important. It is that the flames of self-awareness, of death-awareness, and of evolutionary awareness have been kindled here on earth and probably nowhere else.

The image of man as seen by Pascal and his contemporaries and successors is different from that emerging from evolutionary science. The difference becomes understandable when viewed against the background of the history of science and of its philosophical implications since Copernicus, Galileo, Newton, and Darwin. Here again I am forced to be too brief and, I fear, too dogmatic. The pre-Copernican man felt certain not only that he was the heart of the universe but that the universe was created for him and because of him. The earth was the hub of several concentric spheres: those of the moon, of the sun, of the planets, and of fixed stars. God watched the smallest happenings on earth from somewhere up above. The interior of the earth contained an elaborately engineered hell; a man could avoid becoming its resident in perpetuity only by good behavior during his brief sojourn on the earth's surface, and by the intercession of the properly constituted ecclesiastic authorities. With travel difficult and slow, the earth seemed to be very large. It shrank progressively as it was gradually explored and as travel became easy and rapid. It is quite small in the age of jet aircraft. But whether large or small, the earth existed for man and for the realization of God's mysterious plans for man's salvation.

All these arrangements did not make man free of anxieties. He faced the *mysterium tremendum*—why has God arranged things as he has? This was, however, just one extra mystery—the greatest one to be sure—but mysteries were all around, from the vagaries of weather to the behavior of one's friends and enemies. All these things were the doings of spirits, good or evil. Though spirits were more powerful than men, men were not entirely defenseless against them, because one could secure the assistance of some spirits against others.

The development of science changed the situation. At first sight, the mystery began to recede; but in fact it was relegated to the beginning of the world. Copernicus, after him Kepler and Galileo, and still later Newton, together with their many followers and successors, changed the image of the universe and of man. The earth is a smallish planet revolving around a much grander sun. Instead of the celestial spheres there is only the endless void, in which other planets, suns, and galaxies are as tiny islets on an infinite ocean. Man is lost in cosmic spaces. It is not, however, the dimensional smallness of man that really matters. It is rather the mechanical and inexorably deterministic nature of the universe, and finally of man himself, that changes man's image. Celestial phenomena are calculable and predictable, provided that one has discovered the precise and eternal laws which they obey. Biological and psychological phenomena are less predictable, but only because they are

much more complex and the laws governing them are yet to be
discovered. Descartes decided that the human body was as
much a machine as a clock or other "automation," although he
still believed that man had a non-mechanical soul. Others
found the hypothesis of soul to be superfluous. Man is a machine, and that is that.

God was found to be another superfluous hypothesis. To be
sure, Newton and many other scientists tried to hold onto their
religions. Newton thought that the planets were hurled into
their paths initially by God. But subsequent to this divine act
at the beginning, the planets follow their proper orbits, according to immutable laws and without further guidance. The deists
thought that God was the original creator and lawgiver of the
universe. Having created the universe and set it in motion, God
found it so well made that his presence became no longer essential. Instead of mysteries, we have the laws of nature. Some
people thought that God reserves the right of occasional mirac-
ulous intervention, temporarily abrogating the very laws which
he himself has formerly established. To others such behavior
appears unseemly for the all-wise and omniscient Creator. It is
more convenient to imagine him as a sort of absentee landlord,
who lets things take their "natural" courses.

Mystery driven out through the front door tends to creep in
through the back door. Has the Creator and Lawgiver arranged
things really well? If he is credited with the order, beauty, and
goodness in the world, he must by the same token be responsible
also for the disorder, ugliness, and evil. The machinery of the
world has serious flaws, and this is a mystery defying compre-
hension. An absentee-landlord god can hardly be prayed to,
since he is unable or unwilling to intervene to change the causal
sequences which bring about events.

To this is added the hopelessness of determinism. As stated
by Laplace, the doctrine of determinism is essentially that if one
knew the position and speed of every particle in the universe at
any single instant, and if one could submit this knowledge to

analysis, then one could predict all future events and also retro-
dict all past events. Although this statement contains two pretty
vertiginous "ifs," determinism is an explicit or implicit faith
which is the basis of scientific activity. It leads, however, to an
embarrassing inference: there is nothing new in the world, because all that ever happens was predestined to happen from
the beginning. No human effort, or absence of effort, can
change anything, because the effort or its absence is equally
predestined. This is a far stronger fatalism than the fatalism
sometimes (and mostly wrongly) ascribed to oriental philosophies.

Darwin has been called the Newton of biology, although the
Copernicus or the Galileo of biology would perhaps be a better
characterization. There is as yet nothing in biology analogous
to, say, the laws of gravitation; the Newton of biology may be
yet to come. To say this is not to underestimate Darwin's contribution. He has shown that the biological species, including
man, have not appeared ready-made; their multifarious structures and functions are not mere whims of nature or of a
Creator. Every living species is a descendant of ancestors unlike
itself, and generally more unlike the farther back in time one
looks. It is probable, though not certain, that all beings now
alive are descendants of one primordial life which appeared
some four billion years ago. Presumed remains of living beings
three and one-half billion years old have recently been found.
The organic diversity is a consequence of adaptation to different environments; the endless variety of bodily structures and
functions makes possible an endless diversity of modes of life.
There are so many kinds of organisms because they can exploit
more fully the diverse opportunities which an environment
offers for living than any single organism conceivably could.

The human species has evolved a unique way to cope with
its environments. This way is culture. Culture is not transmitted from generation to generation by the genes, although its
biological basis is so transmitted. Culture has been called

"superorganic," although it surely rests on an organic foundation. Man is an animal, but he is so extraordinary that he is much more than an animal. Darwin and his successor evolutionists have thus extended to the living world, and even to the human world, the principles which were shown to be so supremely efficient in the study of the physical world. Biology has by now exorcized the ghost of vitalism, which wanted to see in life something radically incommensurable with the rest of nature. Mechanism has triumphed in biology. This triumph was what Darwin and the evolution theory were, and still are, mainly acclaimed for. There is, however, another aspect to evolutionism which may be at least equally and possibly more important. It sees the whole universe, and everything in it, in the process of change and development. The universe is on its way to somewhere. Where is it going?

The grandeur of the Newtonian image of the universe was in its serene constancy and the precision of its laws. Planets and their satellites follow their orbits again and again, in predictable fashion. Moreover, since Newton accepted the traditional creation date as well as the apocalyptic prediction of the end of the world, there was little opportunity for change either in the past or the future. The laws of the conservation of mass and of energy were discovered later; here was a break in the constancy, however—although energy is conserved, it undergoes a directional change because of entropy.

What biological evolution is all about, however, is not constancy but change. Darwin and his successors have shown that the living world of today is different from what it was in the past, and that it may become different again in the future. Mankind proved to have a hitherto quite unsuspected kind of history. This is the history of its slow emergence from its animal ancestors, in addition to the recorded history of patriarchs, kings, battles, and empires. And while recorded history goes back only a few thousand years, biological history extends somewhere between one and a half and two million years. But even this history is short relative to that of the life from which man came, which took perhaps four billion years. And back of that are more billions of years, when the universe existed without either life or man.

I do not wish to be understood as claiming that it was Darwin who made evolution into a universal principle. In point of fact, it was recognized before Darwin that the planetary system has had a history of origin from the primitive sun, or from a mass of matter which gave origins both to the sun and to the planets. Human history has been studied at least since Herodotus and Thucydides; late in the eighteenth century Condorcet ascribed to it a directional character—from a primitive barbarianism to an earthly paradise of perfect enlightenment. Darwin's theory of biological evolution is, however, the keystone of the evolutionary conception of the world, beginning with the evolution of the cosmos and culminating in the evolution of mankind. Modern cosmology is evolutionary cosmology. Even the atoms of the chemical elements, hitherto symbols of indivisibility and unchangeability, proved to have had an evolutionary history. In the homely language of some modern cosmologists, the atoms were "cooked" in the Big Bang at the start of cosmic evolution, and they are still being cooked in the furnaces of the interior of the sun and of the stars.

It has been urged by some authorities that the term "evolution" should be restricted to biological evolution only. I do not share this view, because it seems to me important to convey the idea that change and development are characteristic of non-living as well as of living matter and of human affairs. This does not prevent one from recognizing that the processes of cosmic, inorganic, or geological evolution are different from biological evolutionary processes. The causes of biological evolution must be looked for in heredity, mutation, and natural selection. None of these is found in non-living systems, and the analogies which some authors have attempted to draw are at best remote. Other analogues of heredity, mutation, and natural selection have been claimed in human social and cultural evolution with, I fear, even less success. These analogies are more often obfuscating than enlightening.

Nor can I see much of an advantage in the views expounded so brilliantly by such philosophers as Whitehead and Hartshorn. They like to ascribe to inorganic systems, and even to atoms and subatomic particles, some rudiments of life, individuality, and, further, of consciousness and volition. It is almost needless to say that there is no positive evidence, either compelling or presumptive, of any such biological and human qualities in non-living systems. Even as a speculative possibility these views do not seem to me attractive. They really amount to a denial of anything substantially new ever arising in evolution. They are most nearly analogous to the early preformistic notions in biology; some eighteenth-century biologists believed that a sex cell contains a "homunculus," a tiny figure of man. This seemed to make the problem of development very simple—the homunculus had only to grow in size to become an adult man, and a corresponding miniature in an animal sex cell had to grow to become an adult animal of the proper species. But this simplicity was deceptive, since it made the problem of the development of succeeding generations insoluble. One had to believe that homunculi contained second-order homunculi, these had third-order homunculi, and so on, ad infinitum. An analogous difficulty arises with the "minds" of atoms. It might seem at first that human mind could simply evolve by growth of the atomic mind. Human mind is, however, somehow associated with the human brain, and where are the brains of atoms and electrons?

The most interesting aspect of evolution is precisely that it creates novelties. From time to time it transcends itself, i.e., produces novel systems with novel properties—properties which the antecedent systems did not have even as tiny germs. The emergence of the living from the non-living, and the emergence of humanity from animality, are the two grandest evolutionary transcendences so far. Teilhard de Chardin was the evolutionist who had the courage to predict further transcendences, mankind moving toward what he called the megasynthesis and toward Point Omega, this last being his symbol for God. Here is evidently a borderland, in which Teilhard's science has collaborated with his mystical vision. I am not planning in the present discussion to take you on an excursion in this borderland of prophecy.

As already stated above, we do not know for sure whether the transcendences of the non-living to life, and of animal to man, have taken place solely on this planet earth or in many places in the universe. Perhaps some positive information bearing on this issue will come from the progress in space travel. Be that as it may, we do have conclusive enough evidence that these three kinds of evolution, inorganic, organic, and human, have happened here on earth. These three kinds of evolution are not independent of each other; they are rather the three stages of the single Evolution of the cosmos. By calling them "stages," I do not mean to suggest that cosmic evolution stopped when the biological phase started, or that biological evolution stopped when the human phase began. On the contrary, the three kinds of evolution are not only going on, but what is more, they are connected by feedback relations. For example, geography influences the living things which inhabit a given territory; in turn, vegetation, animals, and especially human activities have now become geographic and even geologic agents. Human cultural evolution influences mankind's genetic endowment, and vice versa. In recent years there have been publicized some alarmist views, asserting that human genetic endowment is in a process of degeneration, and predicting dire consequences of this for the future. This matter cannot be adequately discussed in this article; I believe that the dangers have been exaggerated, and in any case the situation is not beyond possible control.

The evolutionary view of the world does not abrogate the classical Newtonian mechanistic view. The change which evolutionism makes is nevertheless of greatest importance for man's view of himself and of his place in the universe. The classical conception stressed the essential permanence of things, at least for the duration of the world's existence. The evolutionary conception emphasizes change and movement. The preevolutionary world view did not, of course, deny all change; but the changes were usually represented as cyclic, and the world as a whole did not go anywhere in particular. Spring, summer, autumn, and winter return again and again at the appointed times; people are born, grow, build families, get old, and die, and a new generation goes through the same succession of stages; plants and animals, like people, produce generation after generation; heavenly bodies follow their orbits again and again; mountains rise, are eroded away, become submerged in the sea, rise up again, etc., etc., etc. . . . But to translate a French adage, the more things change the more they remain the same.

Constancy, lack of change, and regular recurrence seem to be reassuring and comforting to many people. "Like the good old days" is a compliment tinged with nostalgia. Change brings insecurity; one has to become adapted, adjusted, or reconciled to altered situations. Yet changelessness, or eternal repetition or return, is the acme of futility. A world which remains forever the same is senseless. It is what Dostoevsky called a "devil's vaudeville." All the strivings and struggles which a person, or a generation, has to go through are in vain because the next generation, and the one after that, and so on ad infinitum, will have to go through the same struggles all over again.

What difference does the idea of evolution make? Quite simply, it is this: the universe is not a status but a process. Its creation was not something which happened a few thousand years ago, before any of us were born and could have influenced it in any way. The creation is going forward now, and may conceivably go on indefinitely. The view that "there is nothing new under the sun" is in error. In the past there were an earth and a sun different from the present ones, and there will be a new earth and a new sun in the future. An important role in this forward movement belongs to the phenomenon called life, and to one particular form thereof called mankind, which exists as far as we know only on a single and not otherwise remarkable planet.

The evolution of life is remarkably rapid, measured on a cosmic time scale. Ten million years ago, the oceans and mountains, the moon, the sun, and the stars were not very different from what they are now, but the living beings inhabiting the earth were rather unlike the present ones. Ten thousand years ago mankind was quite different from what it is now, while except for the destruction of some biological species, the biological world was pretty much what we now observe. Evolution is a creative process; the creativity is most pronounced in human cultural evolution, less in biological, and least in inorganic evolution.

A creative process by its very nature always risks ending in a failure or being stranded in a blind alley. Every biological species is nature's experiment, essaying a new mode of living. Most species eventually prove unsuccessful and become extinct without issue. Yet some, a minority, discover new or superior ways of getting a living out of the environment which is available on earth. These few lucky discoverers inherit the earth and undergo what is technically known as adaptive radiation. That is, the surviving species differentiate and become many species again, only to repeat the process of discovery, extinction, and new adaptive radiation. Yet this is not another specimen of eternal return. New adaptive radiations do not simply restore what there was earlier; the new crop of species may contain some which have achieved novel or surer ways of remaining alive, or have discovered previously unexploited niches in the environment and have thus augmented the living at the expense of the non-living.

The trial-and-error process of proliferation of ever-new

species and of disappearance of the old ones has achieved remarkable successes. Biological evolution has transcended itself
by giving rise to man. Mankind as a species is biologically an
extraordinary success. It has gained the ability to adapt its environments to its genes, as well as its genes to its environments.
This ability stems from a novel, extragenetically transmitted
complex of adaptive traits called culture. Culture leads to still
another kind of discovery, discoveries of knowledge, which can
be transmitted to succeeding generations again by means of the
extragenic processes of instruction and learning. One of the
discoveries which became known is the discovery of evolution.
Man knows that the universe and life have evolved, and that
mankind entered this universe by way of evolution. With perhaps a bit too much poetic license, it has been said that man
is evolution having become conscious of itself. It is no poetic
license, however, to say that having discovered evolution, man
has opened up a possibility of eventually learning how to control it.

The enterprise of creation has not been completed; it is going
on before our eyes. Ours is surely not the best of all thinkable
worlds, and, we hope, not even the best of all possible worlds.
Man is constantly asking whether his existence, and that of the
universe in which he finds himself, has any sense or meaning.
If there is no evolution, then all is futility—human life in particular. If the world evolves, then hope is at least possible.

An uncomfortable question inevitably presents itself at this
point. Can science ever discover meaning in anything, and is
a scientist entitled even to inquire about meanings and purposes? To a rigorous mechanist who does not wish to think in
evolutionary terms, such words as meaning, improvement, progress, and transcendence are meaningless noises. Everything in
the world, including myself, is an aggregation of atoms. When
this aggregation disaggregates, the atoms will still be there and
may aggregate into something else. Is there an objectively
definable difference between an object of art and a junk heap?

If a virus and a man are nothing but different seriations of the nucleotides in their DNA's and RNA's, then all of evolution was a lot of sound and fury signifying nothing.

One of the exasperating phenomena of the intellectual history of mankind is politely called "the academic lag." This crudely mechanistic world view was acceptable in science chiefly during the eighteenth and nineteenth centuries. It had justified itself by having given a powerful impetus to scientific discovery. It is now being displaced by the evolutionary world view. Yet the representatives of what C. P. Snow has referred to as literary or nonscientific culture have only recently discovered that the world is nothing but an aggregation of atoms. It is a curious experience to hear an artist argue that a junk heap is, indeed, no less worthy of aesthetic appreciation than is the "Venus de Milo," because both are matter wrought into arbitrary shapes; or to have an eminent musician declare that the atonality and certain other characteristics of avant-garde music are merely recognition of the Copernican discovery that man is not the center of the universe; or finally to read in a book by an intellectual pundit that "something pervasive that makes the difference, not between civilized man and the savage, not between man and the animals, but between man and the robot, grows numb, ossifies, falls away like black mortified flesh when techne assails the senses and science dominates the mind."

In reality science is neither a villain debasing human dignity nor the sole source of human wisdom. In Toynbee's words: "Science's horizon is limited by the bounds of Nature, the ideologies' horizon by the bounds of human social life, but the human soul's range cannot be confined within either of these limits. Man is a bread-eating social animal; but he is also something more. He is a person, endowed with a conscience and a will, as well as with a self-conscious intellect. This spiritual endowment of his condemns him to a life-long struggle to reconcile himself with the Universe into which he has been born." The fact that the universe has evolved and is evolving is surely relevant to this reconciliation. The advent of evolution-ism makes it necessary to ask a new question which simply could not occur to those who believed that the world is created once and for all, stable and changeless.

The question is, Where is evolution going? This question can be asked separately about the three known kinds of evolution—cosmic, biological, and human. It has also been asked about evolution as a whole, because the three kinds of evolution can be viewed as the constituent parts, or stages, of a single all-embracing process of universal evolution. This universe, so formidable and so beautiful, is in a process of change. It may be that evolution is merely drifting at random, and is going nowhere in particular. There is, however, also a possibility, for which no rigorous demonstration can be given, that universal evolution is one grand enterprise, in which everything and everybody are component parts. Whose enterprise is this, and with what aim and for what purpose is it undertaken? The four centuries of the growth of science since Copernicus have not dispelled this mystery; the one century since Darwin has made it more urgent than ever.

What role is man to play in evolution? Is he to be a mere spectator or, perchance, the spearhead and the eventual direc-tor? There are people who will shrug this question off, or will recoil from it, considering it an exhibition of insane arrogance. Since, however, man is one and presumably the only rational being who has become aware that evolution is happening, he can hardly avoid asking such questions. For the issue involved is no less than the meaning of his own existence. Does man live just to live, and is there no more sense or meaning to him than that? Or is he called upon to participate in the construction of the best thinkable universe?

# 8

# SPECULATIONS ON THE PROBLEM OF MAN'S COMING TO THE GROUND

SHERWOOD L. WASHBURN

SHERWOOD L. WASHBURN, *professor of anthropology at The University of California (Berkeley), is former editor of the* American Journal of Physical Anthropology *and* Viking Fund Publications in Anthropology. *He is a past president of the American Anthropological Association.*

8

# SPECULATIONS ON THE PROBLEM OF MAN'S COMING TO THE GROUND

*Sherwood L. Washburn*

OVER the last few years, numerous scientists have spent many hundreds of hours observing the behavior of the primates. Although man himself has been observed far more than all the other primates put together, at last there are beginning to be substantial accounts of the natural behavior of several species of monkeys and apes (Altmann 1967; Jay in press; Washburn, Jay, and Lancaster 1965). It is my belief that these studies— and particularly the more problem-oriented ones in progress— will fundamentally change many of the theories about human evolution and the nature of man. Obviously, field studies will not supplant the fossil record; the only direct evidence on the form of our ancestors is the scanty testimony of fossil bones, teeth, and associated objects. Nor will the field studies replace laboratory experiments or genetic theory. I stress this because to some there appears to be an incompatibility between investigations in the field and in the laboratory and a lack of connection between the study of the fossils and the observation of the living forms. These different forms of knowledge supplement each other, and the study of human evolution requires the understanding of genetics, the execution of well-designed experiments, and a thorough familiarity with the behavior of primates—both human and otherwise.

This emphasis on the need for a broad approach is not a personal bias, but stems directly from the synthetic theory of evolution. Evolution is the history of adaptation, in which

This paper is part of a program on the evolution of human behavior supported by United States Public Health Service Grant MH-08623. I particularly want to thank Dr. Phyllis C. Jay for help and criticism, and Drs. Jane Lancaster and Vincent M. Sarich for discussions which helped to lead to the present formulation.

193

reproductive success depends on behavior. Without an appreciation of the significance of behaviors there can be no understanding of evolution. The evidence for reconstructing the behavior of our ancestors comes from the fossils and from observation of the naturalistic behavior of contemporary primates, and both these kinds of evidence must be analyzed experimentally.

The view that the central issue in investigating our evolution is the interpretation of the sequences of behaviors results in two kinds of problems. The first is that no one person can master all the different kinds of evidence and techniques, and in this sense no one person can be an expert on human evolution—let alone the evolution of the primates or of the mammals. This means that the evolutionary syntheses of the future will have to be based on cooperative research, and this is true in most of modern science. The second problem caused by the emphasis on behavior is that the study of different aspects of behavior is now relegated to a wide variety of departments. Universities are divided by nineteenth-century traditions, and the answers to contemporary evolutionary questions lie neither in particular departments nor even in the major divisions of existing universities.

With this introduction, let us consider the problem of our ancestors' coming to the ground, and let us see how the problem is illuminated by what is now known about the behavior of the contemporary primates. The traditional view of how we came to the ground can be summarized as follows. Man's apelike ancestors were living in trees, but there was a long and widespread desiccation that greatly reduced the forests, forcing our ancestors to take up bipedal life on the ground away from trees, and probably in savanna country. Obviously, to state any theory briefly oversimplifies it, but the essential point is that in this view bipedalism is caused by coming to the ground.

A look at the behavior of the nonhuman primates suggests that this explanation is much too simple. For example, of the many different kinds of New World primates, not one has adapted to life on the ground. When New World forests became smaller there was less area available for primates and many forms became extinct. In the New World, at least, reduction in forests led to the extinction of primates and not to their spending more time on the ground. Undoubtedly there are many reasons for this, and a comparison of New and Old World forms suggests a few of them.

No very small primates have adapted to life on the ground. Even on the island of Madagascar, where predator pressure appears to have been at a minimum, only some of the largest extinct forms were ground-livers. It is likely that most of the New World forms are too small to adapt to ground living in the manner of other primates. In addition, direct comparison of the locomotion of *Cebus* and *Macaca irus* in our laboratory at Berkeley shows that *Cebus* is much less efficient on the ground. In the New World form the lumbar region of the back is curved and functions differently, being used less when the monkey moves and especially when it jumps. The curvature in the lumbar region appears to be related to the prehensile tail, which is primarily a feeding adaptation. The tail, while of minor importance in locomotion, enables the animal to feed with both hands while stabilizing itself with feet and tail. The function of a structure as large as a prehensile tail may be easily misinterpreted without field observations; the tail has been considered primarily as a locomotor adaptation rather than as a feeding adaptation used occasionally for other purposes. Only when New and Old World monkeys were put in the same cage and observed as they moved over precisely the same areas and obstacles were the differences in the low back noticed. It is evident that appreciation of behavior as adaptation requires observations in both field and laboratory. Much more information on the behavior of New World primates is needed before this interpretation can be considered more than a suggestion. But I think that the situation in the New World implies that the effect of reduction in forests on the behavior of primates will depend on the precise nature of their arboreal adaptation. If primates are small and adapted to certain kinds of arboreal feeding, the probable result is extinction, not ground adaptation as the desiccation theory suggests.

Turning to the Old World monkeys, at least four and probably more have become adapted to living on the ground—the patas, gelada, baboon-macaques, and entellus. Further, there are species (such as *Cercopithecus aethiops*) that show intermediate adaptations, staying close to trees but frequently feeding on the ground. These forms remain fully quadrupedal, and the arboreal adaptations of the Old World monkeys do not involve the anatomical-behavioral limitations seen in the large New World primates. Adaptation to living on the ground has two advantages —it opens new areas for feeding, and it allows animals to move between isolated trees and so to live in much less densely forested areas.

To adapt to life far from trees requires adaptation for defense against predators, and this has been accomplished in two quite different ways. In patas monkeys it has been achieved by anatomical adaptation to high-speed running and the social adaptation of the adult male's making himself very obvious and running off as a decoy (Hall 1967). In baboons and geladas the anatomical adaptation is in the size and fighting strength of the adult males and the social adaptation of the males' joining in defense against predators, even those as large as cheetahs and leopards (Hall and DeVore 1965; DeVore and Hall 1965).

The Old World monkeys' successful coming to the ground shows that ground living near trees presents only minor problems in adaptation for many of these forms, and that for the vast majority of monkeys ground-living takes place close to trees—this is true even for most baboons. For Old World monkeys the problem is not so much that of ground living, as of the anatomical and behavioral adaptations necessitated by living away from trees. This requires both anatomical and social adaptations, and only three species of monkeys are really adapted to this way of life—patas, gelada, and hamadryas.

Before considering the apes (Pongidae), I would point out that the traditional theory of the origin of man suggests that our ancestors became not only bipeds but also savanna-livers as a result of the reduction of the forests. Judging by the monkeys, this would have required complex anatomical and social adaptations to be made at the same time and under conditions of maximum exposure to predation. The savanna was well supplied with carnivores before our ancestors were there, and there is no evidence that they had the kind of anatomical adaptation seen in baboons—and certainly they did not have the speed of patas. The more one studies the behavior of the contemporary monkeys the less likely seems an occurrence of a direct transition from arboreal life to savanna living.

The behavior of the contemporary apes is of particular importance because they are our nearest relatives among the living primates. It must be remembered, however, that the modern apes are only remnants of a much more diversified and widespread group. Significantly, as the forests were reduced in size during the Pliocene most apes became extinct, and the area the remnant occupied was reduced to much less than half its former size.

Adaptation to ground living differs strikingly in the Asiatic and African apes. The Asiatic apes (orangutan and gibbons) have no structural adaptations for locomotion on the ground and come to the ground only rarely. In marked contrast, the African apes (chimpanzee and gorilla) are primarily ground-livers and have substantial anatomical adaptation to a most peculiar way of locomotion (Tuttle 1967). These apes have been described as brachiators.[1] However, Schaller (1963) never saw an adult gorilla brachiate and although Goodall (1965,

[1] Brachiation is a form of locomotion characterized by swinging under a branch instead of walking on top. The structures making this possible are in the hand, wrist, elbow, and shoulder. Man shares these basic structures with the apes, and man can swing along under a bar using the same motions as an ape.

also motion pictures and personal communication) has seen chimpanzees brachiate, it is not a major part of their locomotor repertoire. Far from being primarily arboreal brachiators, chimpanzee and gorilla are fundamentally ground-living knuckle-walkers.[2] The gorilla is also a ground-feeder, whereas the chimpanzee primarily eats fruits obtained by climbing in trees.

Recent immunological studies (Sarich 1967) show that the chimpanzee and gorilla are more closely related to man than are the orangutan and gibbon. These studies suggest further that the chimpanzee and gorilla may not be any more closely related to each other than are man and chimpanzee. If all this information is put together, it is most probable that the common ancestor of gorilla, chimpanzee, and man was a knuckle-walking ape, spending much of its time on the forest floor. Observations on the actual behavior of the African apes suggest a long behavioral stage quite different from any postulated in traditional anthropological theory.

If it is assumed that there was a stage in which our ancestors were knuckle-walkers, the whole problem of coming to the ground takes on a different form. At the end of the Miocene and the beginning of the Pliocene, forests were much more extensive than they are today. There is no reason why the same species of forest-living ape might not have a range from India to Africa—indeed Pilbeam (1967) has shown that *Ramapithecus* of India was the same kind of a creature as *Kenyapithecus* of East Africa. When the forests were more or less continuous, there was no reason why the same species of ape might not have ranged over this whole area, as is suggested by the very frag-

---

[2] Knuckle walking is an unusual way of moving on the ground where the weight is borne on the back of the middle phalanges of the fingers. This is characteristic only of the genus *Pan*, chimpanzee and gorilla. Tuttle (1967) has fully described this gait and the anatomical adaptations which make it possible. He also calls attention to many features of the hand found in Bed 1, Olduvai, which are reminiscent of the structure of the contemporary knuckle-walkers.

mentary remains. In contrast to the theory that suggests coming to the ground was most likely when the forests were being reduced, the knuckle-walking theory suggests that coming to the ground was most likely when the forests were extensive, when the forest floor was greatest.

In summary, the similarities that man shares with the gibbon and the orangutan are due to common arboreal ancestry, to life in the trees and to the climbing-feeding adaptation, one part of which is the locomotor pattern called brachiation. The greater similarity that man shares with the gorilla and chimpanzee is due to a common knuckle-walking ancestry and a late separation—occurring after this behavioral stage had evolved.

This sequence is, of course, speculative, and even more speculative are the reasons for apes' coming to the ground. Chimpanzees move on the ground in order to go from fruit tree to distant fruit tree (Goodall 1965). If the forest is relatively open and if animals are large, moving arboreally from tree to tree is difficult or may even be impossible. One adaptive advantage of large size is that it permits the chimpanzee and gorilla to compete successfully with monkeys. Judging from the fossil record, there were in Africa many small apes, all of which became extinct. The reason for the abundance of small apes in the Miocene may have been that the highly successful monkeys of the genera *Cercopithecus, Cercocebus,* and *Papio* had not evolved at that time. In Africa today, even the large apes are far less successful than these monkeys, and the great interest in the apes is more because of their relation to man than because of their zoological success. Small apes (gibbons) have survived in Asia, but their primate competition has been primarily from leaf-eating monkeys (Colobidae) and these appear to be less aggressive than the African forms. The Asiatic macaques are primarily ground-living forms, offering much less direct competition than the African monkeys. Also, it is probable that the macaques evolved in Africa in the Pliocene and are late arrivals in Asia.

If our ancestors were knuckle-walkers, then the origin of bipedalism and tool use may be seen in a new way. For a long time I have been puzzled about how a creature could be adapted to partial bipedalism. Man moves so slowly compared to quadrupedal creatures and is so vulnerable without weapons that it has been very hard for me to conceive of a creature any less efficient that could survive at all. A knuckle-walking stage gets around this problem, as shown by the contemporary chimpanzee. The chimpanzee can move very rapidly quadrupedally and then climb out of danger if necessary. The chimpanzee knuckle-walks, climbs for feeding and escape, brachiates, and may walk bipedally for moderate distances, especially when carrying something.

If changed selection pressures favored the bipedal part of the behavior repertoire, then the beginnings of the human kind of bipedal walking and running might evolve while the animal could still move rapidly as a knuckle-walker and escape from danger by climbing. Probably the new selection pressure was for tool use and carrying and, according to this model, the adaptation of climbing for escape could not be lost until weapons had evolved to a level at which they could replace the need for climbing. The human foot must have evolved long after the evolution of simple tools.

These speculations are supported by two lines of evidence, the behavior of the contemporary apes and the fossil record, both of which have recently been reviewed by Lancaster (in press). The amount of object manipulation by the chimpanzee far exceeds that of any other nonhuman primate. Chimpanzees build nests, use sticks to get termites, ants, and honey, use stones to break nuts, and use both sticks and stones in agonistic displays. They throw both underhand and overhand.

It would be a remarkable coincidence if the creature closest to man in body chemistry, chromosomes, and locomotor anatomy should, through chance alone, also be the most similar in object using. (It is not certain how great the difference between the chimpanzee and gorilla really is, because the richness of Goodall's data comes from more years of study and a much more favorable situation for observation than does Schaller's account of gorilla behavior.) Chimpanzees play with objects (Goodall 1965, motion pictures, and personal communication). Our culture tends to belittle the importance of play—but play is the educational system for the nonhuman primates. The acts that will be important in adult life and learned in social situations (Hall 1963; Hall in press) are practiced in play.

Playing with objects is rare among free-ranging nonhuman primates. Most play is social, preparing for social skills such as interactions, sex, and fighting. Tsumori (1967) has demonstrated that in monkeys exploratory-play learning practically stops at maturity. His observations give the first experimental evidence of the great importance of extending the period of protected play-exploration, an extension that greatly increases the chance of the discovery of new adaptive behaviors. In chimpanzees this period is approximately twice as long as in the macaques, and there is object play and exploration, as well as the much more widely distributed social kind. Certainly the study of the contemporary primates shows that the chimpanzee is closer to man in many behavioral capacities than any other living primate.

Turning to the fossil record, it is probable that selected natural stones, chips, and simple pebble tools were used throughout the lower part of the Pleistocene and probably well before that. These were made by several kinds of small-brained men (*Australopithecus*, sensu lato). These forms were living in the savanna, away from trees, and had a fully human, nonprehensile foot. This is certainly not the beginning of tool using, for escape by climbing was no longer possible. Also, even in the earliest specimens the canine teeth are small and their functions in fighting, both in dominance fighting in the group and in fighting outside the group, must have been transferred to tools long before. And, just as in baboon or patas monkeys, the social life had to change from what had been adaptive on the forest floor to meet the problems of the savanna.

If the fossil record gives evidence of two million years of stone-tool use before the advent of *Homo erectus*, and if it took an absolute minimum of an additional four million years for the degree of object use seen in the chimpanzee to evolve into the degree reflected in the early pebble tools—then a minimum of six million years, and probably much more, was required for our ancestors to learn how to be human.

The central problem in the use of objects is psychological; it is the appreciation of the effectiveness of manipulation. And the skills that are learned in the social group, practiced in play, and used by adults are dependent on the brain. The reason that it took millions of years for the adaptive behaviors of apes to evolve to the effectiveness of *Homo erectus* is that the brain had to evolve in a feedback relation with the new behaviors. Through natural selection the success of behaviors alters the biological base of the behaviors, ultimately making new behaviors possible. We learn the skillful use of tools so easily that it is hard for us to appreciate the immense gap that separates our motor abilities from those of even our closest nonhuman relatives.

The relation of the brain to the problem of ground living may be illustrated in a different way. Man's use of the ground, his perception of space, is very different from that of the nonhuman primates. Most monkeys and apes spend their lives within a few square miles, perhaps as much as 15 square miles for gorilla and chimpanzees, but much less for the vast majority of primates. Here are animals with senses like our own, which can see food, water, and other animals beyond their range, but which make no use of this information. Both in gathering and in hunting, man utilizes vastly larger areas, and in the larger area there is a far greater diversity of plant and animal life. The knowledge necessary for human gathering and hunting is of a different order from the comparable activities of the nonhuman primates, and learning the resources, possibilities, and dangers of 300 square miles is utterly different from the knowledge necessary for the kind of adaptation seen in apes and monkeys.[3] Learning to utilize the diversity of a large area requires a brain capable of that learning, and only in man, among the primates, has such a brain evolved.

Probably a major factor in the evolution of human locomotion was the concomitant evolution of brains that were capable of perceiving the advantages of going long distances. The selection pressures that led to the evolution of the human pattern of locomotion came from the evolution of a more successful way of life, and the utilization of space requires far more than bipedalism. It requires tools for offense and defense and hunting and gathering, cooperation, division of labor, planning, and other social customs. It is difficult to imagine how the speed of a patas monkey would be as valuable to the species without the decoy behavior of the adult male; so human locomotion has no meaning aside from the other aspects of the human way of life.

An essential part of the human adaptation to living on the ground away from trees was the use of weapons. When our ancestors could no longer escape by climbing, they had to be skilled in the use of tools and to have had a biology which made it easy to learn to fight with objects. Man easily learns to fight, and throughout most of human history the arts of war were practiced in play, were socially rewarded, and were personally satisfying. And apparently for vastly longer than recorded history, man not only killed for food, and defended against predators, but man killed other men as an essential part of his adaptation to life on the ground. This does not mean that such behavior is inevitable, because man's biology expresses itself

[3] Space can be simplified by limiting the kinds of objects of interest. For example, if a species of animal eats only grass or a few species of other animals, the problem of space and distance is completely different from that for monkeys, apes, or man, which eat a wide variety of things. Also the environment may be highly simplified by built-in limitations of what a species may sense or learn.

in a social system, and the social system gives opportunities and sets limits. What it does mean is that it is very easy to convince men that war is useful—that it is right. What it does mean is that the control of aggressive males depends on social institutions, and part of our present problems is that the old institutions which glorified war are still in control.

In the field studies we see the power of play, social learning, and identification creating adults whose biology and learning have both fitted them for their adult roles. The patas male is built to flee, and he has learned when this behavior is appropriate. The baboon male is built to fight, and he has learned the behavior of his troop. Biology and experience make possible the appropriate behaviors of the species, and there is no contradiction between the juvenile view of life and the adult actuality. Probably the same was the case in the life of our ancestors, but today we do not know whether we are educating for war or peace. Today we are uncertain what sort of institution is to control the land, or whether this is to be left to antiquated customs and the aggressive nature of man.

The study of evolution affords a way of looking at man, a way of seeing some aspects of human nature and the forces which produced them. Coming to the ground was much more than a single event and involved much more than a locomotor adaptation. Changes in behavior and structure probably first made life possible on the forest floor. Later, further behavioral, structural, and social change made life possible on the open savanna. Each way of life lasted for millions of years, and each way depended on the feedback interrelations of biology and behavior. And even today our natures are products of these times long past, so we easily learn to walk, to talk, to play with objects, and to participate in the social life which gives success to the human adaptation.

REFERENCES

Altmann, S. A., ed. 1967. *Social communication among primates.* University of Chicago Press: Chicago.

DeVore, I. and Hall, K. R. L., 1965. Baboon ecology. In *Primate behavior: Field studies of monkeys and apes*, ed. I. DeVore, pp. 20–52. Holt, Rinehart, and Winston: New York.

Goodall, J., 1965. Chimpanzees of the Gombe Stream Reserve. In *Primate behavior: Field studies of monkeys and apes*, ed. I. DeVore, pp. 425–73. Holt, Rinehart, and Winston: New York.

Hall, K. R. L., 1963. Observational learning in monkeys and apes. *Brit. J. Psychol.* 54:201–26.

———. 1967. Social interactions of the adult male and adult females of a patas monkey group. In *Social communication among primates*, ed. S. A. Altmann, pp. 261–80. University of Chicago Press: Chicago.

———. In press. Social learning in monkeys. In *Primates: Studies in adaptation and variability*, ed. P. C. Jay. Holt, Rinehart, and Winston: New York.

Hall, K. R. L. and DeVore, I., 1965. Baboon social behavior. In *Primate behavior: Field studies of monkeys and apes*, ed. I. DeVore, pp. 53–110. Holt, Rinehart, and Winston: New York.

Jay, P. C., ed. In press. *Primates: Studies in adaptation and variability*. Holt, Rinehart, and Winston: New York.

Lancaster, J. B. In press. Primate communication systems and the emergence of human language. In *Primates: Studies in adaptation and variability*, ed. P. C. Jay. Holt, Rinehart, and Winston: New York.

Pilbeam, D. R., 1967. Man's earliest ancestors. *Science Journal* 3:47–53.

Sarich, V. M., 1967. A quantitative immunochemical study of the evolution of primate albumins. Unpublished Ph.D. diss. University of California, Berkeley.

Schaller, G. B., 1963. *The Mountain gorilla: Ecology and behavior*. University of Chicago Press: Chicago.

Tsumori, A., 1967. Newly acquired behavior and social interactions of Japanese monkeys. In *Social communication among primates*, ed. S. A. Altmann, pp. 207–19. University of Chicago Press: Chicago.

Tuttle, R. H., 1967. Knuckle-walking and the evolution of hominoid hands. *Am. J. Phys. Anthropol.* 26: 171–206.

Washburn, S. L., Jay, P. C. and Lancaster, J. B., 1965. Field studies of Old World monkeys and apes. *Science* 150: 1541–47.

# 9

# REVOLUTION AND DEVELOPMENT

*KENNETH E. BOULDING*

KENNETH BOULDING *has published numerous books and articles over a wide range of fields including peace research and international systems. He is professor of economics at the University of Colorado.*

# REVOLUTION AND DEVELOPMENT

*Kenneth E. Boulding*

L ET ME BEGIN by talking about development not only as a
process in economic and social life, but as a process in the
whole universe. What we call economic development is only
one aspect of a larger developmental process in society, and this
developmental process is just the tag end, from our point of
view, of the whole evolutionary process in this part of the universe. Biological evolution and social development, indeed, are
two aspects of an essentially continuous process. Both biological
and social evolution can be usefully described by a mutation-
selection model, even though in its usual form this is a rather
empty theory with not much predictive power. The processes
of social evolution are, of course, different and more elaborate
than the processes of biological evolution. The similarities, however, are great enough to assure us that we are dealing with a
single process in time.

In social evolution, as in biological evolution, we can distinguish between genotypes and phenotypes. On the whole,
the genotype is what mutates and the phenotype is what is
selected, although this distinction is often fairly rough. In social
evolution the processes of reproduction are much more complex
than they are in biology, because we have a lot more than two
sexes. Even though, in a quite literal sense, an automobile plant
is the womb of an automobile, automobiles are not produced
by an orgasm, despite many appearances to the contrary. A
distant observer from outer space might conclude from simple
observation that automobiles were reproduced sexually. We
know, however, that the process is a great deal more complicated; hence the possibility of messing up the genotype material

209

is much larger in social evolution than it is in biological evolution.

The social genotypes are things like blueprints, plans, ideas, symbols, sacred histories, and all the things which organize production both of artifacts and of social organizations. Genotypes are things which have the power of organizing role structures, for evolution, on the whole, is evolution of roles. They are the acts, relations, and structures in society which are social organizers. Then the phenotypes consist of the organizations which they produce: families, universities, firms, churches, states; also commodities and artifacts, automobiles, libraries, microphones, clocks, and so on. All these things are species of the social system and they have a kind of ecology of their own, just as there is an ecological system in the field or the forest. In the larger ecological system of the world, indeed, the artifacts and commodities of man, considered as species, compete ecologically with natural species. The automobile, for instance, has competed very successfully with the horse. In these days man, his artifacts and his organizations have become dominant in the ecological system of the world. Pretty soon nothing will survive which is not in some sense domesticated.

The world ecological system consists not only of ecological equilibrium but also of ecological succession, and it is the latter which constitutes the evolutionary process. This process is not continuous, but exhibits "gear changes." It seems to go on at a certain pace for a long time and then suddenly there is an acceleration and a shift to a new rate of evolution. The development of life was one such gear change; the development of the vertebrate was certainly another one; and the development of man was a very fundamental change, because with the biological evolution of the human nervous system the possibility of social evolution opened up—that is, evolution within the human nervous system itself. This goes on at a very rapid pace. Within social evolution we also distinguish gear changes. The first was the shift from the Paleolithic into the Neolithic with the invention of agriculture and the domestication of crops and livestock. This produced a settled village, an increase in the length of human life, and an acceleration in the growth of human knowledge. The next gear change was the urban revolution, of some five thousand years ago, or perhaps eight thousand. Now we are going through what I have elsewhere called a third great transition, a new gear change in the evolutionary process as a result of the rise of science and social self-consciousness.

In explaining social evolution we have to look for the social genotypes—relationships between people and organizations which are capable of organizing roles and role structures. I distinguish three main categories of social genotypes, which I call the threat system, the exchange system, and the integrative system. More categories might be distinguished but, in our culture at least, everything has to be divided into three parts.

The threat system begins when somebody says to someone else, "You do something nice to me or I'll do something nasty to you." This is a fairly powerful organizer; it is the basis of the urban revolution and of civilization, which, I should hasten to add, I regard as a most disagreeable state of man, which is now in process of passing away.

The threat system is capable of producing a moderately elaborate society. It produced the classical civilizations, which depended on the prior existence of agriculture and the food surplus from the food producer, and on a threat system to take the food surplus away from the food producer and to feed the kings and the priests, the artisans and the soldiers, who constituted the cities. The threat system produced slavery and it produced war, but it has a limited horizon of development. The trouble with slavery, as Adam Smith pointed out, is that it does not produce much economic development because the slave owner has no incentive and the slave has no opportunity. The slave owner has it made anyway, and if the slave thinks of an invention the slave owner thinks he is trying to get out of work and slaps him down. It is not surprising therefore that the threat system goes so far and no further.

Exchange is a somewhat different kind of process. It begins fairly early, perhaps, as anthropologists have described, as "silent trade." The little booths of the merchants spring up under the shadow of the temple, which is a spiritual threat system, or the castle, which is a material threat system, and the network of exchange begins its almost continuous and irresistible growth. Exchange begins when someone says to someone else, "If you do something nice to me, I'll do something nice to you." This is, as economists have always pointed out, a positive game sum, in which everybody becomes better off. Furthermore, exchange encourages the division of labor, and this increases the productive powers of labor, which develops exchange still further, which develops the division of labor still further, and so we go on in an enormous cumulative process.

The threat system is a Sisyphean system. It is like pushing uphill a stone which is always breaking away and running down into destruction, the collapse of empire, wars, and revolutions. Once we get to exchange we push the stone over the top of the hill and we are chasing it. The world is working with us and development is constantly fostered by the famous "invisible hand." As a result the exchange system has a much higher horizon of development than the threat system—a horizon which we certainly have not reached yet.

It is possible, however, that the exchange system does have a developmental horizon, perhaps because we have run into difficulties about under-consumption and secular stagnation, perhaps because a pure exchange system does not develop the kind of integrative structure which will legitimate and support it. This was Schumpeter's great argument,[1] He argued that a market economy had to have sacred institutions which would legitimate it and that the rationality of the market tended to destroy these. It is pretty hard to love a bank much, yet without

[1] J. A. Schumpeter, *Capitalism, Socialism, and Democracy* (New York: Harper, 1942).

a network of affection and support the exchange system tends to delegitimize itself and hence to destroy itself. I think it was Schumpeter who said, "The only thing wrong with capitalism is that nobody loves it." This, however, is a pretty important defect.

My third category, the integrative system, is something of a ragbag without the unity of the other two, but we must have it because there are a number of social organizers which are neither threats nor exchange. The integrative system consists of a number of diverse social organizers, all of which, however, revolve around the establishment of things like community, status, legitimacy, love, loyalty, benevolence, and malevolence. An integrative system begins when somebody says to someone else, "You do something and I'll do something because of what you are and what I am and what we both are, because we are all in the same boat, or because we love each other, or hate each other, or because we are all Seventh-Day Adventists or all Americans or all human beings," though this last is rather implausible. Without the integrative system, neither the threat system nor the exchange system can really operate. If either of these is to have any kind of developmental power there has to be an integrative matrix within which they can be legitimated.

With an unlegitimated threat, for instance, you can be a bandit, and organize a temporary social system by saying, "Your money or your life." If you want to be a bandit twice, however, you have to be either a landlord or a tax-collector—that is, you have to legitimate the relationship in a whole network of acceptance, law, security, community, and so on. Community is perhaps the key word in the integrative system, for it is around this that all the other concepts revolve.

All actual social systems and all actual organizations involve all three of these genotypes. Nevertheless, it is not difficult to classify the social phenotypes according to which of the three genotypes predominates in them. Thus the threat system produces phenotypes in the shape of kings, armies, empires, and some kinds of temples and churches. Not all religions are based on threat, but early religions frequently were. The priest, for instance, says to the farmer, "You give me part of your crops or I won't do the rituals and the crops won't grow." Farmers, being nice, innocent types—at least they used to be— believe this and so they support the priest with part of their surplus crops. Armed forces are still more obviously a phenotype of the threat system, and these, of course, are still very much with us.

The exchange system dominates such phenotypes as firms, banks, corporations, insurance companies, and all those organizations which exist primarily in a market environment— which exist by the transformations involved in exchange and production. Some of these have become very large, like General Motors, which, while it does not rival the United States Department of Defense, is exceeded by only eleven countries in its gross product. The corporation does not use threats or love very much to survive. Nobody says, "Ask not what General Motors can do for you, ask only what you can do for General Motors," because we expect General Motors to do something for us. This is the meaning of exchange.

Exchange, however, as Adam Smith again pointed out, can function as a social organizer only if there is reasonable security of private property—that is, the threat system has to be controlled or organized to the point where property is reasonably secure in the possession of the owner. We cannot have exchange without property, because property is what is exchanged. It is only as the institution of property is legitimated in some way that exchange can develop and organize the division of labor. Property, of course, can be either private or public, and the concept is certainly not abolished by socialism. It is one of the paradoxes of the ideological struggle of our time that whatever success socialism has had has been because it has been able to legitimate property in the form of public property. The weakness of the market economy has often arisen from the difficulty it finds in legitimating the property concept.

What "security" means in this connection is that the people who make decisions should be able to enjoy their fruits and suffer their consequences. Otherwise exchange would not result in development, and would not result in a division of labor and the improvement of the productive powers. Given this security and legitimation, however, exchange can certainly work miracles, as we have seen recently in Germany and Japan, and indeed in the whole extraordinary development we have had for the last two-hundred years.

There are also phenotypes which are dominated by the integrative system: such things as the family and the church, and, even more strikingly, institutions like the Elks, the bridge club, or the little league, which have almost no function except developing integrative relationships.

Just as is true in the biological sphere, as we have seen earlier, organizations have mixtures of genes, which might almost be called social chromosomes—that is, threats, exchange, and love in different proportions. Even the most idealistic utopian community has a little bit of a threat system, at least in the form of potential expulsion; even an organization like an armed force has to rely on a certain amount of exchange, and a good deal of integrative activity, in terms of morale-building and so on. Exchange organizations likewise have to exist in a matrix of a threat system, insofar as law and order and security of property depend on this, and also in an integrative matrix. Even General Motors has to be loved a little. We may not need to be passionate about it, but it has to be accepted in some sense as legitimate before it can really operate in the long run.

The key to all these developmental processes, I argue, is the growth of knowledge properly interpreted. If we ask of the evolutionary process what it is that evolves, the answer has to be some form of information or improbability of structure, and this is the key to the whole process right from the primordial hydrogen atom. Matter and energy are subject to an inexorable law of conservation. Chemistry, for instance, is a moderately dismal science, because in the material world nothing is ever lost or gained in total. We have pure zero-sum games of redistribution of the elements. If one has more, somebody else has less. Matter as such, once the elements are set up, is obviously incapable of development, at least until the social system resumes the evolution of the elements from where it left off some four to six billion years ago. This is why materialism as a developmental philosophy has serious weaknesses.

The contemplation of energy is even more depressing. Thermodynamics is an even more dismal science than chemistry, and, as a matter of fact, much more dismal than economics. Thermodynamics says that nothing you do is any good in the long run. Available energy is not even conserved, but is spent. We are all spendthrifts, living on our capital of potential, of which we cannot even be parsimonious. Entropy goes on increasing all the time, and entropy is everybody's enemy.

The evolutionary process, as Schrödinger describes it,[2] is essentially the segregation of entropy. What this means is that even though we spend our capital of energy potential we build up what is left into more and more improbable forms. Evolution is the development of the improbable. Thermodynamics, of course, proclaims the ultimate conquest of the probable, that is, chaos, unless something funny happens to the universe at the end, as it probably does. Maybe Brahma does breathe the universe in and out every ten billion years.

Once the evolutionary process has produced structures with the improbable capacity for self-reproduction we are off on an evolutionary voyage, destination unknown.

There seem to be two processes at work in evolution, which correspond roughly to the genotype and the phenotype. The first, by which the genotype reproduces itself, might be called

    [2] Erwin Schrödinger, *What Is Life?* (Cambridge: Cambridge University Press, 1951).

"printing." In this process a structure simply reproduces itself in the material world in the way a print shop operates. This is apparently the way the gene reproduces itself. It acts as a three-dimensional printing set which has the capacity of attracting its own pattern into it, producing a mirror image of itself in the material world, and the mirror image then reproduces the gene. The gene, therefore, can print itself on the material world indefinitely, provided it has the material environment around it. The same might be said of the *Chicago Tribune*, which is a kind of gene of Chicago, though fortunately not the only one.

The second process might be called organization, by which the genotype produces the phenotype. We see this also in society as well as in biological evolution. Thus Mr. Harper's idea and Mr. Rockefeller's fifty million dollars in a rather improbable sacred history produced the University of Chicago. The genotypes print themselves and then proceed to organize the phenotypes.

We see the processes reflected in the miracle of teaching itself. After a teacher finishes a successful class, the students know more and he knows more too. This is not at all like exchange in which if I give you something I have less of it. In teaching I give you something and I have more of it. It is a widow's cruse.

Knowledge, of course, is also lost by people forgetting it and by people getting old and dying. Death is an enormous brain drain and all human knowledge is lost every generation. This is why we have to have all sorts of educational institutions to reproduce it. The more easily it can be produced, however, the more easily it can be expanded.

What I am arguing, therefore, is that all developmental processes are fundamentally learning processes—processes by which more and more improbable structures come into being through these related operations of printing and organization. Economic development is just part of this larger process, though perhaps the most visible and the most measurable part. Political and moral and aesthetic development are observable processes but they are hard to identify and measure, and it is often hard even to tell which way is up. There is certainly development, for instance, from Shakespeare to the Beatles, but its direction is not wholly certain.

If we could get a measure of the entropy of structures we might have a pretty good measure of development. An entropy theory of value is by no means absurd, for value is improbability, and the more valuable anything is the less probable it is.

Whether economic development is really measurable or not, it has the great advantage that it has a measure in terms of something like per capita real income or per capita real gross national product. It is tempting, therefore, to take the rate of economic growth as a first approximation of the overall rate of development. A better measure might well be the increase of knowledge or the decrease of entropy, but this is hard to devise. We have some notion of the acceleration of the rate of growth of knowledge; in the Paleolithic it may have taken one hundred thousand years or more to double the stock of knowledge; in the Neolithic it may have doubled every five thousand years, and in civilized society, every thousand years. Today in many fields it is supposed to double every fifteen years, at least in quantity. Similarly, if we look at the per capita real income, this probably took one thousand years to double before 1600, but today in rather slow countries like the United States it doubles in thirty-seven years and in really developing countries like Japan it doubles every eight years. This seems to represent a real shift of gears.

No matter how we measure it, however, economic development is still a learning process. It is not merely a piling up of existing commodities, like agricultural surpluses. Development means changing structures, not piling up stock. It means producing new kinds of things and new kinds of people with new kinds of knowledge and skill. It involves a reorganization of society and a total learning process. We can even define capital as frozen knowledge—an improbable arrangement of the material world depending upon a prior improbable arrangement in the mental world. Thus, the microphone, and still more, the computer, is a fantastically improbable arrangement of matter which is here because somebody thought it up, and was able to think it up because of a long process of development of human knowledge going back thousands or perhaps tens of thousands of years. Man is now imposing his own knowledge on the material world.

The computer may easily represent another gear change. Computers have become almost quasi-biological organisms, without very much in the way of sex. They are, however, developing capacities for producing low-level knowledge. If this represents a really new element in the knowledge-building process it should also produce further acceleration in the rate of development.

The dominance of knowledge over material can be seen quite clearly if we observe how rapidly a society can recover from material destruction if the knowledge structure is unimpaired. Thus, in Japan and Germany where the physical capital was destroyed during the Second World War, it was restored in astonishingly short time because the human capital was practically unimpaired. In Indonesia, on the other hand, which had much less physical destruction, the absence of knowledge has produced a declining society.

Non-economic development also requires a learning process. It involves learning how to live at peace with each other. It involves learning how to make the fruits of virtue reasonably secure and the retributions of vice moderately certain. It involves learning to organize; for learning the skills of organization, perhaps, underlies all social development. The main obstacle even to economic development in countries where it is not happening is the inability to organize. Organization, however, is a skill; it is something that people have to learn. It is certainly not given genetically, but it is something that can be transmitted. Economic development also requires moral development. There has to be a minimum degree of trust. Exchange, for instance, is impossible without this minimum of trust. In a society in which nobody can be trusted unless he is a blood relation it is hard for economic development to go beyond the second cousins. In developed societies, such as the United States, abstract trust has got to the point where nobody checks on your baggage tickets at the airports and we can even have telephone credit cards. We have computerized billings which can be sabotaged in a minute by punching a few more holes in the card. In spite of the extraordinary vulnerability of complex societies to possible betrayals of trust, the odd thing is that we learn not to betray—that is, we learn not to indulge in prisoner's dilemmas and all these other little games that make everybody worse off.

An increase in the rate of development can be called "acceleration." Sometimes this takes place rather suddenly in a society, as it did, for instance, in Japan at the time of the Meiji Restoration or after the Second World War. Sometimes the acceleration may take a generation or more. We have mentioned earlier the acceleration that marked the end of the Paleolithic and the Neolithic periods. Even within the civilized period we can trace minor accelerations. In Europe, for instance, the fall of the Roman Empire seems to have produced one. The Roman Empire itself was technologically stagnant, and development in western Europe did not start up until Rome fell. It may be that one of the problems of China, and the reason why the great breakthrough into science did not take place there, is that it did not fall far enough.

The development of science, of course, is the great acceleration. It is a mutation of the learning process itself. It may, of course, turn out to be a flash in the pan, if it results in the human race destroying itself; on the other hand, it may be a mutation almost as important as the development of life itself. We are only beginning to see the full impact of it. Science did not really affect economic life very much until about 1860. The industrial revolution of the eighteenth century, about which so much fuss is made, was really the tag end of the folk technology of the Middle Ages. The steam engine was actually less complicated than the medieval clock and owed very little to science, though that little, for instance Boyle's law, may have been important. The real theory of the steam engine, which is thermodynamics, did not come until almost a hundred years after the steam engine itself; so obviously the steam engine owed nothing to it. After 1860, however, the story is different. The electrical industry would have been impossible without Faraday, Ohm, and Clerk-Maxwell. The nuclear industry likewise would have been impossible without Bohr and Einstein. Today it is quite likely that 75 per cent of the output of the economy is science based.

To come now, rather late in the day, to the second part of my title—a look at the role of revolution in the developmental process—revolution is a term which is used very loosely and sometimes means simply a large change in the system. It is sometimes used to mean what I have here called an "acceleration"; that is, a change in the rate of change. In the narrower and perhaps more exact sense of political revolution, it means some kind of overturn in the power structure by means of which an old elite is displaced by a new one, usually, though not necessarily, with a certain amount of violence and upheaval. Political revolutions sometimes, though not always, produce an acceleration. An acceleration tends to be produced if the incoming elite has a higher level of knowledge and organization relevant to development than the outgoing elite. If, before the revolution, those who have the will to develop do not have the power and those who have the power do not have the will, the society is likely to be fairly stagnant. In those circumstances a revolution which gives those who have the will the power is likely to produce an acceleration.

Revolutions, however, are costly. If they are violent they

produce a lot of émigrés, and one of the major products of revolution seems to be refugees. This represents a great waste of the talents of the society and an actual loss of the knowledge structure which it sometimes take a generation or two to recover. We might even classify revolutions into those that cost two generations, those that cost one, and those that cost none. The Russian Revolution was a two-generation revolution—that is, the country did not get back to the position of 1913 in terms of per capita income until the early 1950's. The French Revolution also was probably a two-generation revolution. The American Revolution seems to have been a one-generation revolution. It was costly in the sense that the refugees, that is, the Tories, were on the whole hard-working, respectable, and knowledgeable people, and American economic development did not really get off the ground until after 1815. The best examples of the costless or no-generations revolution would be the Glorious Revolution in England in 1688—though if we include Cromwell, that also was a two-generation revolution—and the somewhat equivalent Meiji Restoration in Japan in 1868. The Japanese experience is perhaps the best example of an acceleration without a revolution, which seems to me almost the ideal way of initiating development.

Under some circumstances, of course, acceleration may be impossible without a revolution, simply because the existing political structure of the society is so corrupt and ineffective. On the other hand, a country with a reserve bank of legitimacy in the shape, say, of an emperor, like the Japanese, is very lucky because it can achieve the transfer of power to a developmental elite with much less cost. Thus, I would always regard revolution as a cost, even if sometimes a necessary cost, and never as a gain in itself. A real obstacle to development is what might be called a revolutionary sentimentality, as one tends to get it on the Left, which idealizes the process of revolution itself. This can be a serious obstacle to development, as we see it, for instance, in Indonesia and in Cuba.

In the early days of the Cuban Revolution I was invited to give some lectures on development in Havana, an invitation which I, unlike many of my fellow economists, found it impossible to resist. It was during what might be called the New Deal phase of the revolution, before it turned to the extreme Left, and the people who invited me, I regret to say, mostly had to flee the country shortly afterward. I tried to point out on that occasion that while revolution was like an orgasm, if you wanted development you had to have a womb, because development was a learning process which required peace, quiet, and long uninterrupted growth. I am afraid this doctrine was not popular, because on the whole the mystique of revolution is a masculine mystiqe. I am inclined to think that what development requires is a feminine mystique, and that the masculine mystique is on the whole an enemy to it. The United States was fortunate in that its revolutionary leaders, with the possible exception of Jefferson, were not very revolutionary. Very often, however, the people who can lead a successful revolution, such as Sukarno and Castro, are not suited to lead the developmental process which should follow. If you have to have a revolution, there is a lot to be said for having a revolutionary leader who has the gift of dying young, and can be succeeded by a developmental leader who has very different qualities.

In conclusion, I would like to try to apply some of these considerations to one of the major problems of our own day, the so-called ideological struggle and the cold war, which revolves around the question of the relative merits of the capitalist free market development on the one hand and the socialist centrally planned development on the other. This is an argument which arouses such fierce emotions that it is hard to deal with it rationally. Nevertheless, I think we have to admit that there are many ways of developing, and the distinction between developing and stagnant societies cuts across the distinction between socialist and capitalist societies. We can perhaps distinguish four types of societies in the modern world following these two classifications. There is first the successful market society, like Japan, most of Western Europe, and the United States. Japan has actually had the highest rate of development known in human history, about 8 per cent per annum per capita in the last twenty years. Many other capitalist societies, however, have been in the 5–6 per cent class, and even the relatively stagnant ones, like Britain, have a slow development to some extent by choice.

The next category might be called the successful socialist societies, which include the Soviet Union and the Eastern European countries. Their rate of development has been less than the most successful capitalist societies, and rarely exceeds 6 per cent per annum; and this has been achieved also at a high social cost in terms of inefficient investment, a distorted price system, and a certain amount of political oppression.

The third category is that of the unsuccessful capitalist societies, which would include most of the colonial and ex-colonial countries, even those like many Latin-American societies which have been free from formal colonialism for a long time but have retained a colonial structure.

Then at the bottom of the list we have the unsuccessful socialist countries, where there has been not merely stagnation but retrogression, as we have seen in Indonesia, Burma, possibly Ceylon, Syria, and Perón's Argentina. One is almost tempted to call the Asian group, at any rate, the Laski countries, because many of their leaders learned their economics from Harold Laski in London in the 1920's. What they learned from him, unfortunately, was how to destroy the invisible hand without providing a visible hand—which merely leads to a capacity for getting the worst of all possible worlds. These countries have managed to destroy the developmental processes of the market without substituting the developmental processes of a genuine centrally planned economy. The case of China is ambiguous. After a rather successful period in the 1950's, it has had a severe setback as a result of its essentially sentimental revolutionism, which has tried to create a perpetual revolution rather than getting on with the sober business of growth.

My general conclusion, therefore, is that while there is occasionally a case for revolution, there is practically no case for revolutionism as an ideology, and that as an ideal, revolutionism should always be regarded as a cost, not as a gain, provided that our real objective is development. One should always leave the possibility open, however, that the objective may not *be* developmental. The revolutionist is frequently motivated by malevolence; that is, there are certain people or certain classes that he hates and will damage even to his own cost. Malevolence means that you are willing to make somebody else worse off even if as a result you are worse off yourself. This is an unfamiliar concept to economists, who are astonishingly nice people, and who have the naïveté to believe that the world is ruled by selfish behavior. Selfishness, however, is a high moral virtue compared with malevolence and envy, and a great deal of human behavior unfortunately falls far below the selfish ideal. Only economists, surely, could have thought up the Pareto optimum, which implies that I will approve of a situation in which somebody else becomes better off even if I am no better off. This no doubt reflects the eighteenth-century character of economics and its descent from a moral philosopher, known as Adam Smith, who, while he was skeptical about undue altruism, did not approve of malevolence.

A great deal of revolutionism, however, is motivated by spite. The first collectivization in the Soviet Union, for instance, did enormous damage to their developmental process because of spite against the kulaks. By contrast, development is fostered by non-malevolent attitudes, and by what I have sometimes called the presbyterian virtues: honesty, punctuality, temperance, the keeping of promises, and a mild benevolence toward others. This is a moral climate which fosters development—not the moral climate of spite which is so characteristic of revolutionism. I think I am prepared to say, therefore, that even where revolution may be necessary as a prerequisite for development it is always a symptom of a low state of moral and political development. Where revolution succeeds it is because it is a teacher; it is, however, an expensive teacher, and the search for a better one is a highly rewarding enterprise.

# 10

# THE PEASANT REVOLT OF OUR TIMES

WILLIAM H. McNEILL

WILLIAM H. MCNEILL *is professor of history at The University of Chicago. Among his books are* The Rise of the West: A History of the Human Community; Europe's Steppe Frontier, 1500–1800; *and* America, Britain, and Russia: Their Cooperation and Conflict, 1941–46.

# THE PEASANT REVOLT OF OUR TIMES

*William H. McNeill*

A MONG the many dimensions of the sweeping changes of our time, I propose to dwell upon an aspect that was borne in upon me during 1966 in the course of travel in Greece and other parts of Europe. I refer to the sharp change in traditional relations between town and country, a change which may be summed up in the title I have taken for this lecture: "The Peasant Revolt of Our Times."

The revolt is probably worldwide, although my own personal knowledge and observation are limited to parts of Europe and North America. But from what I read in the newspapers it very much looks as though similar feelings to those I have observed in Greece, for example, lie behind the fighting in Viet-Nam as well as anticolonial movements elsewhere in the world. The peasant revolt is, in fact, one of the major axes of political development in our time—or so I have come to believe; and it is one of which we who live in great cities are not often aware.

The peasants' revolt against their traditional, disadvantaged status has excellent and most rational grounds. Civilization was built upon the backs of the world's peasantries. Traditionally, in all civilized societies, the few have taken goods from the many, either as rents and taxes, or in less stable situations, as booty and tribute. The few have then gathered together in cities, partly for protection and partly for the pleasures of social intercourse with each other. Around the predatory few in turn arose a circle of servants and caterers—artisans and other specialists—who ministered to the wishes and wants of the lords of the land, and in doing so created the material goods and specialized skills we associate with civilized society.

When it is described in this way, most of us may feel that the lords and masters were somehow wicked and that civilization was a creature of social injustice. In a sense this is so. Poor farmers certainly think that way, and poor farmers still constitute a majority of mankind, taking the world as a whole. But the predatory city was also a great social invention, now about five thousand years old. It allowed rapid technical advances; increased social variety; opened up interfaces within society between men of different skills and habits of mind, across which invention and innovation of the most diverse sort might arise; and, finally, provided the matrix within which religion, art, and literature flourished.

Moreover, the predatory city survived so long because it allowed men to construct a more formidable society than could arise on the basis of undifferentiated villages. The masters of the land were often political-military specialists in their own persons—or else they hired professionals to fulfill these functions on their behalf; and the existence of such specialists in violence permitted the organization of comparatively large regions of the earth into great empires or smaller kingdoms. Such political organizations proved more powerful than alternative modes of social organization—in most places and times. Hence the innumerable jacqueries, with which the pages of history abound, always failed. Efforts to undo the central injustice at the heart of civilized society never succeeded for very long. Even when rebels succeeded in overthrowing one set of exploiters and rent-collectors—as happened often enough—the victors were quickly compelled to imitate the wicked ways of their predecessors by collecting taxes and establishing a government, for if they did not do so, defense against professional men of violence was not possible.

Five thousand years of history do show some important variations on the underlying theme of inequality and injustice. Instead of the usual system, whereby individual landlords owned private estates and exacted heavy rents but comparatively light taxes, collective exploitation of a more distant hinterland was sometimes possible. This was the way the Athenians sustained their much-admired democracy in the fifth century B.C. The Vikings of the ninth and tenth centuries A.D. did the same. So did the innumerable tribes of steppe cavalrymen who raided the civilized communities of farmers and cities that lay south of the Eurasian steppe. But this sort of collective exploitation of comparatively distant regions and peoples was usually a transitory phase: viable only as long as rude (usually barbarian) equality held the raiders together, and yet they were not strong enough to conquer and hold the land they raided.

Another variation saw individual landlords leave the cities and take up residence amid the villages and fields they controlled. This was true, for example, of Iranian barons between 200 B.C. and A.D. 600; of medieval knights in western Europe; and of Japanese samurai after the end of the Nara period. Such a pattern was usually a reaction to a low level of public order, and involved making rents almost all-important (at the expense of taxes). Sometimes it allowed towns to achieve greater autonomy *vis-à-vis* the landowning class than was possible when the landowners lived in the town and dominated its life from within.

A third variation from the historical norm leaned toward the opposite excess; for when taxes eclipse rents a bureaucratic exploitation of the peasantry becomes possible without the mediation of private landowners. The late Roman Empire and the Ottoman Empire from the seventeenth century are two classic examples of this mode of social organization. The bureaucratic pattern is more relevant to our own day—when the assault upon private landlords is worldwide—than we perhaps usually recognize. But I will come back to this point later.

For the moment, my argument can rest upon the observation that these three different ways of departing from the norm that prevailed most widely in civilized societies are merely different ways of slicing up the same pie. Economically unrequited goods and services were provided by the peasantry; and fluctuations in absolute amounts wrung from them, or in the hardship particular communities had in paying whatever was demanded of them, were relatively small compared with the fluctuations and ranges of choice that existed at the top of the social scale for distributing the "take" between officials, priests, individual aristocrats, or some combination of these groups.

The naked collision between peasant and lord that lay at the very heart of civilized society was modified in a more fundamental way by trade. Interregional trade between cities enhanced the range of effective exploitation of the world's peasantries. Local magnates could compel their subordinates to perform corvée in order to produce goods needed by foreign merchants from the cities. In return for the ores, timber, wool, or other raw materials produced in this way, the chieftain collected city goods from the merchants. But seldom did such luxuries reach the hands of those who did the labor. Instead, long-distance trade acted as an opening wedge for social differentiation and specialization—the onset, in short, of civilization, with its central injustice.

Trade between city artisans and local peasants did sometimes arise, but was a far more slender thing than we, with our experience of the modern American relationship between town and country, are likely to imagine. First of all, the peasants had to have enough left after paying taxes and rents to be able to sell some of their products. This involved an oversight, so to speak, on the part of the rent- and tax-collectors that seldom lasted long. Secondly, the artisan products of the town had to be clearly superior to what could be had from within the village itself. Itinerant smiths, for example, could usually provide plowshares and other essentials without bringing peasants into town markets.

I conclude, therefore, that economic reciprocity between town and country is very rare in human history, and does not exist very widely today despite the spread of market economies and the elimination of private landlords across wide portions of the earth's surface. Indeed, instead of asking why economic reciprocity does not develop naturally or spontaneously all round the globe, we should ask: How can the exploitation of rural populations *fail* to develop? How can city folk be induced to invest in facilities to produce goods for the peasants' use when they can so easily take the surplus produced in the fields, and use that surplus for their own satisfactions? "Modern" armies, monumental buildings, social welfare schemes for city workers, and modern factories that hire city folk to produce high cost and low quality goods are no less effective ways of exploiting the peasantry than old-fashioned individual consumption by aristocratic landlords or royal courts.

With this effort to adjust habitual presuppositions as preface, it is time to ask, What are the changes in rural-urban relations that we can recognize in our time? I propose to speak of two regions in Europe that I visited during 1966, and to contrast them with the American Middle West in which we find ourselves. Generalization from these examples may be a bit more plausible than would be the case if I continued in the vein of these opening remarks.

First, then, North Wales—not more than fifty miles from Birmingham, Liverpool, and Manchester, where the industrial revolution began nearly two hundred years ago. The remarkable thing, however, is that rural life continues even today in a way that struck me as amazingly stable, conservative, and traditional. Local social patterns of deference and class distinction survive: the gentry are a cut above farmers and farmers rank far above mere hired hands. I had the sense that many rural folk felt themselves morally or in other ways superior to city people, whose ways seemed soft and corrupt, untrustworthy and strange—and who were, for the most part, hired hands, dependent on wages like the lowest stratum of rural society.

In other parts of Western Europe where I had less entry into
local life, a casual tourist's eye still catches evidences of similar
conservatism—perhaps partly affected, as when villagers in
Holland or in Austria dress up in traditional costumes on special
occasions, but also, I suspect, partly real.

Presumably what allows this conservatism in Western
Europe is the comparative gradualness with which modernity
and industrialism affected the countryside. Over decades and
centuries, men from the bottom of rural society went off to seek
their fortunes in town. Those who stayed behind were the more
fortunate, richer, more propertied groups. How could they fail
to feel themselves superior to urban types who had left because
they had nothing to stay for? But the surprising result, it seems
to me, is that peasant life in Western Europe, closest to the
hearth where modern industrialism first was forged, survives
even today. Men have not generally repudiated the hierarchical system of society that gives each of them a place and rank
and defines mutual relationships up and down the social scale
with an exactitude surprising to a city man like myself.

By comparison, the American Middle West has seen far
greater disruption of its far more egalitarian rural tradition in
the last three or four decades. American farmers have worked
technological miracles; only 5 per cent of the United States
population now produces the food consumed in this country
and the surpluses sent abroad. The rest of us do not raise our
own food—but then, neither do the farmers. They have become
businessmen in their own right, still harboring a considerable
suspicion of the city, but absorbed almost entirely into its exchange relations. The American farmer's activity is part of the
flow of goods and services in which we all find ourselves im-
mersed, regulated by credit and taxes, supply and demand,
price supports, export subsidies and other governmental programs and policies. The city-centered web of economic
relationships, in other words, has reached out and engulfed the
United States farmer almost entirely, and deprived rural life

and society of its autonomy and of most of its differences from city ways.

Yet within the scope of my own direct observation, the place where the sharpest change and disruption of rural traditions has taken place is Greece. Here the impact of modernity was delayed, but when it came—in the shape of radios and bus connections with Athens—the effect was extraordinary. In 1944–46, when I first saw Greece, a stranger was an event and village hospitality was limited only by poverty. Traditional hand-made costumes distinguished the inhabitants of one village from those of the next; and within each village a very precise gradation of rank and status, based mainly on possession of land, but partly on personal qualities, assigned everyone his place. Dowry and marriage negotiations reaffirmed and defined the gradations of status, and provided an inexhaustible topic for gossip among the women at church and the men at the village *taverna*.

In the seventeen years since warfare ceased in Greece, this age-old traditional social structure of village life has been almost destroyed. The drastic experiences of the war years, when as much as one-seventh of the entire Greek population was officially classified as refugees from their villages, introduced the women and the young girls to the great wide world beyond village limits; and with this the great conservative force which had kept village life going suffered critical disruption. Official government policy, supported by United States aid programs, delivered the coup de grace by opening wide the channels of communication between Athens and the countryside. As a result, the great urban world presented itself in siren shape to the dazzled villagers of Greece. Almost to a man, the peasants decided to abandon traditional ways and aspired to escape rural idiocy by getting to the city where the bright lights glittered and life was so much easier.

The desire to escape village limitations was partly founded on economic fact. City folk in Greece do live better and often work less than peasants have to do. But the urge to leave the land went beyond strictly economic limits. Success and energy came to be equated with leaving home. Only failures or persons who had some unlucky disadvantage stayed behind. Or so it seemed in some of the villages I visited that summer, where emigration to Germany and to Athens had eaten the old structure of village life almost completely away. Other rural communities have suffered less disruption, of course, and the land is still fully occupied and farmed. But the psychological and emotional autonomy which struck me so forcefully in Wales and Western Europe among the rural people I encountered was definitely gone from even the most prosperous Greek villages. Real improvements in rural standards of living—which in some communities have been truly remarkable since 1949—count for little when village life has become an exile from the land of heart's desire, even when that land turns out in fact to be a shabby slum in Athens or a dismal workers' barracks in Germany.

The result, I thought, was an all but universal restlessness and discontent in the villages, and scarcely less dissatisfaction in the towns, where the men and women who had started life as peasants found the uncertainties of city life hard to get used to, but could not very well give up and go back home again without surrendering the dream that had brought them to town in the first place. Old values had been rejected; new ones that were in the least adequate to real experience of town life were hard to find.

Political instability, which has since resulted in an army coup d'etat and the establishment of military dictatorship in Greece, was the result. When so many persons rejected traditional patterns of conduct and escaped from traditional village hierarchical relationships into the anonymity of city life, traditional political life was disrupted also. Too many options opened. Too much tinder for demagoguery lay scattered through Greek society. Government by consent and through the ballot box broke down—at least for the time being. Given the prior breakdown of some ten thousand village communities, the recent course of public events in Greece ought not to be so very surprising.

One of the frustrating aspects of the Greek peasants' position was the absence of any tangible enemy against whom to direct feelings of frustration and hate. Landlords disappeared in most parts of Greece with the overthrow of the Turks. In those regions where the Greek landlords established themselves, land reform between the wars removed them. Even governmental taxation is not very apparent, since it comes mainly indirectly in the form of high-cost goods whose sale prices bring excise taxes and different forms of industrial subsidy home to the consumer, whether urban or rural.

Where private landlords have not yet disappeared, a discontented peasantry does, of course, have an immediate and obvious target for its wrath, and since no one is much inclined to come to the defense of receivers of rents, the position of landlords who do not command immediate and personal armed force becomes utterly untenable. Contemporary weaponry is such as to make it all but impossible for a landholding class to monopolize effective violence—as used often to be possible in times past when weapons were fewer and the skills needed for their use were harder to learn than today.

But the elimination of landlords means the removal of the private siphons that brought goods from village to city in traditional societies. This in turn opens three theoretical possibilities. Cities might simply melt away and peasants consume everything they produce. This sort of social structure appeals to naïve peasant feelings, but in a day when organized armed forces and transportation and communication are more effective than ever before, the idea that peasants could somehow make good their escape from the toils of city exploitation by simply refusing to feed their exploiters seems more utopian than ever. The Russian peasants tried something like it in the early

1930's and saw their stores of grain seized by main force, with the result that it was dispersed peasants, not organized city populations, that did the starving.

A second theoretical alternative would be for the city populations to keep going by borrowing from abroad while the peasants supported themselves. Something close to this has in fact occurred in India, where recent American shipments of food feed some ninety million persons—that is, just about the urban population of India's big cities. But this is a sadly unstable posture for any community to find itself in. Survival rests upon the will of distant outsiders who may find other uses for their surplus food—or worse still, find their surplus disappearing.

The third alternative is therefore the only one that seems in the least practicable, namely, to step up taxation so as to take up the slack produced by the elimination of rents. In our world, by far the most reputable and popular form of achieving this result is industrial development. Building new plants, and then allowing them to sell high-priced and poor quality goods in a protected national market, can give employment to city folk and keep innumerable government officials busy planning new investment or regulating what already exists. Other and more old-fashioned forms of taxation have, of course, not been given up. But nothing commands such enthusiasm as forced savings to finance further building of factories, unless it be the diversion of resources to the support and equipment of armies.

In effect, therefore, I think what we are seeing in the so-called underdeveloped world is the rapid emergence of new patterns for the exploitation of the peasant majority. The great virtue of the traditional landlord system was that the number of rentiers tended to be limited by the extent of arable land. When a man inherited only a small portion he sank toward the level of an ordinary peasant. Rents also tended to freeze into traditional payments, and everybody knew what to expect.

The new, indirect, bureaucratic forms of exploitation of the world's peasantries are not so obviously limited. Governmental and private bureaucracies have an almost indefinite power to expand. The need for coordinators of coordinators, and for liaison between the hydra heads of separate bureaucratic offices, generates its antithetical counterpart in the form of expediters who know how to penetrate bureaucratic thickets and shortcut normal channels to get things done in a hurry. Indeed I can see no effective brake upon the multiplication of bureaucratic and administrative personnel other than their capacity to collect food from the countryside or credits from abroad.

Indirect, collective, and bureaucratic exploitation of the peasantry has some serious problems therefore, and may not be stable for very long. The problem is how to prevent city folk from using the advantages of their position in society to squeeze the peasants too hard; for with the technological resources a modern bureaucracy and army possess, old limits upon exploitation of the countryside have weakened or disappeared.

Lest I leave you with too smug a sense of our own national advantages when compared with the problems faced by poor, predominantly peasant lands, let me say in passing that the American pattern of urban-rural relationships has its risks too. The productive efficiency of our farms has been purchased at the price of vulnerability to any sort of disturbance to the flow of goods across half a continent and more. Without a supply of gasoline, electrical power, chemicals, spare parts, and literally hundreds of other items, our farmers could not produce a crop. Any breakdown of the industrial web of exchanges that lasted six months or longer would therefore involve an immediate breakdown of agricultural production too. In former times, disruption and temporary paralysis of city exchange relationships was not so serious. Life on the farms went on more or less as usual, because the routines of cultivation did not depend on the economy of the city—at least not in the short run. But this is no longer true in the United States. Sudden and drastic food shortages are perfectly possible precisely because techniques of American farming have become so efficient and complex.

In the world as a whole, however, our style of urban-rural relationships is rare indeed. Two-thirds or more of mankind is instead experimenting with bureaucratic exploitation of the peasant majority by an urban minority. The peasant revolt of our time, repudiating traditional subordination, seems therefore headed for failure, just as the jacqueries of the past failed, even though the elimination of private landlords in ex-peasant lands seems all but certain to become universal. And the disappearance of private landlords certainly will constitute a major landmark in human history. From the time when men first learned how to erect civilized societies on rain-watered land until our own time, landlords and peasants have constituted the fundamental polarity around which the rest of civilized society revolved. The shift from peasant to farmer and from farmer to agricultural businessman is recent and still local. Only parts of Europe ever broke the peasant mold, and then not always completely. American, Australian, and Argentinean forms of rural life are eccentric indeed to the principal experience of mankind, and it is hard to imagine a time when 95 per cent of the Chinese or Indian peoples might depend on the mechanized food production of the other 5 per cent.

What I am driving at is this: our own national experience of bringing the food producers almost wholly within an urban-centered market system is rare and extreme. There is no reason to think that the rest of mankind will "catch up" and eventually arrive at a similar definition of rural-urban relationships. Instead, most of the world seems likely to try a new form of exploiting the peasant majority, and to postpone anything like economic reciprocity between town and country indefinitely. As long as poor countries need armies and defense systems, not to mention new factories and improved communications, compelling and respectable reasons for exploiting peasants will not disappear.

In Russia and China, as well as in lesser countries, Marxism has been used to organize and justify this kind of social structure. It is indeed a striking and ironic fact that a doctrine intended to apply to the most developed industrial lands of the world has in fact been applied only in predominantly peasant regions, by men whose own emergence from peasant status was in most cases quite recent. The all-embracing character of Marxian doctrine certainly appeals in important ways to the minds of men who, in rejecting traditional status and values, need a substitute guide to action. The vigor and venom of Marxian denunciation of landlords and capitalists also fits in well with peasant sentiment. But most of all, I suggest, Marxism gives the leaders and rulers of Communist societies a plausible excuse for exploiting "their own" people with all the rigor that bureaucratic manipulation of economic processes allows. More than that, the doctrine allows men to act harshly in good conscience—working for the future when, they fondly think, the injustices of exploitation of man by man will cease.

It is, however, not only Communist lands in which bureaucratic exploitation of peasants exists. The impressive development of Greek industry in the last twenty years almost entirely rests on subsidy, tariff and quota protection, and special legal privileges of the most diverse sort. The effect is to raise prices for local consumers, and to shift resources from those who produce the basic export commodities—tobacco, currants, etc.—to those who work in the new factories, or who own, manage, plan, regulate, or merely record what goes on in the new urban segments of the economy. I believe that substantially the same occurs in all of Latin America and—so far as the new African governments are yet capable of carrying through plans of industrial development—also in Africa.

Perhaps the world's peasants will acquiesce. Their predecessors did, most of the time. And the splendors of independence and of new factories, national armies, and diplomatic representation all around the world are vaguely satisfying to those who know about such things. The splendor of vanished royal courts and ancient temples was similar—a spectacle that may have pleased humble peasants so far as they were aware of it.

Perhaps, on the other hand, there will be recurrent outbreaks of peasant anger at the continued frustration of their hopes for fuller participation and an equal share in civilized life. But in such cases all the advantages lie on the side of organized, urban-based armies. More than ever before, the peasantries of the world are at the mercy—and not very tender mercy it seems to be—of distant rulers and their servants. Modern weapons and the moral righteousness of those who strive by every possible means to develop national industry and military strength give overwhelming advantages to the bureaucrats. By comparison the simple, silly peasant ideal of local autonomy and equality, and the justice that says "In the sweat of thy brow shalt thou eat thy bread," stand no chance.

In the longer run one can of course believe that a truer equality and more real economic reciprocity between town and country may dawn over most or all of the world. But projection of a future whose characteristics contradict observable trends and development seems utopian. In our public debate and common assumptions about the economic development of backward peoples we, as well as the Russians and Communists generally, seem to me to have been utopian. In reacting against this common habit of mind I may have been guilty of exaggeration, as I have certainly been of oversimplification. Yet I submit to you that the peasant revolt of our time is central to the history of the world in the twentieth century; and that its containment and frustration by bureaucratic, indirect forms of taxation—if I understand rightly what is happening—constitutes one of the fundamental worldwide social transmutations of our age.

11

# TRIUMPH AND FAILURE IN ANCIENT EGYPT

JOHN A. WILSON

JOHN A. WILSON, *whose books include* The Culture of
Ancient Egypt *and* Signs and Wonders upon Pharaoh, *is Andrew MacLeish Distinguished Service Professor of Egyptology at The University of Chicago.*

11

# TRIUMPH AND FAILURE IN ANCIENT EGYPT

*John A. Wilson*

THIS SERIES of Monday Lectures began with two talks about
our perception: "Language and the Mind," and "The
Nature of Consciousness," and has just dealt with revolution.
From such critical modern problems, we may seem to shoot
off into the empyrean with the present talk on ancient Egypt
and the earlier one on astronomy.

Perhaps the series is not as disjointed as it appears. Perhaps
remote time and remote space have some external play on modern problems. They are not escapes, to permit us to avoid problems, even though their focus is away from the immediate scene.
But properly taken, they provide perspective. One form of
perspective is the vast universe in which we live, in which our
earthly role is a small integral part of a tremendous cosmos.
Another perspective comes out of the long sweep of human
history, in which our current problems take their small place
in the great movement of man's social, economic, and political
process.

Perspective may give the setting for making judgments and
decisions, but it does not necessarily provide specific answers.
The study of astronomy will not tell us flatly whether the heavy
expense of landing a man on the moon is justified, or whether
we should now explore out toward Mars and Venus; nor will
the study of ancient Egypt provide crisp answers about the
American role in world affairs. If you know the history of the
pharaoh Amenhotep IV, who changed his name to Akhenaton,
and decide that he was the "first monotheist in history," it need
not help you to make up your mind whether or not God is dead.
The fifty-year-long inflation in Egypt in the twelfth century

B.C. is interesting to us who worry about modern inflation, but it does not tell us what to do about it.

Yet it is paradox of human history that you have to know where you are if you are going to leave your position. You have no room before you unless you are aware of the room beside you and behind you. You need perspective.

You might say that we Americans are about three hundred years old, if you take the stretch of time in which we have been conscious of being separate and distinct. You might more appropriately say that we are only two hundred years old, if you take the stretch of time since Americans decided to divorce themselves from Europe and moved toward the distinctly American form of government and society. Over against those two or three centuries, remember that the ancient Egyptian system lasted three thousand years, if you take the outer limits from 3000 B.C. to A.D. 200, within which it maintained itself, or it lasted two thousand years, if you take the inner limits of 2700 to 500 B.C., within which it was a successful expression. Mere arithmetic is no criterion of quality, and status might be equated with stagnation. Yet to endure so long a time, it must have had an extraordinary adaptation to environment, a suitability to the time and place. Certainly the culture was admired and respected by others. It was successful for a remarkable length of time, and we cannot ignore that.

It is impossible for me to think of a fixed lifetime for ancient Egypt, in the terms which are offered by such cyclical historians as Spengler and Toynbee. In the activities of the mass of the people, ancient Egypt was still the same only a century ago. In terms of the cultural expression of ancient times there was strong continuity and constant change. You could say that it was always the same, and you could say that it was always different. The more it changed, the more it remained the same. There were three great cultural periods of ancient Egypt, and each of them had its own lifetime. The Old Kingdom lasted from 2750 to 2250 B.C. and died. The Middle Kingdom lasted from

2050 to 1800 B.C. and died. The New Kingdom lasted from 1550 to 1100 B.C. and died. Either there were brief cycles or there were no cycles at all.

Let us characterize each of the three great periods. The Old Kingdom, or Pyramid Age, saw the cultural expression laid down, so successfully that later Egyptians maintained it, insisting that there was no change. Its people invented the idea of a nation. They developed art and literature. They were the first great builders in stone. After only a century and a half they built one of the most triumphant monuments of all time, the Great Pyramid, a perfection of technique. This mountain of rock, thirteen acres in area, lies upon a natural stone platform, which was smoothed off to 99.996 per cent of true levelness. The four corners of the pyramid were within 99.94 per cent of being exact right angles. Working within the mighty mass of stone, with the primitive building machinery which they commanded, they achieved almost superhuman exactness. Neither they nor any of their successors ever again achieved such architectural conscience.

The Great Pyramid was built for eternity—to denote the never-dying power of Egyptian rule. As far as we know, it may last forever. It will vastly outlast our age, and may even outlast man himself.

The Old Kingdom laid down the principles of government, social organization, religion, architecture, art, and literature in terms of the concept of *ma‘at*, "proper order." That order was eternal; and the Egyptians attempted to repeat the principles for three thousand years. The emphasis was on the continuation of the past, not upon change and movement toward new good. They did continue it, but the technical conscience exemplified in the Great Pyramid did not survive. You might look in vain for such skilled and exact building in later Egypt. You might then say that the Old Kingdom lived and died, and that later ages were a new and different life.

There was a period of breakdown, when the emphasis of the

Old Kingdom upon material achievement and success was negated. The power of the king was challenged. When a new age appeared, the Middle Kingdom, it was decidedly different in its basic expression. It was a feudal period, when the king was only *primus inter pares*, sharing power with others. There was an approach to the idea of social equality. In a religious text the creator god is quoted as saying: "I made the four winds that every man might breathe of them like this fellow. . . . I made the great inundation that the poor man might have rights in it like the great man. . . . I made every man like his fellow." Other texts of the period exalt the poor man and impose social responsibility upon the ruler. Egypt had a brief glimpse of the essential worth of every human being. It was a great promise, but it did not last. With returning power and prosperity, this glimpse of egalitarianism died.

There was another period of confusion, this time marked by foreign conquest of Egypt. Then the country moved into the New Kingdom, an imperial age in which the pharaohs went out and conquered the nearby world. This was the height of Egypt's political power and wealth. There were exciting new winds of internationalism, and Egypt's parochial gods became universal.

In the interest of new achievement, emphasis changed from a concern for a bland eternity to a relish of the exciting present. Art changed from an idealism of the blessed eternity to telling stories about the here-and-now. King or noble was shown at a specific ceremony or battle, not in blissful remoteness.

Within the rapidly changing world, one pharaoh, Akhenaton, focused upon a single god to the exclusion of others—the warm and life-sustaining sun. If this was not an absolute and categorical monotheism, it was the world's first approach to monotheism.

This also lived and died. The monotheistic pharaoh was a blend of genius and insanity; he could not transmit his warm new faith to others. Egypt went back to polytheism. When the

Egyptian empire finally collapsed, the interest in the present day was again replaced by an emphasis on the next world. Each of the three great ages had a truly great character. None of them survived in that character long enough to influence later ages or other peoples.

After 1100 B.C. Egypt had a long, slow decline. We might suggest reasons why a culture became static and inert after great strength, but we shall never be able to isolate one central reason. There were sporadic attempts to regain power, but generally there was weakness and division for more than a thousand years. Egypt was taken over by the Libyans, the Ethiopians, the Assyrians, the Persians, the Macedonians of Alexander the Great, and finally by the Romans of Julius Caesar.

The Romans used Egypt as their granary and held the country by military power, denying the land the self-government enjoyed by Roman provinces. Egypt was bled white by taxes. When, in the second century A.D., the Christian message came that patient poverty in this world would be rewarded by triumph in the next world, Egyptians went over to Christianity in great numbers. The ancient Egyptian system was finished.

A number of very valid claims may be made for Egyptian culture. The Egyptians did work out the world's first nation, the world's first architecture in stone, a year of twelve months and 365 days, and a highly sophisticated art and literature. When Egypt was in its slow decline, the Greeks in a positive way and the Hebrews in a negative way paid high tribute to the force and brilliance of Egyptian culture.

In its highest expression, the cultural achievement of Egypt was supreme. A prime example would be the technical perfection of the Great Pyramid. Dr. Breasted urged a similar high appreciation of Egyptian medicine as characterized by real scientific insight. A specialist on art has stated flatly that the art of the Old Kingdom was better than anything else in the ancient orient until the time of the Greek flowering. If we judge any people by its best, Egypt must stand very high.

The extraordinary stability of Egyptian culture, successful for two thousand years and continuous for three thousand years, must be appreciated in view of the observation that there were competitions and challenges. Babylonia, Assyria, the Hittites, the Canaanites, and the Hebrews were different and presented other ways of expression. Even later, the strong new winds of thought and expression from Greece left Egypt essentially unchanged, but left the Greeks in clear admiration of Egypt. There has to be great poise and balance in such stability. Perhaps one could say that Egypt was solid enough to resist change and yet flexible enough not to be broken by change, as a tree will bend with the wind and yet remain rooted.

With the possible exception of the Minoan culture in Crete, ancient Egypt presented the liveliest face of antiquity. Egyptians had a gay relish for life. Tombs and temples, instead of being remote and austere, are full of color and movement and humor. One can point to the picture of the mischievous monkey on a tomb wall or the water-logged Prince of Aleppo on a temple wall. The prince had been driven in battle into the water of a river, and his adherents had to hold him upside down to drain him out. Religious texts are full of puns, often of the most atrocious kind, and none of the Egyptian gods could escape satire on their foibles. A culture which was brilliant with color and humor was not obsessed with death; it clung lovingly to its rich life.

The direct transmission from Egypt to later cultures might seem to be in form, rather than essence: columns with floral capitals, which later cultures used, but in different ways; techniques in mathematics and medicine, which later cultures advanced to the point of abstraction and prediction; and literary forms, which one can see in the Hebrew Bible. Whether the idea of a single god passed from the Egyptians to the Hebrews is debatable. Yet one can still claim that Egypt introduced monotheism into a world which was nearly ready to receive it.

Against any claims for triumph, one must list the failures visible in Egyptian history. The brilliant success of the Old Kingdom, when the bases of the cultures were laid down, meant that Egypt was retrospective, rather than prospective. It looked back and tried to recapture old glory, instead of moving on to new forms. This made no difference as long as there was an atmosphere of successful power. In the last thousand years, however, it meant mere repetition, without inner motivation. No culture can survive indefinitely on its past.

The psychology of pre-Greek cultures appears in their religions, which were entirely god-centered. Every phenomenon, good or bad, might be ascribed to the activity or intervention of the gods. They thought in terms of myths and miracles. This gave man little scope for independent activity. It was demanded of him that he conform to the *ma'at*, the created order laid down by the gods. Thus there could really be no questioning and experimenting state of mind, no scientific attitude. Environment controlled man; he made little attempt to control environment. Even though the system had enough flexibility to permit some slight initiative, it ultimately reduced man to the plaything of the gods. It remained for the Greeks to free man for independent thought and action, to ask questions about nature, and thus to work out a partnership between men and gods.

The lively and witty Egyptians were not a profound people. They relinquished the deeper problems to the realm of the gods and did not speculate about the ultimate realities of life and death, man and nature, man and god. Over in Babylonia the Sumerians did ask some profound questions, as in the Gilgamesh Epic the problem of death was faced with sobriety. The Egyptians were too tolerant to match the Hebrews in categorical ethics. A light people, they asked only a good life.

The impact of the Greeks and the Hebrews was so strong

that the world did not forget them. They had something to say to any later generation. When the Egyptian system disappeared in the first Christian centuries, it disappeared from human thought, except insofar as the Bible or the classical authors had something to say about Egypt. The pyramids might still be visible, but the voice of Egypt itself was silenced. It had had nothing continuous to say. It was not until the nineteenth century, when Napoleon, Champollion, and their successors rediscovered ancient Egypt, that a remarkable chapter of human history could be understood again in its own terms.

There is a further factor of importance to our generation. Egypt and Babylonia invented human civilization about five thousand years ago. They invented forms and ways which controlled man for five full millenniums—up to the twentieth century A.D.

Let us take some of the forms. Most of us still live in that ancient invention, a house—a cubical box with holes in the sides to form doors and windows, with fixed rooms, stairs, and a chimney. Most of us still use those ancient inventions, chairs, tables, and beds. These are four-legged machines, originally devised to give dignity. The man of position and rule had to sit stiffly at a higher level than his subjects, clients, and servants. These machines were the uncomfortable signs of his social and political height.

Perhaps today you sat on a chair at a table, using an ancient Egyptian invention, paper and pen. You dated the letter in terms of a twelve-month year, and sealed it, as the ancients might have sealed it. You gave it to a national authority to deliver. The twelve-month year, the sealing, and the nation were invented five thousand years ago by the Egyptians. Until recently the carriage of the letter was entrusted to the muscles of a man or animal or a sailboat.

Within our own lifetime we are experimenting with the change of these ancient forms. The house may be no longer cubical, but cylindrical, suspended from a central column. That column may be a bank of elevators, which have replaced the stairs. Architects are experimenting with rooms whose walls may be moved easily. Most important, the holes in the box, the windows, have become walls, so that the entire side of a building may be open to view. This has had important psychological consequences. It is difficult to sit in a living room with a huge picture window and insist that a man's home is his castle. The defenses of the castle are coming down.

Your chair and your table may no longer have four animal legs. They may have one or three legs, or be suspended from the ceiling. They may no longer be oblong in surface. There are posture chairs and kidney-shaped tables. In place of pen and paper, you may typewrite your letter, or telephone or telegraph the message. For other purposes your record may be punched in holes on cards for a business machine. Your letter may be carried by international postal service, by airplane, or by pneumatic tube. You may no longer feel the same about a nation, as is suggested by the abusive term "nationalistic." Perhaps you are an advocate of a thirteen-month year, instead of the traditional twelve months.

Most important, the essential concerns of man have altered radically. In our Western world the majority of citizens are no longer on the farm; they are interested in the movement of goods, rather than the production of goods. This has been permitted by the revolution in power. The common unit of power is no longer the muscles of man or animal, but a machine of some internally projected power. It is ironical that we continue to talk in terms of horsepower, when a majority of Americans have lost direct experience of the muscular power of a single horse.

We might go on to detail other aspects of this revolution, as in the field of communications and world-wide interrelations. Another notable example would be the contrast between our kitchens and the kitchens of our grandmothers. It is clear enough, however that our current revolution is a major crisis in human history. Back in prehistoric times there was an agricultural revolution, when men gradually settled down with cultivated crops and domestic animals. At the beginning of history, back in Egypt and Babylonia, there was a professional revolution when the new urban centers developed factors to carry on the complexities of civilization. These factors were rulers and merchants and makers of goods; they were priests and artists and teachers. The farmers fed them, and they carried on professional services for that vast mass of the population which consisted of farmers. This interplay of activities is still present, but the current mechanical revolution has already changed the emphases of the past in the West, and is slowly changing the emphases in other parts of the world. The present mechanical revolution is taking place at a far greater speed than the old agricultural or professional revolutions did. We seem to be discarding five thousand years with frantic speed.

Let us not argue whether the change is good or bad. The change is here, and we must ride with it. But if we are in the process of wholesale change, we may throw out the baby with the bath. Do we know enough about the process of setting up civilization five thousand years ago to think intelligently about revolution? Do we know enough about the values in those ancient choices to think about values in our present choices? We certainly have to move into the future, but we might move with more confidence if we had a stronger sense of the past. We need a springboard for our leap forward.

# 12

# THE TYRANNY OF PROGRESS

ROBERT GOMER

# THE TYRANNY OF PROGRESS

*Robert Gomer*

CHANGE has been the permanent condition, in fact the pre-condition, of man. Nevertheless, the most striking feature of the world today is the rapidity with which it is changing. The changes we are experiencing are clearly man-made, but it is not totally clear what their real nature is, and it is very unclear what their effect on man is and will be; nor is it clear whether they are controlled by man or are controlling him. In speculating about these matters, I do not hope to find answers but perhaps some of the questions will come into sharper focus.

Many of the following remarks are based on situations in the United States, not only because my ignorance is even greater about other societies, but because our problems will probably be encountered sooner or later by most of mankind. For better or worse, almost the whole world is committed to technology and materialism. This premise transcends boundaries, and its problems outweigh ideologies and political systems.

Just what are the changes that are reshaping the world, and what are their causes? In a somewhat restricted sense, the answer to the latter question is short and simple: science and technology. It requires only a moment's reflection to realize how much these have changed life within our own memory. The motorcar has transformed living patterns, enabling the rise of the suburb and the decline of the city as it was thought of for centuries; the airplane has shrunk the globe and has transformed war; nuclear weapons and missiles have lifted general war from the category of rational policy; chemistry and genetics are transforming agriculture; modern medicine and public health are decreasing death rates and are increasing world population; automation is transforming the job spectrum from production to service; television has added a new dimension to politics, and to entertainment, if that is the right word.

These are just a few examples of the more obvious effects of technological change. While scientific and technological innovation are causal in a certain sense, the resultant social, political, economic, and cultural changes in turn lead to further change, even in the development of science and technology, so that there are numerous complex and interlinked feedbacks. Beyond a certain point it becomes difficult to distinguish cause from effect. If we are not to be overwhelmed completely by what we have set in motion, it would be well to understand more clearly this complex interplay and the forces governing it.

It is interesting to look at the most significant changes produced or triggered by modern technology and science in a little more detail. To begin with the obvious, technology has made possible a higher living standard—more and better food, shelter, health, and material comfort and more leisure—for a larger fraction and a vastly increased absolute number of people in the "developed" countries, notably our own, than was even conceivable fifty or a hundred years ago. There is no obvious sign that prosperity will not increase in the rich countries, and there is hope that, despite some very tragic times ahead, even the most bleakly overpopulated and underdeveloped countries will succeed, or be helped in curbing population growth, becoming industrialized and achieving a sufficient measure of prosperity to bury their dead and feed and house their living.

Such advance has not been achieved without a heavy price paid by past generations. One need not be a Marxist to appreciate the hell of nineteenth-century England for working people, including small children, or to realize what conditions were in nineteenth-century America for immigrant labor, also including children. Although in very different ways, we continue to pay a price. The most important is without question the enormously rapid rise in world population, a direct result of dramatic decreases in death rates because of elementary improvements in public health, unaccompanied by decreases in birth rates. Even in advanced countries, notably our own, where population rises at a mere 1.5 per cent per year instead of the dizzying 3 per cent of poor countries, the effects, while less dramatic than the prospect of mass starvation, are not altogether attractive. The expanding population is increasingly urban, because technology is revolutionizing agriculture with a dramatic decrease in manpower required, and a corresponding increase in the minimum acreage that can be farmed economically by one man. The consequent urban expansion is enormously rapid, but quite haphazard; for the most part it is degrading the environment in which the inhabitants of megalopolis must spend most of their lives. To appreciate this one need only look at the suburban sprawl of housing developments, shopping plazas and overburdened "freeways" around which they have sprung up. A few years ago 1 per cent of the land area of the United States was covered by highways, and the figure is obviously rising. As the countryside near population centers is increasingly covered with concrete, outdoor recreational facilities are being overtaxed, to put it mildly. The following is taken from an advertisement by *Forbes Magazine* in the *New York Times* of May 3, 1967:

### Our National Parks Are Becoming Our National Slums

Like a barbarian horde, they swept into the valley, thousands on thousands of them, men and women and yowling kids.

They came in automobiles belching exhaust and on motorcycles that roared up and down the highway like tanks. They came dragging trailers and carrying tents.

Soon, the floor of the valley was carpeted with autos, motorcycles, trailers and tents; and the smoke of 10,000 campfires poured into the air until it almost blotted out the sky. The blaring of radios, the shouting of drunks, the bickering of children went on most of the night.

When dawn crept in, there were 57,000 people in the valley. It's a small valley, only 7 miles long and 1 mile wide, which means that 8,143 people were crowded on every square mile. The highway was choked with traffic, the river with garbage.

The time: The Fourth of July 1966. The place: Yosemite Valley in Yosemite National Park. The 57,000 people had come to Yosemite to enjoy the beauties of nature. They had managed to convert the valley into a slum.

Congress never anticipated anything like this when it established the first national park in 1872. What congress wanted, says Forbes, was to create a living museum to preserve for posterity the wonders of nature.

Today, the U.S. has 32 living museums that cover 26 million acres.

The national issue: how to use them? As a playground? Or as a living museum?

Doesn't the park system belong to all the people? To the 57,000 who crowded into Yosemite Valley on the Fourth of July just as much as the handful who hike into the surrounding mountains to watch the deer graze?

The conservationist, says Forbes, depicts the controversies as a simple matter of greed vs. God. But, Forbes points out, the problem of our parks is not as simple as the conservationists would have the nation think.

Forbes believes there's room in the U.S. for all: out-door museums, family recreation areas and exploitation of national resources.

Thus the prospect of an additional 150 million Americans by the year 2000 is not altogether pleasant to contemplate.

There are other consequences of technology linked fairly directly to population growth. The most obvious is the pollution of our environment. From time immemorial earth, air, and water have been used by man as garbage dumps and we continue to use them so, but on an enormously expanded scale. Everyone is familiar with the pollution of rivers and lakes by industrial effluents, by sewage, and by pesticide, fertilizer, and detergent residues. It is perhaps not so well known that thermal pollution, a rise in river temperatures because of water heating in reservoirs, is reaching a point where the survival of many fish species is questionable. We are all too familiar with the pollution of the atmosphere by car exhausts, by industrial wastes, soft coal and by garbage-burning. It may not be quite as well known that the carbon dioxide content of the atmosphere is rising rapidly because of man-made combustion processes. The estimated increase in $CO_2$ content by the year 2000 is 25 per cent; this will produce marked climatic changes over the entire globe. Most of us are also familiar to some extent with soil pollution, the accumulation of copper, arsenic, lead, and organic poisons, notably chlorine and phosphorus compounds, in soils and in produce because of chronic use of pesticides. Needless to say, man is not the only species affected. Protestations by the concerned industries to the contrary, pesticides are not harmless. A few years ago I was involved in the problem of how to detect the clandestine manufacture of chemical warfare agents in the context of arms-control agreements. It turned out that the more potent agents differ so little from agricultural products that they could easily be manufactured in the same plants, and this could not be detected by analysis of effluents or raw materials.

There have also been less tangible, if even more far reaching, psychological and social changes, not all of which can be directly associated with technological change, although they probably could not have occurred without it. The most apparent is a wave of egalitarianism which is worldwide, although it takes many different forms. I would class what has been called the revolution of rising expectations in the poor countries, as well as the widespread antiauthoritarianism of the Western world, as part of the same phenomenon. There can be little question that its manifestations in the West are the result largely of prosperity, and in the poor countries, of seeing what technology can accomplish. It is ironic that this particular result of technology is also likely to be doomed by it, since the ever-increasing specialization of knowledge and skills militates against equality. To take a very minor example, I wonder how many voters in the next presidential election have even a superficial understanding of the technical aspects of ballistic-missile defense, without which its political implications cannot be understood? The example may be minor, but it is typical. Decisions are influenced more and more by "experts"; even if the final choice is made by Presidents, the alternatives presented to them are shaped by specialists. It is hardly the fault of the experts if their expertise is not matched by the wisdom which is more and more demanded of them, but it is certainly our loss just the same.

Part of the egalitarian wave has been a liberation of mores and a widening of intellectual horizons. To cite just one example, sexual freedom has become practical through technology and is therefore becoming acceptable within the expanding moral framework. Perhaps the most important psychological change is a new sense of power, a feeling that man can accomplish anything he sets his mind to. In the extreme, this is dangerous arrogance and will continue to have unfortunate effects, but it has positive aspects as well—flexibility, a willingness to experiment, the nerve to tackle new problems. On the other hand, the feeling that anything is possible for mankind as a whole is also accompanied in many people by an increasing sense of personal impotence, by an acute feeling of being left behind in a too rapidly changing world. While this is most tragically true of the poor and unskilled, who are getting relatively poorer and more unskilled, it is also true of the engineer who graduated twenty years ago, of the middle aged scientist, in fact, of almost everyone.

Closely related to such feelings is an increasing sense of alienation, most apparent among the very affluent young and the very poor young. Even when there is no open rebellion, something often seems to be missing. Religion in the traditional sense had been inadequate for many people in a world so patently man-shaped, so influenced by scientific rationalism, even before God was declared officially dead last year. On the other hand the new age has little solace to offer the soul, either in explicit Weltanschauung or in terms of beauty, peace, and order.

No assessment of where technology is leading us would be complete without mentioning modern weapons. These give us, for the first time in known history, the means of wiping out the human race; possibly I am being too optimistic in feeling that we are unlikely to avail ourselves of the opportunity. Whether used or not, their mere presence contributes to a sense of great helplessness.

Even this cursory glance is enough to show that we are paying a stiff price for material well-being in decreasing privacy, in the ever more pervasive ugliness of our environment, and quite possibly in health; indications are that things will get considerably, possibly catastrophically, worse in the not very distant future. Is this a necessary price for prosperity? Can an economy be prosperous only if it is constantly expanding? Can it be expanding only if population continues to increase? I do not pretend to have absolute answers to these questions, and in other contexts than our own they are meaningless. Clearly, the problem of India is not lack of population growth. I believe, however, that once a certain level of prosperity has been reached, once a country or region has a degree of technological and economic muscle comparable to that of the United States, there are no prohibitive physical or economic obstacles to shaping its destiny with decency; yet there is very little assurance that this will happen, at least in the United States.

To understand, even to describe in any detail, the complexities that shape our society would encompass the life-work of many eminent social scientists, but perhaps it is worthwhile to attempt a few generalizations. In social as in physical systems, change occurs as the result of driving forces and is inhibited or reversed as the result of other forces. Often the changes themselves provide the forces which inhibit or stimulate further change, so that the changes can be damped out or can rise explosively, can overshoot and oscillate. While cybernetic analogies are much overworked, the idea of feedback is very useful because it emphasizes that only those changes which produce sufficiently strong inhibitory responses can be self-correcting, while others will continue unchanged or be magnified. (The exponential growth of scientific knowledge is itself a very interesting example of positive feedback, and it is not difficult to devise mathematical models to explain it, or to predict negative feedbacks that will slow it.)

For the technological revolution, negative feedbacks have so far been feeble or lacking, in large measure, of course, because the gains have been enormous and visible, while the ill effects have been slower to make themselves felt, and have been obscured or justified by the gains. On the other hand, there are strong positive feedbacks which tend to spur uncontrolled, unplanned expansion. Chief of these is economic pressure; pressure for doing things most cheaply regardless of ultimate cost to the society, and pressure for stimulating population growth in order to increase consumer markets. If it is a little cheaper to build a steel mill on a lake dune, no matter how unusual, chances are the mill will be built there. If it is cheaper to buy a few state legislators than to install expensive scavenging equipment, chances are that water and air will be polluted. As long as an expanding population can pay for goods, there will be strong pressures against population planning and against planning of any kind which might reduce profits.

More subtle, but possibly as important a feedback is a blunting of sensibilities and increasing, rather than decreasing, public apathy, as we get used to smog, unusable lakes, overcrowding, loss of privacy, and loss of the power to do something about these things. Ignorance, apathy, shortsightedness, greed, and manipulation of public opinion, and of legislators contribute in varying measure not only to the degradation of our lives but to the way we react to it. Governor Reagan's famous dictum, "What's so special about a tree? You've seen one, you've seen them all," may reflect majority opinion in California right now.

Last but not least among the factors militating against constructive response is human inertia; this usually takes the form of looking the other way in the hope that unpleasant problems will go away. Such behavior is true of individuals, and unfortunately also of governments, whose proclivity for taking paths of least resistance in the short term need hardly be emphasized. It is plain that problems can elicit both constructive and inertial responses in proportion to their severity, but it is not always obvious which will predominate. Inertia and denial are perhaps most likely to occur if the problems are either so overwhelming as to kill all hope of solving them or so slight as to be considered only a nuisance, but this merely restates the question.

At the moment constructive counterpressures are relatively feeble and disorganized. The crucial question is to what extent they can or will be strengthened in time. In a democracy, such a strengthening can consist in the end only of aroused public opinion, and arousal can occur only if the sting is sufficiently severe and severely felt by enough people. The need for legislation to control the drug industry may have been apparent to a few enlightened medical men and legislators like the late Senator Kefauver, but his bill would very probably have been defeated had it not been for the thalidomide tragedy. Public opinion has not become noticeably aroused about pollution where it poses no immediate and severe health hazard, but is merely hideous, as in southern California. It therefore seems unlikely that constructive feedback through aroused public opinion will occur where the deleterious effects of change are slow, slow to be felt, or where they are subtle and affect human happiness in less tangible ways than acute respiratory disease. To a large degree this reflects accurately the values of our society, and it seems idle to talk about planning without a profound restructuring of cultural values. The imminent expiration of the billboard law, which will have died without removing a single billboard, is not only an example of greed but of public unconcern. The issue of the *New York Times* which carried the *Forbes* advertisement already quoted also carried the following editorial comment:

### Shortchanging the Future

In its work on the budget for the Department of the Interior, the House Appropriations Committee has just provided a dazzling display of how to waste money while preaching economy.

With land prices rising sharply and the receipts of the Land and Water Conservation Fund falling below expectation, President Johnson asked Congress to advance $32-million to the fund to buy land for new national parks and seashores. The request was only a token gesture since a much larger sum is needed now if the public is not to pay sky-high prices for the land in later years. But the Appropriations Committee, after stating in its report that it is "especially concerned with the unabated escalation of land prices," cut the President's request to a mere $9.5-million.

To arrive at this illogical figure, the committee made several unwise cuts, including the elimination of all funds for the Indiana Dunes National Lakeshore.

It seems very unlikely that this congressional action would have been taken against determined public opposition.

At first glance, wise planning would seem much easier in authoritarian societies. Up to a point this is probably true, but leaders of no society operate in a vacuum or are heaven-descended. Stalin and Hitler were as much products of their world as shapers of it, and were fully imbued with its myths, tastes, and prejudices. Thus the real problem—to become sensitive to all human needs—is not so very different in different societies, although it can take different guises.

It has already been said that change may blunt reaction to further change, but fortunately there are also forces working in the opposite direction. More wealth and more leisure could provide more scope for an upgrading of tastes and sensibilities. In my opinion, the preoccupation with machines, with mechanical devices, even in our leisure, unfortunately does not increase aesthetic sensibilities rapidly. It is not yet known how many outboard motors must simultaneously be operating on a given area of lake to make even their users uncomfortable, but the number is clearly very high. On the other hand, only when people are liberated from the drudgery of hard labor (by servants in the past, by machines in the present), are they able to appreciate the sweetness of *some* work, of doing something under one's own power. Perhaps the outboard motor market is saturable.

The problem once again is to maximize, by whatever means possible, awareness and sensitivity to human values and needs. It is not entirely clear, of course, if a consensus could ever be reached on what constitutes happiness or the preconditions for happiness, but it seems less difficult to list the preconditions for unhappiness. Granted that it is possible to define broadly values and goals, how are these to become imbued with sufficient force in a mass culture? I have no very clear ideas, and no desire to become embroiled here in the arguments of education from the bottom up versus from the top down. It is often true, however, that latent feelings may be far more widespread than anybody realized until they emerge, crystallized by some nucleating agent. Certainly attempts at education in humanistic and human values must be pursued with vigor at every possible level. If even the single idea that having more than two children is sinful could be established sufficiently to permit punitive taxation of larger families, we would have come a long way.

Frankly, I am not terribly optimistic. Quite apart from all other considerations, time is running out very rapidly, and many effects of technological change will be almost impossible to reverse once they have occurred. Even if pollution can be halted, many animal species may be extinct; even if planning can be instituted, it may be almost impossible to unbuild the past. How will people adapt to a world in which there is little privacy, very little in the environment that is not man-made or man-modified, and little that is not ugly or monotonous?

How will people adapt to a world of shrinking initiatives and challenges but much more leisure—something that seems likely even in the best of probable worlds?

The distinguishing feature of man is his adaptability and the great variety of cultural patterns under which he can exist. Had we but time enough (world enough is out of the question), I am confident that social and cultural norms, attitudes, and even our psyche could shift enough to cope with almost any situation. It may not be pleasant for someone of my generation and tastes to contemplate that my not very distant descendants may never see a maple blazing against an autumn sky, but for all I know that may be all right. (On the other hand it may not: nobody really understands our atavisms, knows what contact we require with the world from which we came, or knows how much identity we need with earth, sky, water.) The trouble again is that there may not be time enough. Although enormously adaptable, man changes very slowly, and the deeper the change the slower it is. The world, on the other hand, is changing fast, so fast that we may be unable to catch up. I do not know if psychologists feel that they understand the relation between speed of change and psychic stress; the beat movement and the psychedelic drug cults suggest that the stresses are considerable already. It is not obvious just how we will attempt to adapt. An elite of decision makers, managers, scientists, artists, and intellectuals will still find challenge and fulfillment in their work. Even these groups may not be too happy with the quality of their lives. Others less fortunate, and this will probably constitute a vast majority, may respond increasingly in what we would call neurotic ways today: withdrawal, singly or in groups, *à la* North Beach; denial, for instance by clinging to meaningless conventions and rituals; escape, either by elaborate games and make-work activities, or escape into the shadow world of drugs. Who is to say that these responses would be neurotic in such a world, or more neurotic than managerial rites and the elaborate fantasies of governments in the world of today?

The picture I am sketching may be overly bleak. It is possible that World War III will postpone the relevance of these speculations by a century or two. Even without general war the imbalance between rich and poor, developed and underdeveloped countries, may create stresses and pressures which will lead to a considerably different shaping of the future. It is even possible that I am vastly underestimating the ability of man to adapt rapidly if the pressure is great enough. However, one conclusion seems inevitable. To a much larger extent than we may realize or acknowledge, we are caught up in an evolutionary stream, of our making but beyond our control. Even under the best of circumstances we will have to accept the fact that man must change to meet changes he has himself set off. Can the process of change be halted? Almost certainly not. It seems most unlikely, for example, that biological research will stop if and when it reaches the verge of creating life or modifying man himself. Even if it should stop we would live in the uneasy knowledge of an artificial restraint. The best we can hope for is a little wisdom and much luck. For better or worse, for a little heartbeat of eternity, until the sun blazes to its death, we, who are also part of nature, are taking over from nature and are thus becoming our own slaves. Is the tyranny of progress better or worse than the tyranny of nature? I do not know.

13

# MAN AND MANKIND IN THE DEVELOPMENT OF CULTURE AND THE HUMANITIES

RICHARD McKEON

RICHARD MCKEON *is Charles F. Grey Distinguished Service Professor of Philosophy and Greek at The University of Chicago. His books include* Freedom and History *and* Thought, Action, and Passion.

# MAN AND MANKIND IN THE DEVELOPMENT OF CULTURE AND THE HUMANITIES

*Richard McKeon*

THE DELPHIC inscription "Know thyself" has the polished opacity of antiquity, prudence, and wisdom. What does man know when he knows himself? What does he study when he studies man? How is the knowledge of human nature related, as instrument and as end, to his problems and his aspirations? Human nature might seem to be a determinate subject for study, much as inanimate nature is; and a knowledge of the nature of man might provide a basis for understanding what man does and what he makes—his institutions and values, his arts and sciences. The probing questions of Socrates concerning the study of man and of nature initiated philosophy and the study of man in the West by shattering the simplicity of that expectation. We often forget the Socratic paradoxes, but the new simplicities which we construct by new methods encounter new forms of his ironic problems. Man's knowledge of man is a reflexive relationship in which man is both knower and known, and the knowledge of man provides him with new powers or virtues, and new environments or rights and values, that is, with second natures in character and society. The developing knowledge of man finds its heuristic force paradoxically in knowledge of his own ignorance. The reflexivity of man's study of man breaks down the limits which set the study of man apart from the study of other subjects. The human includes what man has said and done and thought; the study of communities, and arts, and sciences is part of the study of man.

When the Monday Lectures were started, two years ago in the Spring of 1965, their subject was "New Views of the Nature of Man." The new views were expounded "in the hope of initiating a new discussion for our times on the nature of man, his place in the universe, and his biological, intellectual, and social potentialities." It was to make use of "new scientific and philosophical and humanistic ideas."[1] We have returned to a pre-Socratic expectation that new scientific, philosophic, and humanistic ideas of the nature of man will provide insight into what man does or has done and indication of what he can or should do. The Socratic paradoxes that knowledge is virtue or power, and that wisdom is knowledge of one's own ignorance are transformed into a dubious and unfruitful anxiety that that expectation will be thwarted by the creation of two (or more) cultures, and that the humanities and the sciences (and the social sciences) are distinct fields cultivated in isolation from each other.

I have given my contribution to this new discussion of the nature of man a title which can be read in this genetic sense— man and mankind have developed culture and the humanities —but I shall interpret the genesis reflexively, since man and mankind are the products as well as the creators of culture and the humanities, and in that reflexive genesis the meanings of "mankind," "culture," and "the humanities" will not be derived from "man" defined by a fixed antecedent human nature, but they will enter into the definition of "man" as coordinate functional synonyms. The development of mankind, culture, and the humanities is not a linear motion to a literally defined end, but an interaction of motions in a unity of reflexivity and an interplay of meanings in a comprehensiveness of synonymity.

A well-ordered genetic hierarchy seems plausible and possible in the study of man. Man has a physical body in a physical world; all the physical sciences study phenomena which have a bearing on understanding the nature and functions of man. The biological sciences are physical sciences extended to include organic processes and animal functions. The behavioral

[1] *New Views of the Nature of Man.* (Chicago: University of Chicago Press, 1965.) *Preface*, first page.

sciences concentrate on actions and functions which lay the foundations of individual and social action and control in habits and institutions. The humanities turn to man's disinterested pleasures and satisfactions, the development of his taste, appreciation, and judgment. In this reductive hierarchy, in which higher functions are specifications and extensions of basic universal processes, it is reasonable to expect that the study of man might be divided into specific inquiries concerning particular aspects of his activities and organized in a stratified series of interdependent functionings and malfunctionings. The steps of interconnection are clear as one moves in good order from anatomy and physiology and the departments of clinical medicine to psychology and psychiatry, to the study of human values in historical and psychoanalytic anthropology, of man's associations and segregations in sociology, of his wants, productions, and exchanges in economics, of his inclusive institutions and constitutions in political science, of his records of achievement and conflict in history, to his expressions or presentations in literature, music, and the arts, and his analyses or speculations or systematizations in science and philosophy.

Any such simple distribution of interests and subject matters encounters the reflexivity of man's study of man first in the tendency of each of the ordered interdependent disciplines to claim dominion over the fields and problems of the others. The two or more "cultures," like other independent dominions, establish their independence by aggression. The psychologist and the sociologist of knowledge explain men's philosophies; and the philosopher analyzes the methods and assumptions of psychologists and sociologists. The mathematician makes use of aesthetic criteria of elegance and analyzes unities, proportions, and structures; and the poet makes use of proportions of harmonies, rhythms, and analogies, and expresses profound substantive truths. The historian and the theologican demythologize accounts of human happenings and expressions of human destiny; and the psychologist and the cultural historian examine the myths that underlie men's accounts of what really happened and men's knowledge of the nature of things and of the ideals of aspiration.

The problems of reflexivity extend from the region of human behavior to the region of biological functions. The functions of the body have a physical basis and an organic structure: the functions of the cell may be analyzed into the operations and interactions of their biochemical constituents; the functions of the organ may be seen in relation to the cell, the functions of organic systems in relation to organs, and the functions of the psyche in relation to the organic body. But it is not an additive relation of interdependent parts: one organ may assume the functions of another in an organic system, and there is no simple answer to the question whether cell or psyche is prior in analysis and explanation. Indeed, as a result of progress in the science of genetics and of the analogies provided by cybernetics, the coded structure or formula has taken precedence over the constituent part or matter; and the function of the psyche has been seen in the programming of cells, organs, and organic bodies.

The reflexivity of man's study of man extends into his study of nature. Our knowledge of things is based on experience, observation, perception, and sensation. But, as William James observes in his *Psychology*, a pure sensation is an abstraction never realized in adult life, and a perception of a *thing* is not a compound of separate sensations but a fusion of sensations and ideas. In the Middle Ages, when grammar was the art of interpreting literature, Bernard of Chartres included among the functions of grammar improvement not only of our ability to understand what others say and to express ourselves but also to perceive, for understanding what a poet has set forth opens our eyes to the perception of facts, relations, and values which would pass unnoticed in untutored experience. Man's knowledge of man is not a simple two-termed relation or one-way process in which an inquirer or learner, man, comes into contact with an independent, formed subject matter, also man: it is a reflexive process in which the nature of man is formed by the study of man, and man's self-knowledge is an essential ingredient in all that he does, or makes, or knows. "Know thyself" is a precept not only in man's moral and social prudence and wisdom, but in all his arts and sciences, in his knowledge of other things and other selves, of systems of statements and thoughts, of communities of men and other beings, and of the cosmos which encloses and conditions man and his activities.

The word "man" is not an unambiguous word designating a unique field for study. The extension of words derived from "man" to cover all fields of knowledge and activity is a semantic sign of the reflexivity of man's study of man. The nature of man is revealed by his values and achievements as well as by his needs and by his bodily and psychological functions. "Mankind" is more than the sum of all men; it embraces and conditions the communities of men and it maximizes common values and minimizes divisive differences. "Humanity" is more than the sum of traits displayed by men; it is seen in the great achievements of geniuses who give sensed values expression and transform man and mankind by the values they manifest explicitly. The "humanities" are more than literature, music, and the fine arts; they are the body of values made by man, which exhibit human nature and include the humanistic achievements of the natural sciences and the social sciences. The "liberal or human or humane arts" are more than humanity or the humanities in the narrow sense; they are the disciplines by which man attains his full development and dignity, and they are therefore the arts proper to the free man and the arts which make men free. "Encyclopaedia" is more than a ready reference compendium of facts; it is the "cycle of learning" or the "cycle of culture" which embraces and orders all the liberal arts and all the arts and sciences. "Philanthropy," like "charity," is more than almsgiving; it is love of man, based on knowledge of his values and achievements and mediated by charity, or love of God. "Humanism" is more than the rediscovery of man in Greek art or the refurbishing of literary criticism by consideration of human values; it includes all study of man and all concern for human values in the sciences and literature. "Humane" and "humanitarian" undergo like changes, for the semantic mark of the tension between the reductive and the reflexive modes of conceiving man's study of man is a balance between the tendency to separate the study of man from the study of other fields and the tendency to define the study of man not by a field but by an effect in transforming man and his values; approaches to the knowledge of man are distinguished by a semantic balance between the reductive tendency to give terms like "philanthropy" and "charity" restricted material meanings and the reflexive tendency to use them as terms of comprehensive relations. The study of man employs a universal art of reflexivity and synonymity or paronymity which provides bases and connections for the particular arts of specificity and univocity suited to the study of different fields, things, and functions.

"Culture" and "humanity" are at the apex of this structure of reflexivity and synonymity which man has built in the study and development of himself. "Paedia," or culture, or education, is part of the etymology of "encyclopaedia," or the cycle of learning or culture, which consists of the liberal arts, or humanity, or the humanities. Culture and the humanities move as a theme through all the institutions, arts, and sciences of man, but the variations on the theme are specific accounts which separate the humanities from the sciences, and give "culture" specific meanings in the humanities and in anthropology. Among the accomplishments of man are the invention of language and the construction of institutions, arts, and sciences. The complex of meanings attached to words preserves a record of the synonymities which connect experience and things in structures, and what man has made in association, production, and knowledge contributes reflexively in turn to make man. In recent phases of the theme, culture and humanity have been united in the science of anthropology. In 1965 Clifford Geertz expounded the reflexivity of culture in his lecture on "The Impact of Culture on the Concept of Man." He attacked what he called the "'stratigraphic' conception of the relations between biological, psychological, social, and cultural factors in human life."[2] He argued that the evolution of man was not divided into two stages, biological and cultural, the first completed before the second began,[3] and he defined culture as a set of symbolic devices for controlling behavior.[4] Culture entered into the evolution of man long before the appearance of *Homo sapiens* in protohuman *Homo australopithecus*.[5] Culture shaped us as a single species and shapes us as individuals.[6]

The development of the theme culture and humanity, and the changes of the meanings of both words and of the reflexive interconditioning of what was signified by "culture" and what was signified by "humanity" prior to the variation of the theme in anthropology, is illustrated by the treatment of "culture" in a modern encyclopaedia. A few years ago there was no article on culture in the *Encyclopaedia Britannica*. There was an article on "Civilization and Culture" written by James Harvey Robinson in 1929. It is an excellent article, conceived from the point of view of what was then known as the New History. Robinson recounts the revolutionary effects which the study of civilization had had not more than fifty or sixty years before. Civilization was a new word; Dr. Johnson had refused to put it in his *Dictionary* in 1772. Man, beginning with his animal nature, produced, as other animals did not, "civilization." Culture is the accumulated product of the development of civilization.

The editors of the *Encyclopaedia* decided to retain the Robinson article and to add an article on culture from the anthropological point of view. According to the article "Concepts of

[2] *Ibid.*, p. 98.
[3] *Ibid.*, p. 109.
[4] *Ibid.*, pp. 106–7, 115.
[5] *Ibid.*, p. 111.
[6] *Ibid.*, p. 116.

Civilization and Culture" by David G. Mandelbaum, all tribes or societies have "culture," and civilization is a particular kind of culture. "A culture is the way of life of a human group; it includes all the learned and standardized forms of behavior which one uses and others in one's group expect and recognize."[7] ". . . civilization is that kind of culture which includes the use of writing, the presence of cities and of wide political organization and the development of occupational specialization."[8] Both terms came into something like their current use about the eighteenth century.

Both articles express a modern viewpoint and find recent beginnings for the concepts of culture which they expound. They make use of recently discovered data and recently established facts. Their accounts of the development of culture depend on advancements in the knowledge of man, but they also expound themes which had been given plausibility and continuity in other versions based on other data and facts established and related in similar distinctions and orientations by similar methods and assumptions. Robinson's theme of the civilization which separates man from other animals and which reaches its culmination in culture is in the long tradition in which the history of culture placed by Lucretius at the end of his *De Rerum Natura* is a distinguished example: the account begins with the evolution of the universe and of animals, and the evolution of human society is traced step by step on the basis of that account. Mandelbaum's theme of the development of culture to satisfy needs and to promote the associations of men is in the long tradition of accounts of the gifts of the gods such as Protagoras traces in the dialogue Plato named after him: Prometheus' gift of the mechanical arts and fire was distinguished from Zeus's gift of the political arts and justice by a difference in their mode of distribution—all men must share in the political arts whereas they may differ in the other arts.

[7] *Encyclopaedia Britannica*, 1967 ed., vol. 5, p. 831A.
[8] *Ibid.*

There was little hint in either article of culture in the sense it was given in the dialectical histories of culture of the nineteenth century, which emerged as *Kulturwissenschaften* to be compared and contrasted to *Naturwissenschaften*. This theme of culture as knowledge or science, distinct from or identical with natural science, and closely related to history or religion, also had earlier beginnings. *Cultura* and *cultus* are both Latin words, and philosophers and students of the arts in the Western world had long speculated on the relation of the cultivation of their gods and of their fields and cattle to the cultivation of their minds and their souls. I was asked to fill in this lacuna with an article on "Culture and the Humanities." It was no less modern than the other two—indeed its philosophic emphasis on communication places it in the wave of the future—but it is a theme in which the beginnings of the terms and of the phenomena are found in antiquity. "The development of the idea of culture centered about three related problems: the relation of culture to nature; the relation of the cultivation of man to the cultivation of God; the use of the arts and literature to achieve 'humanity,' both in the sense of individual perfection and in that of mutual love."⁹ The final sentence of the article relates the culture of the humanities to man and mankind: "Humanists finally continue to ask how culture, in the sense of the cultivation of the arts and literature, may further the self-realization of individual men and the mutual understanding of peoples."¹⁰ The three articles are not an expression of controversial oppositions among the ideas of culture in history, anthropology, and philosophy or the humanities, but an illustration of the pluralism of the manifestations of culture which are encountered in the study of man and in the underlying phenomena of culture to which history, anthropology, philosophy, and the arts and sciences contribute and of which they are parts, products, and productive forces. Man, mankind, culture, and the humanities

⁹ *Ibid.*, p. 832B.
¹⁰ *Ibid.*, p. 833A.

have a range of synonymity because they define each other and because they reflexively make and are made by each other.

Since the synonymity of man and culture develops many aspects and characteristics of man and many meanings of "man," the reflexivity by which man makes man is not exhausted in a single process. Philosophy first emerged in Greece from the study of nature and man. Science is knowledge of that which is, but the Eleatics observed that whatever can be said or thought is, and argued that motion and change are not; Democritus treated being and non-being in the plural, and responded that what is not, the void, is as truly as what is, the atoms; Plato set the ratio of being to becoming in proportion to knowledge and opinion, and found an intellectual structure reflected in change. The nature of man for Democritus was a congeries of atoms operating according to laws of motion. Virtue is action according to the laws of nature, and education is therapy by knowledge to remove inhibitions and errors induced by external influences and passions. Virtue is knowledge according to the Platonic Socrates, and self-knowledge is knowledge of one's own ignorance, which is a starting point for education which leads through mathematics and dialectic to the idea of the Good. Man is the measure of all things, of that which is and of that which is not, according to Protagoras, and a *metron* or measure contributes to making what it measures. Virtue is power, and education is the acquisition of arts and skills of expression and of making, which are inseparably conjoined and often indistinguishable. When Aristotle constructed his philosophy as an organization of all the sciences, he made the study of man the reflexive connecting link between the physical and the biological sciences, the theoretic and the practical sciences, and the universal arts and the productive arts or sciences. The motions of inanimate bodies, including the constitution of homogeneous bodies (we would say compounds) from simple bodies and organic bodies from compounds, are studied in physics. The psyche is the natural principle of motion of organic bodies. Aristotle places the study of human psychology before treating the problems of animal motions in the transition from physics to biology because man shares many functions, such as reproduction, growth, nutrition, local motion, and sensitivity with animals; and in the study of science, as in foreign exchange, it is wise to base inquiry and calculation on a familiar scale. The practical sciences are based on a minimum knowledge of the nature of man; and, reflexively, science is one of the intellectual virtues studied in ethics, and the scope and content of science are conditioned by social and intellectual circumstances and sanctions studied in politics. The universal arts are arts of discourse, dependent on the opinions of men, while the productive arts are arts of making, originating in and satisfying pleasures of men.

The beginnings of culture as a cycle of learning were in the *philosophic* "encyclopaedia" in which the Greek philosophers built a theory of nature and a theory of man reflexively one on the other. The accumulations of knowledge resulting from the speculations of poets and philosophers, and from the contacts of peoples after the campaigns of Alexander gave culture a new turn in the *learned* "encyclopaedia" in which the Hellenistic scholars and librarians organized classifications of man's knowledge and literature and constructed empirical sciences and histories of facts reflexively one on the other, in the cultural context of a literature of aphorism, lyric poetry, and romance, and of mystery religions. Culture received its characteristic turn and its name, however, in the *factual* "encyclopaedia" in which the Roman orators and statesmen paused to philosophize on the past and its uses in the present, and wrote textbooks of antiquities and of disciplines organizing the rules of man's words and his deeds reflexively one on the other, in the cultural context of a world empire in which Roman civil law was adapted to the law of nations and Greek literary forms were adapted to the Roman tastes and ideals. The Romans were fearful of the refinements and pedantries of the Greek arts, but they were also convinced that they were useful to reinforce and advance the native virtues of Rome. The encyclopaedia of the wise man and the encyclopaedia of the learned man were adapted in the encyclopaedia of the prudent man. The humanities and culture, in their long history since Rome, have continued to have this double aspect, which has been interpreted as a virtue or as a fault in the endless battles of the books and the recurrent cultural and educational reforms concerning arts and letters, humanities and the sciences, ancients and moderns—they are the indispensable bases of rebirth of culture and science, or they are the deadweight of tradition employed to resist needed innovations.

The Greeks invented the liberal arts; the Hellenistic men of learning equipped them with technical terms and distinctions and systematic rules and organizing principles; the Roman orators and teachers of rhetoric adapted them to use in courtrooms, legislative bodies, and learned, polite, or popular assemblies. The nine liberal arts enumerated by Varro contain the seven liberal arts which were fixed in the encyclopaedism of the Middle Ages, and their liberal characteristics were explored by the Scipionic circle of politicians, generals, historians, poets, and philosophers. As Cicero reports their conversations in the *De re publica*, they held that men are properly called men who are perfected in the arts proper to humanity—*artes propriae humanitatis*.[11] They are liberal arts—arts appropriate to free men—and arts of policy and civility. They are a part of general education and, as such, essential to the practice of law, for forensic oratory needs a man who has some training and is not unacquainted with "general literature and more polite education"—*communium literarum et politioris humanitatis expers*.[12] The more polite studies of humanity have a bearing on policy and civility which is lost in the more restricted associations of the modern words "polite" and "civil," and the members of the

[11] Cicero *De re publica* 1. 17. 28.
[12] Cicero *De oratore* 2. 17. 72.

Scipionic circle who are clearer in glory, weightier in authority, and politer in humanity—*humanitate politiores*—are evidence of the openness of Rome to the influence of philosophy and learning.[13] Students of oratory should be well trained in the study of civil law, grounded in a general education in which they engage in every right study and humanity—*in omni recto studio et humanitate serventur*.[14]

The theme of the liberal arts and culture was explored systematically and diversely in the course of the Roman Empire. One version of the theme was given a simple popular presentation in the second century A.D. by Aulus Gellius in the *Attic Nights*. *Humanitas*, humanity, does not mean what the common people think. It is not a translation of the Greek word *philanthropia* but of *paideia*. It means erudition and instruction in the good arts—*eruditio institutioque in bonas artes*. Those who earnestly desire and seek after these arts are in the highest degree most human—*maxime humanissimi*. The pursuit of this kind of knowledge and the training it affords have been bestowed on man alone among animals, and for that reason it has been called *humanitas*. It was in this sense, Gellius goes on, that earlier writers like Varro and Cicero used the word, and he quotes Varro's *Roman Antiquities* for an explanation of "humanity." Praxiteles, because of his surpassing art, is not unknown to anyone who is more human or cultured—*humaniori*—more human. Varro explains, not in the sense of more "good-natured, amiable, and kindly" but in the sense of being somewhat more erudite and learned—*eruditori doctorique*—to the extent of knowing who Praxiteles was from books and history. *Humanitas*, Gellius adds, is also the *enkuklios paideia*, the circle or cycle of learning or knowledge. General education and the encyclopaedia of knowledge trace the same circle. In *paideia*, in education or culture, all the arts which pertain to humanity have a common bond and are held together by a certain kinship, as it were, to each other.[15]

---

[13] *Ibid.*, 2. 37. 154.     [14] *Ibid.*, 1. 60. 256.     [15] Gellius *Attic Nights* 13. 17.

Gellius gave one version of the theme of the liberal arts and culture. There were other versions, some of them contradictory, which were variations on the same theme and contributed together to the formation and evolution of culture and the humanities. Gellius said, in Latin, that *humanitas* was a translation of *paideia* not *philanthropia*. Themistius, who wrote in Greek, used *philanthropia* in a sense which could be translated by the "humanities." Themistius was a teacher, orator, and politician in Constantinople in the fourth century under a succession of emperors beginning with Constantius; he was Senator in 355 and Prefect of Constantinople in 384 on the nomination of Theodosius. He was fearful of the effects of Christianity on culture and society, and he argued, against the Christians, that *philanthropia*, the love of mankind, is essential to the training of a statesman and that it is achieved by the study of literature.

The study of man is the study of the good arts or of humanity, which makes men more human—more polite, more politic, more civil, more prudent, more learned, and more wise. Men use the arts of humanity to achieve individuality, polity, civility, science, and wisdom. It is general education which bases innovation on tradition, but it may also, in the evolution of the theme of culture and the liberal arts, be an alien study subversive of national culture and integrity, antagonistic to religion and the preservation of spiritual values, or a distraction from economic and social progress and scientific advancement. It may be made an adjunct of the rhetoric of the assembly and the law court and flower in the stylistic extravagances of the Second Sophistic and the moralizing literature of popular erudition, examplary history, and satire; it may be made an adjunct of the scholastic method of canon law and theology and flower in the imaginative expansions of lyrical, cosmological, and mystic poetry and the controversial complexities of the problem of the universal; it may be made an adjunct of the study of Greek art and literature and flower in the over-all adornments of the Baroque; it may be made an adjunct of the study of arts and literatures and flower in the literary universalisms of the stream of consciousness, of the phenomenally given, and of stochastic juxtapositions.

Different conceptions of man have been reflected in the different encyclopaedias of humanity. "Man," "humanity," and "culture" were used reflexively in defining each other, and the resulting definition was sometimes inclusive of all men or "mankind," sometimes restricted to a selected portion of men who illustrate the more advanced culture which is the model and definition of man. The Greek philosophers wrote philosophy in the form of encyclopaedias which set forth the principles and the organization of all knowledge. They sometimes limited culture to the Greeks, sometimes took into account the contributions of the barbarians; and Socrates was early distinguished as having turned philosophy from the study of *nature* to the study of *man*. The librarians of Pergamon and Alexandria wrote bibliographical treatises which were encyclopaedic guides to all that was available of the arts and the sciences in the books in their libraries, set forth for the use of scholars and scientists. The character of their collections and classifications of books provided two bases for the organization of knowledge and the study of man, in poetry and in philosophy, that is, in *literature* and *science*, and the Hellenistic age saw the development both of universal histories and of histories of the arts and sciences. The Roman encyclopaedias were ready-reference handbooks to facts and statements and programs or textbooks of study for the formation of experts in all fields; they were collected commonplaces of *words* and *deeds*. They reflected the development and codification of Civil Law and *Jus Gentium* or the law of nations or of mankind. The contacts of peoples and the dawning consciousness of mankind in the structure of the relations of peoples gave concreteness and specificity by rules of operation in general questions and in individual issues to the organization of learning, both as bodies of knowledge and as courses of education.

The three great monotheistic religions of the West—Judaism, Christianity, and Islam—built their cultures and educations on the Greek and Roman encyclopaedias. In all three, from the beginning and throughout their histories, there was controversial opposition between those who argued that there was nothing in common between Athens and Jerusalem, and those who argued that the example of the Hebrews who took utensils and raiment with them in their flight from Egypt justified a like purification and use of the pagan arts. In Western Christianity the development of theology and canon law was inseparable from the development of the seven liberal arts of the trivium and quadrivium, and in the high Middle Ages the philosophers and theologians of the three religions discussed the same problems and achieved an unprecedented degree of communication and common culture.

The revolt of the Renaissance was a revolt against the medieval liberal arts and encyclopaedia. It was a return from the technicalities of the verbal logics and speculative grammars of the late Middle Ages to a renewed use of rhetoric to effect the shift from verbal structures and consequences to structures of expression and communication. The study of man was reoriented from the ends formalized in theology to the ends expressed in Greek art and in the Scriptures conceived and interpreted as literature and history. The arts became fields rather than disciplines, and *literae humaniores*, the more human literature, became the distinguishing mark of man, not as superior achievement in the use of language which distinguished him from animals, nor as the exercise of disciplines distinct from those used in the interpretation of divine letters, but a branch of learning distinct from the emerging new sciences. The Renaissance encyclopaedia developed into the modern encyclopaedias, in which facts increased and fields fragmented and new universalisms are sought in inter-disciplinary research and learning, in universalisms of statement and operation, of words and deeds.

The theme of the liberal arts and culture may be recounted as an evolution or as a series of revolutions, as a creative emergence or as a series of rebirths. Historians of culture and proponents of the liberal arts choose their variations on the theme and find their facts and values in data which are given meaning reflexively by the ideas produced in the development of culture or sought in the use of the liberal arts. Since these various accounts and programs of culture and education are facts of the culture of any time, however, the theme itself of the development of culture and the liberal arts is not a choice of one but an interplay of all accounts and programs. Two of the variables which determine the formation of an encyclopaedia or cycle of culture, or learning, or education are the external conditioning circumstances which extend in widening compass from society to contacts of peoples to mankind and internal conditioning functions which extend in culminating power from natural abilities and inclinations to acquired skills and tastes to liberal arts and critical judgments. The cultural problems of the present are problems of mankind and of the arts. The recognition and treatment of those problems must use and effect changes in the conception of man, adapted to larger associations and more diversified activities, and consequential changes in the arts which make him human and free, and which achieve at once a revolution and a renaissance, an abandonment of opaque ideas and ineffective arts, and a recreation of heuristic ideas and liberating arts.

There are two ways in which the theme of the liberal arts and culture is elaborated: in the evolution of culture itself by what men say and do and think, and in the accounts of that evolution which are particularizations of the theme and at the same time factors in its ongoing development. The elements in any consideration of the theme, in statement or in action, are facts and ideas, but they are not independent elements: each conditions the other reflexively—ideas enter into the determination of facts, and facts are the source and basis of ideas. Our accounts of the cultural problems of our times are colored by a compulsive recognition of the vast increase in the facts known, which is made the defining sign of a consequent vast increase in knowledge. This new synonymity of facts and knowledge is facilitated by an associated tendency to ignore the facts of other cultures, for they are not facts in the light of our ideas, and we busily reconstruct the facts of past cultures and other cultures in our cultural histories and cultural sciences. No neutral and unambiguous census of the facts known in different cultures and no comparison of the extent of the different sciences or the efficacy of the different values of different cultures can be made, since the facts recognized by the census taker and the opinion surveyor are conditioned by their cultural ideas. When our accounts of the cultural problems of our times turn to the consideration of ideas which are no longer respected or used, it is either to exhibit them as untrue or ineffective or to advocate a return to former customs, aspirations, arts, or beliefs. Accounts of cultures and programs of policy are relative in their orientation and controversially opposed, but they are also effective instruments in the formation and advancement of culture and their operation in a culture may be considered without the distortions and delimitations introduced by adherence to or skepticism concerning particular accounts and diagnoses, by considering the functional interactions of ideas and facts and the institutional interdeterminations of man and societies of men.

A theme is a structure of ideas and facts, of functions and operations. The theme of culture and the liberal arts is an evolving structure determined by the external conditions of societies of men and their institutions, and the internal conditions of human functions and arts. Culture took a characteristic turn in Rome as a result of the contacts of other peoples and cultures, which set it sufficiently apart to justify the definition of a special word to name it and the formulation of special arts to state the rules of discourse and operation to develop it. The cultures of subject peoples brought their bodies of customs and laws to bear on the formulation of Roman law; and the culture of one subject people, the Greeks, brought their liberal and intellectual arts, their eloquence and wisdom, to bear on the formation of the Roman conception of the cosmos as a commonwealth of gods and men. The Roman encyclopaedia was an organization of the more human arts in a rhetoric applied to legislation and adjudication. The contacts of peoples and the emergence of new peoples had a like influence on the formation of the arts and culture of the Renaissance. The rediscovery of man emerged in the formation of new nations, new religions, and new sciences; and the liberal arts and fine arts of antiquity provided the model and impetus for new creative expression and new liberal arts. The Renaissance encyclopaedia was an organization of the more human arts or letters in a rhetoric applied to aesthetic creation and appreciation. It is mankind and the contacts of peoples, again, which give our problems today their characteristic turn. We have seen colonial peoples become self-governing, independent nations and influential members of the United Nations, and we have sensed the emergence of a world community; we have built on and applied what we think to be sound in the arts and the sciences. The controlling art of our encyclopaedia is still an art, not a practical legal art, nor a poetic fine art, but a theoretic scientific art which we have disguised by joining "science" and "art" in naming it "technology"; the modern encyclopaedia is an organization of the more human arts and sciences in a rhetoric of technology and communication.

Since the development of the arts and culture by men does not depend on ideological agreement on one conception of cultural life and values, the pluralism of conceptions and programs, of arts and institutions, such as is found in earlier instances of cultural transition or perfection, of revolution or renaissance, reflects an interacting pluralism of conceptions of man and mankind. The freedom of man is a freedom of spontaneity, of self-determination, of self-realization, and of self-perfection. In the theme of the development of culture and the arts these are four interacting aspects of freedom, but they also reflect basic-ally different, and often opposed, philosophic conceptions of the nature of man. We have more diversified data and more estab-lished facts concerning the nature of man, but the continuity of theme and problem emerges in a continuity of structures in which the nature of man is discovered and made and the knowl-edge of man is formed and interpreted. To act spontaneously is to act without determination; to act by self-determination is to act according to the rules of one's nature; to act for self-realization is to take nature into account as potentialities-rather than determinations; to act for self-perfection is to act under the guidance of a transcendental ideal. While philosophers and scientists offer evidence for conflicting theories developing con-ceptions of man and his actions which present him as a maker or creator of himself and his environment, as a nature operating by action and reaction among other natures, as an agent de-veloping the potentialities he finds in himself and his environ-ment, and as a knower perceiving a rationality in things which he adapts in his knowledge and actions, the contribution of their ideas to the progress of culture is found less in the accept-ance which any one set of ideas achieves than in the interaction of men as spontaneous creators, self-determined natures, self-realizing agents, and self-perfecting intelligences.

The theme of culture and the arts is an amplification of theses concerning the nature of man and mankind in interaction; and reflexively it is restricted and delimited by the same theses in opposition and conflict. The problems of our times take their particular character from this alternation of amplification and diminuation more than from the compelling force of facts or from the attractive truth of ideas. Newly liberated peoples, alienated classes and races, and assertive and negative youth have learned to practice new freedoms of spontaneity. It would be reasonable to examine the possibilities and consequences

opened up by their actions, but their theses encounter ready-
made and persuasive opposed theses according to which the
new spontaneities exceed the limitations properly imposed by
considerations of nature and human nature, individual satisfaction and common good, or truths and values. Advancements
in the knowledge of the nature of man have made possible new
freedoms of self-determination which are put into practice, but
the extension of their use encounters oppositions resulting from
theses according to which they substitute coercion for spontaneity, destroy privacy and freedom of choice by public intrusion
and control, and confuse facts with values. The maximization
of rights and liberties has opened up new freedoms of self-
realization, but questions are raised concerning their desir-
ability on theses which hold that they destroy self-initiation,
ignore natural differences, and run counter to knowledge of the
possible and ideals of the desirable. The contacts of cultures and
the resultant spread of rights and knowledge have established
new freedoms of self-perfection, but they are seen according to
opposed theses as the establishment of new restrictive imperial-
isms, which substitute other ends for those of individual impulse
and desire, ignore the bases of action in nature and human
nature, and abstract from the circumstances which condition
thought, action, and communication. The liberal arts should
make man more human according to the opposed theses by
making him more spontaneous, more natural, more just, or
more rational; the theme of culture and the liberal arts is developed in our times by the oppositions of these theses in statement, program, and action, and by their interaction in
increasing spontaneity, self-determination, self-realization, and
self-perfection of individuals, of groups, and of mankind as a
whole.

The basic reflexivity of the study of man which is also the
making of man is of peculiar importance in the problems of
culture and learning today. They are not problems to be solved
by waiting for the sciences and the humanities to develop theses

which will secure universal acceptance and lead man and mankind to their salvation. Reflexively man and mankind reform the sciences, humanities, and cultures which form man and mankind. Communication and technology—man understanding men and man applying knowledge and embodying values —provide means of guiding action by reason and intelligence which put the theses of science, religion, the humanities, and culture to effective use without reducing the oppositions and dynamic differences by which they open up new problems and new possibilities. The reflexive study of man is a cycle of knowledge and learning, an encyclopaedia. Arrested at any stage and viewed in a still shot of what is known, it is complex to the point of chaos and indefinite to the point of infinity. It has a structure in its formation, however, which is sometimes overlooked in the calculation of its complexities. That structure is dynamic and ongoing in its operations and functionings. As it grows and forms man, it opens up new dangers and new confusions as well as new opportunities and new satisfactions. To those threats and perplexities there is no remedy other than the study of man, which itself ceases to exist when it ceases to be an ongoing process, the development of humanity or of a cycle of learning, or an encyclopaedia, which is the education of mankind.

# INDEX

295